Fifty Years in Cricket

Fifty Years in Cricket

LEN HUTTON
with
ALEX BANNISTER

STANLEY PAUL
London Melbourne Sydney Auckland Johannesburg

Stanley Paul & Co. Ltd

An imprint of the Hutchinson Publishing Group

17–21 Conway Street, London W1P 6JD

Hutchinson Group (Australia) Pty Ltd
30–32 Cremorne Street, Richmond South, Victoria 3121
PO Box 151, Broadway, New South Wales 2007

Hutchinson Group (NZ) Ltd
32–34 View Road, PO Box 40–086, Glenfield, Auckland 10

Hutchinson Group (SA) Pty Ltd
PO Box 337, Bergvlei 2012, South Africa

First published 1984
© Len Hutton 1984

Set in Linotron Sabon
by Input Typesetting Ltd, London

Printed and bound in Great Britain by
Anchor Brendon Ltd, Tiptree, Essex

ISBN 0 09 155220 6

Contents

Acknowledgements

In writing this book, I was particularly fortunate to have the collaboration of my long-standing friend Alex Bannister, who was cricket correspondent of the *Daily Mail* for thirty-two years, and who saw so much of my cricket both at home and abroad. As cricketers everywhere know, he is much respected for his knowledge and fairness throughout his distinguished career

Photographic acknowledgements

For permission to reproduce copyright photographs, the publishers would like to thank Central Press Photos Ltd, the *Daily Express*, Patrick Eagar, Ken Kelly, Keystone Press Agency Ltd, the Press Association Ltd, Sport and General Press Agency Ltd, Sporting Pictures (UK) Ltd and the *Yorkshire Post*

Foreword

It is an honour to be offered an opportunity to open the innings in front of the many great names whose immortal deeds are described in this book. Indeed, I feel confident that I can risk playing a few shots of my own without endangering the rest of the innings.

The book is a testament to a career which, though ending in playing terms about twenty years before mine finished in 1974, continues to survive in the memory, and shames my own into virtual oblivion. If anything, living with the name has become harder since I stopped playing first-class cricket. As I move now in another world I am confronted and confounded by the uninitiated. 'Did you play cricket?' they ask, and then, to underline their total ignorance: 'Is your father still alive?' The answers are provided in this book, which, far from being a life story, is a series of fascinating reflections on those events and individuals my father has been closely associated with over a period of fifty years.

It is his third effort at authorship and, with the aid of modern practices, has been produced with considerably less inconvenience to myself. I remember the previous one in 1957, when for months I had to suffer the intrusion into my normal home life of the ever spreading litter of reams of laboriously hand-written manuscript.

The book says more about my father's career as a cricketer than as a parent. This may not be surprising because he was not often at home, and when, after his retirement, he was, I was not. During my childhood I discovered most about my father through the back page of the daily newspaper; quietly leaving my bed in the early morning, I waited patiently by the letter box for its arrival. I learned to read by picking out my father's name and his score from the scoresheet.

Often they were in the headlines, which made it easier. Eventually I moved on to the match reports, and thence to taking cricket books to bed. By then I was devouring every written word about my father; he had become greater than God. To be sure of seeing him when I wanted to I had to go to the cricket ground. For hours I would sit enthralled as I compiled his score in my own scorebook, anguishing over every ball in the fear that the apparent frailty of his play, which I failed to recognize as artistry, would let him down. How little I knew, and I wonder if he had any idea of the torture I suffered.

At the age of ten I disgraced myself, my mother and my school in public on that awful day at Headingley when Lindwall bowled him out second ball. It was made worse by the fact that, as far as my young eye could judge, there was an easy single off the first ball. Before too long, however, I was bathing in the reflected glory of the Ashes victory and then the successful defence in Australia.

After his retirement there seemed to be little left to follow. Instead, the nature of his influence shifted, and my adolescence met the hand of paternal discipline, as if the returning hero felt the need to make up for lost time.

The book contains many anecdotes but omits one story which I must tell, because it is probably the only occasion when I scored any runs off my father other than in the garden. During my school holidays, aware of my desire to play cricket, he arranged for me to play for Bradford Second XI in the Bradford League. In the following summer I graduated into the first team as an opening bat and in my first match scored a 50, so qualifying for the traditional collection. Returning home with my pockets overflowing with coppers, three-penny bits and sixpences, all donated by a generous crowd, my great joy was in no way lessened by my father's expression of horror that his son, and a schoolboy at that, had actually received money for playing cricket.

The next match was an away game at East Bierley, and at lunch-time it was still not decided whether my father would drive me to the ground. Pointing out that I could get on just as well without parental support, I got the bus into Bradford and caught the trolley out to East Bierley, arriving in time for what I thought was a 2.30 p.m. start. In fact the starting time was 2 p.m. and as the match had already begun and Bradford were batting, I was put down at No. 6 as a punishment for arriving late. In the meantime and unknown to me, my father had decided to go to the match and, in the comfort of his motorcar, had arrived before me to find that Bradford were 0 for 1 (last man 0). Seeing that I was not at the crease and assuming that mine was the wicket to fall, he went straight home without showing himself to anyone.

Eventually when my turn to bat came, I was fortunate enough to make another 50. The collection was even more overwhelming than the week before and, since the after-match activities held no interest for me then, I hurried home in total ecstasy to display my proud winnings for the second week in succession. Opening the kitchen door I was confronted by my father who posed the clever question: 'So, where's the collection this time, then?' Seeing my moment, I emptied my pockets, and hundreds of coins cascaded across the kitchen floor, rolling to rest in every nook and cranny. The superior grin facing me altered its shape to open-mouthed amazement and remained so as if set to stone until he found the wit to say that it is quicker to travel by car than by bus!

If this was one of the best moments of my life, probably the worst also involved my father through his own exquisite sense of timing. By 1968 I was just about holding a Yorkshire place when I had an appalling day at Lord's in a match against Middlesex, which was also John Murray's benefit game. To put the varied careers of my father and myself into perspective, I suppose I could say that my bad days were as numerous as his good days, and my good ones about as infrequent as his bad. On this dreadful day I could find neither length nor line, and Murray himself, as befitted the occasion, took full advantage and was on his way to a large score. As I trudged off to my field position, after one particular over in which he savaged me for several boundaries, including a 6, I heard the public address system being put into operation. 'This is Sir Leonard Hutton speaking,' it said. I was suddenly panic-stricken with the appalling thought that I was about to receive a public admonishment for improper bowling. A snigger went round the ground, and I stood breathless as I prepared for the worst. What followed was an appeal on behalf of John Murray's benefit fund, which hardly relieved me – but the Yorkshire captain did.

There has always been a certain eccentricity about my father; particularly one can never be sure of the response he might make to certain situations. I was abroad at the time when I telephoned him to announce my intention of getting married. There was a deafening silence as though the shock had killed him. Eventually, in his woe-ridden manner, he informed me that only on that very day the Government had been forced to take over British Leyland and the rates were doubling. Nevertheless, I said that I was still going to get married. The conversation concluded with his remark that he would be having trouble with my mother that night!

My mother, who, of course, was delighted with the news, has never been any trouble to anyone. As a representative of the Dennis family, another Yorkshire cricketing name, throughout she has been the rock upon which we have all depended. Without her strength, forbearance and understanding, none of us would have achieved much.

Now another generation of Huttons is with us. In a reversal of roles, two small boys are adored by their grandfather. I hope they develop without feeling the pressures of carrying on the name of their famous forebear, that in doing so they enjoy the great game as much as I have, and that the author of this book will have many happy times watching them.

Richard Hutton
Ashurst, Kent
November 1983

1
364 and All That

No more remarkable exhibition of concentration and endurance has been seen on the cricket field than that of Leonard Hutton in a match which ended in the defeat of Australia by an innings and 579 runs. Record after record went by the board as Hutton mastered the bowling in calm, methodical fashion for the best part of two and a half days. At the end of 13 hours, 20 minutes the batsman of only twenty-two passed the highest individual score in Test history and had taken part in two record stands – 382 with Maurice Leyland for the second wicket, the best for any wicket by England, and 215 with Joe Hardstaff for the sixth wicket. This Test, which enabled England to share the series, will always be remembered as 'Hutton's Match'.

Wisden Cricketers' Almanack, 1939

Fifty years on, as I write, from my Yorkshire debut, and armed with the hindsight of a lifetime as a player, Test captain and selector – not to mention my years in the press box – I sometimes wonder if it was not the second worst happening of my career to become a record-breaking national celebrity at an age when I had just qualified to vote.

It was not that I lost my head in the clouds; quite the reverse. Proud as I was to have scored 364 against Australia and to have overtaken Don Bradman's record, which I had watched spellbound as a schoolboy at Headingley eight years before, I was still capable of being overwhelmed by the suddenness of fame and worried by its penalties.

No doubt some might deem it highly implausible that a young batsman able to stay for almost fourteen hours in a Test match could be vulnerable to pressures and private misgivings. The public might have seen me as a dedicated, single-minded, perhaps even ruthless, scoring machine, but the truth was that I was shy and retiring by nature. By upbringing and instinct I was highly practical, a Yorkshireman in heart and soul, but reluctant to voice an opinion. There was never any danger of my feet leaving the ground. Indeed, the more praise to come my way the more I fretted that I might not be able to live up to my reputation as a record-breaker.

I was also an unashamed hero-worshipper and I could never bring myself to believe I could enter the world of Jack Hobbs, Don Bradman and the entire Yorkshire team of the thirties. My first meeting with Sir Jack literally left me tongue-tied. I gaped and no words came. I shudder to imagine what he must have thought of me. When I went into the Yorkshire dressing room I felt like a youthful interloper, a boy among men, and I can say with honesty that when I opened the batting for Pudsey St Lawrence in the Bradford League at the age of fourteen, I did not think I was anything better than above average for my years.

A year later, one bitter February night, I was invited by George Hirst, the Yorkshire coach – known in the cricket world as George Herbert – to the Headingley nets – the famous old Winter Shed – to bat against Bill Bowes and Hedley Verity. George wanted their opinion of 'this promising lad from Pudsey'. It was my first meeting with two great bowlers who were to play an important part in my career and my life as true friends.

Bill's opening words almost cost him my eternal devotion. 'It's about time tha had a new bat, isn't it?' he asked after looking me up and down. To me the very suggestion of discarding my Harrow-size bat, personally selected for me by none other than Herbert Sutcliffe, was like asking the owner of the Kohinoor diamond to throw it in a dustbin. With it I had made my first half-century and century, and many a night I had taken it to bed with me.

At the end of the session George Hirst put a kindly hand on my shoulder and said, 'Well done.' Simple words to lift my heart, but on the way home I realized: Bill's right. I do need a new bat. Not for the last time, I had cause to be grateful for his advice.

Among Hirst's priceless teachings was a shrewd little piece of advice given to me when I was fifteen and travelling to the Winter Shed on a tram (I always used to meet him and carry his bag). As the old tram swayed and clanged he said: 'Whatever tha does, doan't get like Victor Trumper.' As any batsman, young or old, would have given anything to be another Trumper, I asked why. 'He was so superstitious that he made his life a misery' was the reply. From that moment I resolved to shun supposedly lucky or unlucky numbers, grounds, bowlers or whatever. My one concession to superstition was to put my left pad on first – and that was only because I had heard Hobbs always did so! Apparently Trumper used the same batting trousers throughout his career. They became threadbare.

Herbert Sutcliffe, who had lost his parents at an early age – his father from the effects of an injury on the rugby field – came to live at Pudsey with two aunts, who ran a confectionery business. He was a friend of my father, Henry, and lived only a boundary throw away. He was, therefore, well acquainted with the cricket of the young Hutton. Not long after I had begun with Yorkshire, he presented me with a book in which he described me as 'a marvel, the discovery of a generation'. I thanked him, but privately I wished the words had not been written, as I was but eighteen, still uncapped, and I did not think I had done enough to justify such flattery.

I survived the burden of premature publicity, thanks to my mentors, Herbert Sutcliffe, George Hirst, Bill Bowes, Hedley Verity and others, including my parents, plus Yorkshire's careful nursing – but I think if my Test record had come later than it did I might have accepted it more philosophically. As it was, it was not until I saw my face staring back at me from newspapers and advertising hoardings, and became the centre of attention wherever I played, that it dawned on me that my life and career had taken a new course. To my consternation I was bracketed with Don Bradman and Jack Hobbs. I could not bring myself to think I was in their class.

The thought of the public actually going to grounds to watch me, and of fathers taking sons to see the record-breaker, bothered me no end, perhaps needlessly. Even the best batsman in the world, which I acknowledged as Bradman, could miss a straight ball or a full toss from the worst bowler in the world. I came to appreciate the awesome burden Bradman had carried from his earliest days, and, from my own point of view, I realized with some apprehension that only a century, or a good innings against good bowlers in testing conditions, satisfied my professional ego. I needed the spur of a challenge, and I never enjoyed taking easy runs off second-rate bowlers.

The more I was in the public eye and the more responsibility to come my way, the more I marvelled how Bradman had coped over the years. He had scored his 334 at Leeds when he was also very young – and even younger when he made 452 not out for New South Wales against Queensland. But Bradman was Bradman, unique, a cricketer beyond comparison, and with deep reserves of character to support his talents.

At the Lord's centenary match in 1980, Bob Wyatt was asked how he rated Bill Ponsford, the other half of Australia's greatest batting partnership. 'A very great player indeed' was the response from a deep student of the game, who was often in opposition to Ponsford. If Ponsford was 'very great', how then can Bradman be measured?

Perhaps my niggling fear of letting youngsters down after the Oval was prompted by a chord of memory from my own experience. I must have been the picture of dejection as I made my way home to Pudsey from Bradford Park Avenue early in July 1930, a few days after my fourteenth birthday. I had counted the days to Yorkshire's game with the Australians, but, to my dismay, Bradman was out leg before to Emmott Robinson for a single. Years later, when I mentioned it to Don, he replied without a moment's hesitation: 'Yes, I nicked it!'

Jack Hobbs also played a single-figure innings on the same ground (I prefer Bradford to Headingley because of its intimacy), and it has to be a measure of my admiration for the two batting masters that I wished them well against Yorkshire!

A few days later, however, I was lavishly compensated for my disappointment at Don's early dismissal when, from my place behind the square leg boundary on the opening day of the third Test at Headingley, I saw him score 309. The following morning he went on to 334, a number to be seared in my mind in years to come; incredible to relate, his innings lasted only 336 minutes. I was enthralled. No aspiring ballerina at a first sight of Pavlova could have been more uplifted and transported to a land of wonderment than I was on that July day.

In the first two Tests Bradman had scored 131 at Trent Bridge, and 254 at Lord's – sometimes considered to be his best innings, with his shots bringing whistles of amazement from the England fielders – and I am grateful to have seen the finest of all batsmen at the height of his powers. The memory will never fade. I am convinced that between 1930 and 1940 Bradman saw the ball earlier and moved his feet quicker than any other batsman in the world, and probably before or since. In 1934 he still produced huge scores although he was fighting ill health, and by 1938 he had, by his own standards, sobered down fractionally. All things are comparative. Once, discussing batsmen with Wilfred Rhodes, the grand old man said with emphasis: 'I bowled against them all from 1900 to 1930 ... Hobbs, W. G. Grace, Trumper, Ranji and many more, but Don Bradman was the greatest.'

Rhodes was within a month of his fifty-third birthday when he played against Bradman in his last match at Scarborough in 1930. 'I should have had him out when he was 10 if I'd had a mid-off,' he used to tell me. Bob Wyatt, in fact, was mid-off and he tells the story against himself. Wilfred would continue: 'If David had been there, he'd have swallowed it.'

David Denton was a renowned Yorkshire fielder, who once found himself in the long field to Rhodes. Three times Wilfred waved to Denton to move, and three times Denton stayed put – a defiance almost tantamount to disobeying a royal command. As Wilfred knew to an inch where he wanted his field, and was invariably right, he would not bowl. Finally he called over: 'Why don't tha move?'

'I'm staying here,' was the response, rather in the tone of Sam the musket man. And by way of explanation: 'Here I can see the ball all the way from the bat. Where you want me to go it's going to take me a quarter of an hour to find it!'

I never discovered the result of the dialogue, but Edgar Oldroyd had the temerity to signal a 6 against Rhodes with a wide grin. 'All right. All right. A 6' was the huffy response. 'But don't stand there grinning like a Cheshire cat!'

The speed of Bradman's footwork and the ease with which he found, and even created, gaps in the field were a revelation, and an abiding memory. He could put the ball exactly where he wanted it to go – and that is no exaggeration. England's captain Percy Chapman admittedly did not have the fleetest of fielding sides, but no matter how he tried, he could not plug the holes. They appeared everywhere, and no sooner was one filled than another was exposed. For example, if third man was placed square, Don would steer between second slip and gully. If Chapman tried to move third man finer, Don would trump the move with a fierce square cut, a stroke he played to perfection. And so it went on.

No fielder could be hidden; no bowler spared the energy of the chase. Bradman aimed for the maximum result from every stroke, and he saw no advantage in hitting hard and straight to a fielder.

He must have memorized the exact position of every fielder to an inch, and his movements at the crease were precise and quick and ending in the perfect position to make the stroke of his choice. Whenever I read an expert analysis of Don's technique, I go along with every observation about his footwork, balance, early sighting of the ball, his positioning and his ability to shut everything from his mind but the task at hand. Yet it is often overlooked that he was the ideal height for a batsman as his head was in line with the ball, and he was in the right position to make his shot without adjustment. He was also a superb fielder, as good as any in his prime, with speed, pick-up and a deadly return.

Bradman had the considerable advantage of learning his cricket on matting surfaces with a concrete base, and later to play on bulli surfaces. At a comparable age English batsman have to contend with slow pitches, often of a doubtful quality. The practice wicket at Pudsey St Lawrence in my time was so bad that Herbert Sutcliffe moved to Pudsey Britannia, which was comparable to crossing the floor of the House or transferring to Lancashire. Australian wickets have changed a lot over the years, indeed from series to series, but I recall the Melbourne Test of 1947 for two main reasons: the deafening reception given to Cyril Washbrook and myself when we went out to open the innings, and a pitch so hard that I could not make a mark for my guard with my bat. 'You have to scratch it with your bootstuds,' Don Tallon, the Australian wicketkeeper, told me.

The noise of that huge crowd was a new experience for me, and it continued until Ray Lindwall was within a few strides of the wicket. Then there was a sudden hush so deep that the thud of Ray's hoofs could be heard.

Good pitches breed confidence. You see the result not only in Australia, but the West Indies and South Africa. Bradman's confidence, helped by his early trust in pitches, amounted to a psychological advantage over bowlers. Once during his innings of 334 at Headingley he slipped while moving down the pitch to the leg-spinner Dick Tyldesley. Instead of accepting the inevitable stumping, he brought his bat from nowhere and cut the ball firmly for a single while George Duckworth stood with gloved hands on hips shaking his head in disbelief. Tyldesley could be excused the wry simplicity of his comment at the end of the day: 'Bradman's no ruddy use to me!'

I had the luck to play in three series against the Don, and I was at Adelaide in 1946–47 when he was bowled by Alec Bedser for a duck by perhaps the deadliest ball I have ever seen. The ball moved into him with conventional swing, and as Don shaped to run it down the leg side it hit the pitch as a fast leg break and found the middle and off stumps. Paradoxically, the average good batsman, not picking the ball up as quickly, might not have lost his wicket.

During his first visit to England in 1930 it was fashionable to say that Don was unorthodox, a law unto himself, and that his bat was not as straight as it ought to have been. A genius to confound all theory, but not one to copy. Yet from Headingley onwards, and certainly later when I was better able to judge, I never saw any part of his technique which could not serve as a model for any batsman from school age upwards. His movements were so right and so emphatic. To the straight good-length ball he would go either forward or back with precise judgement, never across the pitch, and at the crucial moment, his bat would be as straight as a Scotch fir.

Genius, however, is a born talent and a very special individualism. Wilfred Rhodes, who rose from No. 11 to set records as Jack Hobbs's opening partner, always prided himself on being able to spot leg breaks and googlies. On the other hand, according to Wilfred, Hobbs was not able to do so and preferred to play the ball off the pitch. In a Test with South Africa, when the White–Faulkner–Vogler googly trio was much feared, Hobbs and Rhodes were batting together and Wilfred was congratulating himself that he was coping better than Jack. Then, glancing at the scoreboard, he read: Hobbs 75, Rhodes 17.

The Bradman effect on me on that unforgettable occasion at Headingley was magical. I rushed back to Pudsey, recruited two willing bowlers, and practised until the night closed around me. I was not to see another Test match for seven years, and then only because I was selected to play against New Zealand at Lord's. Unfortunately it was an inauspicious start and I completed a hat-trick of ducks in maiden appearances: o for Yorkshire Second XI, o for Yorkshire – run out by Jack Davies who once bowled Bradman – and o for England. As Maurice Leyland said: 'Well, tha can only get better, lad.'

One short summer later, after my Test debut, I was on the opposite

side to Bradman, the captain of Australia, in the first Test of the
1938 series at Trent Bridge. In fact, the first time I ever spoke to
him was in the middle during my opening partnership with Charlie
Barnett, who went off like a rocket and was 98 at lunch. I told Don
that I had watched him at Headingley eight years previously, but,
as far as I recollect, it did not become a dialogue as he did not
answer. Maybe he had heard the same words so often that he was
wincing inside, or maybe he was too preoccupied with trying to
break a stand which went on to 219 with both Charlie and me
scoring centuries. Two months later, when I passed Don's record,
he beat everyone in a race to shake my hand, and he could not have
been more generous in his praise.

At Trent Bridge I was so elated when I reached 100 in my first
Test against Australia that I lost my head and made such a wretched
shot that I was deservedly leg before to the left-arm googly bowler
Fleetwood-Smith. Denis Compton also got himself out as soon as
he arrived at the magic figures, and had a severe telling-off from
Wally Hammond. 'You don't do that against Australia,' he said,
as if the first commandment of English cricket had been broken.
Fortunately I escaped a similar reprimand. Possibly Wally thought
that a Yorkshireman did not need to be told the facts of cricket
life, but I was duly mildly admonished by Herbert Sutcliffe. 'Never
willingly get out at 100,' he advised. 'It looks bad. If you feel you
can't go on to 200 at least, add 20 more or so.'

Normally if I did anything to incur Herbert's disapproval I had
his imperious look, before which many a fellow player quailed.

On my twenty-first birthday, just after I had been selected for my
first Test, Herbert and I took 315 off Leicestershire at Hull in the
four hours up to tea. As we walked out for the final session, Herbert,
in his most matter-of-fact tone, announced: 'We'll go for 556.' He
might have said: 'We'll catch the 7.12 train to Leeds.'

The 556 target was 1 run more than the record held by Herbert
and Percy Holmes and set up at Leyton in 1932, but whether they
actually passed the previous record of 554 by their Yorkshire predecessors, Brown and Tunnicliffe, is open to doubt. While the new
record was being celebrated the scores did not tally, and a no-ball
was discovered and added. No doubt Herbert wanted to bury the
argument once and for all, but his almost peremptory order so
alarmed me that I was bowled without addition to the total. I could
feel Herbert's eyes boring into my back as I made my departure.

Oddly, Herbert and I put on another 315, this time at Sheffield off Hampshire, but mercifully Herbert was first out. The scorebook read:

H. Sutcliffe b Heath	116
L. Hutton not out	280
W. Barber not out	91
Extras	6
Total, one wkt, dec	**493**

Herbert was never averse to putting his name to records. During the Leyton saga when Percy made a risky shot, Herbert called down the wicket: 'Percy, do you, or do you not, want to go for this record?'

I did not learn the secret of his immaculate appearance until I went into the Yorkshire dressing room and saw him and other seniors arrive with a flat case in addition to the old-fashioned cricket bag. Unlike me, the custom was not to stuff flannels into a bag but to carry them separately. Flannels and shirts were thus kept spotless and creases remained razor sharp. Those were the days when fielders stayed on their feet and did not fling themselves full length at the ball. In recent years I have seen players leave the field presenting a sight which must have gladdened the hearts of dry cleaners. It would not have appealed to Herbert.

He was an extraordinary man, a great Yorkshireman and patriot, and self-possessed almost to the point of infuriating his opponents. On one occasion when he was hit and refused to stop for repairs, he announced: 'We Sutcliffes do not feel pain.' I owed a lot to his promptings and wisdom and, though our styles were different, it was an enriching and invaluable experience to bat with him. His running and understanding with Jack Hobbs have never been surpassed and, as the junior in our partnership, I naturally and gratefully accepted his judgement. I was never in any doubt that if he called for a run, I would make it comfortably. Herbert and Geoff Boycott would have been an impossible partnership. One or the other would have had to go, and I have a strong suspicion that it would not have been Herbert!

Had Geoffrey played in the thirties, however, I believe his attitude would have been different and he would have been a much better player as a result. With a captain like Brian Sellers, and stiff competition for places, Geoffrey would have been obliged to use the strokes he undoubtedly possesses. He is a fine player, but he bats with the one thought in mind of not getting out. While Bradman, Hammond, Compton and myself, to name but a few, looked for a scoring opportunity as the bowler ran in, Geoffrey is absorbed with the defence of his wicket. Defence is his first thought; attack is his second. Therefore if the ball is hittable, he has to change his mind after the ball has been delivered. Often he is not in a position to be able to change from his original intention to stop the ball to be able to attack. I cannot think of a batsman in his class who has allowed more bad balls to go unpunished.

I can claim, in all truth, that records as such were never my special interest. I was never under a compulsive influence to prove myself a better batsman than the next man. If records came, they came, and that was splendid. As for my Oval innings, it just grew and grew. Contrary to stories I have since heard and seen printed, I did not receive any direct orders from Hammond to go out and stay until 1000 runs were on the board. He did not give me any specific orders for none were needed, and 1000 is such a distant target that it would be said only as a joke. The pitch was perfect, the match was to be played to a finish – therefore time was not important – and no prewar Yorkshireman began a match without a clear purpose in mind. To have started an innings with any idea of specifically going for Bradman's 334 score would have been patently absurd, and it was only when I was 300 at the end of the second day's play that it began to register that the record was within my grasp. Then I had all evening, and some of the small hours, to reflect upon the situation.

At breakfast the newspapers confirmed that Neville Chamberlain, Hitler and the others temporarily had a back seat, and the Opinion column of the *Daily Express* provided a typical example:

The thoughts of millions throughout the Empire centre on Hutton, steadily batting at the Oval. For the third day he stands before the wicket as his score mounts to within reach of the Test record of 334 runs set up by the great Don Bradman in 1930.

Can Hutton do it? The strain on his nerves and body is terrific. He is only 22, slim, almost frail in appearance. He shows no sign of weariness,

so his appearance is no guide to his stamina. In all the great crowd at the
Oval he is the only one showing no excitement. His nerves are good.

In the offices clerks and managers share the interest and excitement, and
in the factories, too, master and man follow Hutton's grand stand.

Already England has put up her highest total, and still Hutton is batting
with astonishing skill. The Yorkshiremen in the crowd talk of 'Yorkshire
grit'. The excitement soars until at last Hutton breaks the record, and
cheers hold up the game. England finds her Bradman.

My main concern was to start again on the third morning without
error, to get a sight of the ball, and not to relax my concentration.
Fortunately I was always blessed with the natural ability to concentrate without conscious effort. I also had to get it into my head that
it was no longer a case of Hutton playing a big innings against the
old enemy but a batsman now carrying the good wishes of his team-
mates, the hopes of 30,000 spectators inside the ground and, to judge
by the incoming mail and telegrams, the prayers of all Yorkshire and
places far beyond. I still cherish the messages, now safely in a box
at home. Over five hundred were delivered to the Oval at the tea
interval after I had broken the record.

I felt I had gone too far by then to let everyone down, and if any
at the time saw me as a committed record-chaser, shameless in my
pursuit of glory, they can take it from me they were widely wrong.
I was only too conscious of my position and it became very
important for me not to let down the dressing room. In those days
the presence of old England players in the dressing room gave a Test
a very special flavour – a happy mixture of nostalgia and geniality.
Throughout my innings I had been wisely and gently encouraged by
Jack Hobbs, among others.

I was grateful to them all, but there was one man I could not fail,
and to whom I owed the kind of debt one can never fully repay:
Hedley Verity. As my innings developed it was obvious that something out of the ordinary was in the offing, and the ever kindly and
wise Verity made it his duty to stay with me during every lunch and
tea break while I nibbled at a sandwich and sipped tea. We both
knew that the most likely way I could lose my wicket was by sheer
fatigue, or by a lapse of concentration causing a careless stroke.
Hedley sat by my side like a faithful ally to make sure that my
thoughts did not wander, and that I concentrated and disciplined
myself as never before. His quiet, natural dignity was an immense

source of strength to me throughout those long hours. Even on the Sunday, the rest day, he slipped me off to Bognor Regis, for a few relaxing hours by the sea and to have lunch with Dr Swain, a real Yorkshire cricket enthusiast. And what did we do after lunch? We played beach cricket.

Years later, when the young batsman who had been steered to a record innings had become captain of England, and MCC were en route to Australia, a small band of pilgrims made their way to the grave of Captain Hedley Verity of the Green Howards. Hedley lies in the military cemetery at Caserta, Italy. The liner *Orsova* had docked in the Bay of Naples under a warm September sun. The Sicilian skies must have been as blue when Hedley was mortally wounded leading an attack in a cornfield on that fatal day in 1943. He died from his wounds in a POW camp. We stood in a respectful line in front of the headstone. There was Bill Bowes, who had heard of the death of his old friend and constant companion while a POW himself from a Canadian airman who had just been shot down ('From what I hear he must have been a great guy'), Bob Appleyard, Johnny Wardle, Abe Waddington, representing an older generation of Yorkshire stalwarts, Bill Edrich and Alec Bedser.

I placed a spray of white roses, held together by a Yorkshire County Cricket Club tie, around the simple stone cross. No words were spoken for there are times when words can be gross intruders into intensely private thoughts. If I had spoken I would have said: 'I loved that man.'

In his unobtrusive way Hedley did much to further my career. I admit I was an unashamed eavesdropper whenever he and Bill Bowes talked cricket for it was like being a privileged pupil attending an advanced seminar. The ranks of deep-thinking cricketers are now too thin for today's youngsters to enjoy a similar privilege.

As I have said, Hammond did not give me any direct orders in the Oval Test, but he quickly made my role clear to me when I jumped out and drove Bill O'Reilly over mid-on when I was 140 or so. Before the ball had reached the boundary Hammond appeared on the players' balcony signalling his orders to cool it. I was not to be permitted any attacking luxuries and, inevitably, the tempo and length of the innings led me to being typecast as a slow and cautious batsman. I never successfully exorcised that particular ghost, though, in passing, I might add that less than a year later, in the first Test at Lord's against the West Indies, Denis Compton and I scored 248 in two hours twenty minutes, and it was reported I outscored Denis!

I have never felt the need to defend my scoring rate at the Oval, or on any other occasion, and I have always thought it faintly absurd for critics to suggest they preferred my innings of 37 in twenty minutes in Sydney in 1946–47 to my 364. Two separate innings cannot be related. To criticize me at the Oval was, in effect, to condemn the conception of playing a Test to a finish, and had I played a brief but exciting innings I would probably have been taken to task. The huge advantage of winning the toss on a pitch that 'Bosser' Martin, the Oval groundsman, had 'built to last to Christmas' might have been thrown away.

England had to win to share the series, and the first priority was an impregnable total. As for Australia's bowling, I smile when I read that they *only* had Bill O'Reilly and Fleetwood-Smith to concern the batsmen. Australia, too, were brilliant in the field, saving scores of runs; once Bradman accepted that I was not going to give it away, he quite properly had an appropriate run-saving field. Bradman often did that to me, especially when he used Ernie Toshack, the left-arm bowler, in between the bouts of fast bowling. I am not complaining. I would have used the same tactics myself.

I had opened with Bill Edrich, who could not master 'Tiger' O'Reilly. He should be forgiven as O'Reilly was a supreme bowler if ever there was one. Even if the conditions were loaded against him, he was still formidable, and even more so when adversity fired his Irish blood. After a few overs I heard him growl to umpire Frank Chester: 'Where's the groundsman's hut? If I had a gun with me I'd shoot him!'

Edrich was inclined to play O'Reilly's action when he was three or four yards from the crease, and accordingly moved fractionally across before the ball was delivered. Consequently he went across the line of the ball, and he did not last long.

O'Reilly is accepted as the greatest of the spin bowlers of his time, but he was sometimes less effective against left-handers. It was an astute move to send in Maurice Leyland at No. 3 at the Oval. I had not seen the batting order when I left the dressing room, and O'Reilly stood in the middle of the pitch, arms akimbo, waiting, like myself, to see who was coming in. Soon the unmistakable thickset figure of Maurice emerged, rather like an old dreadnought steaming to battle. As always, he wore his Yorkshire cap when batting for England.

When O'Reilly recognized Maurice, he exploded: 'Good God, it's that Yorkshire bastard again.' At that moment I knew all was well for England. Some time later, when we had taken the total from 29 to around 200, Maurice confided to me: 'I'll tell you something. I've got O'Reilly taped. And I'll tell you something else – he knows it!'

Australians always brought out the best in Maurice, and at thirty-nine he was as good as he had ever been. From the other end of the wicket his bat seemed to be as broad as his shoulders, and he obviously relished the position and every run he scored. The only way he seemed likely to go was to be run out, and that was how he got out, going for a second after Lindsay Hassett had originally misfielded.

One of the interesting points to me was the careful way the senior batsmen like Leyland, Hammond and Hardstaff played themselves in. When Hardstaff arrived he said: 'These Aussies have had their games with me, and now it's my turn to have a little game with them.'

The closer I crept to Don's 334, the better the Australians bowled and fielded, and I could almost sense the tension in the crowd. My final testing moment came with my score at 331. As I had expected, Bradman responded by crowding me. I had fielders on top of me, and breathing down my neck. Don put himself at silly mid-on, and before each ball from the brilliant but erratic Fleetwood-Smith, I looked at him and he looked at me. A psychological duel which I had to win. Fleetwood-Smith began dropping the ball spot on a length, and I figured that if I could hold out he would eventually send down a loose ball which I could hit to the boundary. As it was, he bowled better than at any time in the match, and twice appealed to Chester for leg before.

The first, as wicketkeeper Ben Barnett sportingly agreed, was snicked onto my pads, and Chester said the second was too high and would have cleared the stumps. To put it mildly, both were unnerving moments, but a long hop came along which I was able to cut for 4. Then Don was pumping my hand and the players, swarming around me, were generous as cricketers always are and should always be. I also heard umpire 'Fanny' Walden say: 'Thank God that's over.' I felt like adding 'Amen' to that. My mother was doing the family washing with a radio by her side in the final moments and I'm told there were proud tears when the crowd broke into 'For He's a Jolly Good Fellow'.

When I was at last out Leyland led me through the Long Room straight to the bar, followed by Verity, Bowes and the ebullient Arthur Wood, who had the time of his cricket life as a late substitute for Leslie Ames, the wicketkeeper. Yorkshire were playing at Scarborough when his call came and he jumped into a taxi intending to go to the station. Instead, he gave the exultant command: 'To the Oval.' On arrival at the England's headquarters he had to borrow from his Yorkshire team-mates to meet the fare! Leyland, who was suspected of setting up the whole affair, offered him fourpence.

Now Maurice ordered two bottles of champagne. 'One for me and one for thee,' he said. The Yorkshire contingent could be forgiven their celebration. Indeed, it had to be a Yorkshire celebration. Back at Pudsey the parish church bells rang a peal of 364, and on the following Sunday that number was the most popular hymn in the services at many Yorkshire churches. The more adventurous members of the choir adapted the first two lines to sing:

> All hail the power of Hutton's name
> Let Aussies prostrate fall.

Between us the Yorkshiremen scored 612 runs, took 10 of the 16 wickets to fall and Wood, who was spraying wisecracks around like verbal confetti, held three catches. Arthur Wood made 53, returned to the pavilion with England's score at 876 for 7 and remarked: 'Just like me getting out in a crisis.' How the pendulum swings. In 1982–83 there was not a single Yorkshire player in England's party to Australia and New Zealand.

I think Bosser Martin took it as a personal slight that England did not go on to make 1000. Hammond might well have done if Don Bradman and Jack Fingleton had not been injured while fielding and were unable to bat. Bosser kept asking if we thought his wicket better than the one at Trent Bridge for the first Test, and Wood teased him by saying he had noticed holes in the wicket when he had batted. 'Yes,' Bosser replied. 'Three at each end where the stumps go in.'

The Oval match changed the pattern of my life in many ways. I found a public reputation can be something of a nuisance both in one's private and professional life. The genuine cricket lovers were little trouble, but the other kind could be a bit hard to take with their inane and persistent questions. I felt I had done a job to the best of my ability and the important fact was that England had won. I am still asked if I really enjoyed batting for over thirteen hours, and I am tempted to quote Hedley Verity's simple maxim: 'If you play for England you have a duty to fulfil.' Hedley's words in this more cynical age might have a platitudinous ring, but that was the way we felt. Ultimately in Hedley's case he gave everything for England. An officer and gentleman fulfilling his duty.

The innings I played at Sydney which appealed to the purists so much ended with the last ball before lunch when I lost my grip on the handle with my weakened left arm and my bat fell onto the stumps after passing over my left shoulder. I had gone in to bat still annoyed by the previous Test at Brisbane where England had been routed on an impossible wicket, and there had been the upset over the Don Bradman catch which had been disallowed. At 117 for 5, and early in his innings, Bradman had, to English eyes, been legitimately caught at second slip by Jack Ikin off Bill Voce. 'What a bloody way to start a series' was Hammond's comment at the end of the over. I was determined to show the Aussies that their bowlers might not be as good as they thought they were. Both the pitch and the conditions were right for a counter-attack, and every shot I attempted came off; not one went in the air or was even uppish. I have since heard that Don was not too worried as he did not believe my innings could last. Yet it took a freakish dismissal to end it, and deep down I suspect the Aussies were relieved at their stroke of luck.

At lunch an elderly gentleman entered the England dressing room, shook my hand and said: 'My name's Charlie Macartney. I would just like to congratulate you on your innings.' With that he turned on his heel and left, before I had time for it to sink in that I had shaken the hand of an immortal batsman. I wished he had stayed to talk.

For parts of my career, and for most of the time when I had a weakened arm and England's post-war batting was fragile and depended on a few, I was belaboured for slow scoring. Often, I thought, unjustly. The critics expected the impossible, and shared a weakness for ignoring excellent bowling, more defensive field placings and my special responsibilities which I felt keenly. If I went on the defensive, it was not through choice for I believed firmly in trying to get on top and not allowing bowlers to dictate. There were times when it was not possible to attack.

That long, long innings at the Oval did have its advantages, however. At the start of the 1939 season I bought my first car, a bullet-nosed Morris, for £125, and on the Sunday of the Middlesex match at Lord's, with my constant companion, Cyril Turner, and two others, I went to Windsor in the hope of seeing George Hirst, then cricket coach at Eton College. I parked the car as near the castle as I could get as we went for lunch. When we returned one of the tallest policemen I have ever seen was standing by the wind-screen with a notebook already in hand.

'Is this your car?' he asked.

'Yes,' I admitted.

'You should know you can't park here,' he said.

As he began to write, Cyril politely asked: 'Officer, I wonder if you could direct us to George Hirst?'

'Do you mean little George, the cricketer?' The pencil stopped writing. 'Yes, of course, it's the second house by the college.'

Cyril then turned towards me and said: 'Do you know who this is – Len Hutton.'

The notebook snapped shut and a big fist was extended in my direction. He asked me for my autograph, had a bit of a chat and we parted company on the best of terms. When we told George of the incident he said: 'Oh, that'll be Lofty. We often have a glass of ale together, and I'll thank him.'

George showed us around the college grounds, the wicket, the dressing rooms, and so on, and said: 'They ought to produce cricket-ers here.' I must say I agreed and felt a touch of envy for boys presented with such opportunities. George loved being with the boys, and when he had gone to the headmaster to confirm the job they had talked cricket for well over an hour. Only after he had left did he realize that no mention had been made of wages!

At the start of that 1939 season George had been at the nets at Headingley when I went for a knock. I had just come back from my first MCC tour to South Africa, and it was less than a year after my score of 364. I had made two other centuries for England off New Zealand and Australia and I was on my way to 10,000 runs in first-class cricket.

While I was batting, a member of the Yorkshire committee went to George and said in all seriousness: 'Look, George, I've been watching this fellow in the nets and I think he's worth a trial in our Second XI.'

George passed the story on to me with a twinkle in his eye: 'Just to let you know, if you didn't know already, what good judges we have on our committee.'

The time was soon to come, however, when I lay in a hospital bed anxiously wondering if I would ever hold a cricket bat in my hands again.

Those long, long days which stretched into long, long weeks within the gravely quiet hospital walls was my private hell, the darkest passage of my life. I had no way of knowing if I had a future as a cricketer. After my wife and family, cricket was my love and had been as long as I could remember. As I lay there with my thoughts, I could not imagine a worse fate to befall me than the accident in an army gymnasium, which left me with a 50 per cent disability pension. I think that should be remembered by those who believe I sold myself short with my technique after the war. That I ever played again at Test level was a miracle of medical science and of the skill and devotion of the surgeons and nurses. I can never thank them enough.

My injury was, of course, a handicap to me. At one stage of my recovery the plaster went on and off no fewer than twelve times, and one of the consequences was that I had a reduced power in my grip. My left arm, which is the guiding arm for a right-hander, was not quick enough to take back for the hook shot which I had used profitably before the war. In the early part of the 1946–47 tour of Australia I tried to hook, but found I lacked the strength and the speed to bring the bat back in time, and accordingly I had to eliminate the shot.

Sir Don Bradman in his *Farewell to Cricket* was good enough to include me in England's leading four batsmen – that is, up to his retirement in 1948–49. The others are Hammond, Hobbs and Compton, and he listed our Test records against Australia up to that date as follows:

	Innings	Not out	Runs	Average
Hammond	58	3	2852	51·8
Hobbs	71	4	3636	54·26
Compton	26	3	1235	53·6
Hutton	21	1	1232	61·6

Bradman's verdict is that Hobbs was technically the best-equipped batsman, without a detectable flaw either in attack or defence. He goes on to write:

In a way I cannot help comparing Hobbs with Hutton. Hutton is certainly the best technician amongst modern players, and his chief fault lies in his lack of aggression. .... I know it has been said that Hutton's arm injury is the reason, but I cannot altogether subscribe to such a viewpoint. Firstly, Hutton had the same failing before his arm was injured, and, secondly, for brief periods since that injury, notably the second Test at Sydney, 1946, I have seen him play the most gloriously aggressive cricket that one could imagine.

I think he is still capable of rising to probably the most superb heights, but believe the constant demands of professional cricket may have taken the edge off his enthusiasm. It is extremely difficult to maintain a light-hearted aggressive spirit of batsmanship for years on end and when playing cricket every day. All the more so when the fierce spotlight demands runs in addition to style. Hutton has no weaknesses. As with Hammond, he does not like being forced to hook, but he can if he wants to. He is more at home to slow than fast bowling, but the difference seems psychological.

I feel distinctly flattered being compared with Sir Jack ('The Master'), especially as Bradman has always weighed carefully his words and opinions. In the matter of techniques and styles a comparison may be in order, but, as we played in different eras, I suggest a comparison of performances is not possible. Even the laws were different, including the highly important LBW change in 1935 (after Sir Jack had retired) and the size of the stumps (1931), not to mention a different quality ball. For all that, I am sure that if Hobbs had played in my era, and I in his, the end result would have been pretty much the same. After all, one of the great features of the genius of Hobbs was that he was able to overcome the challenge of the new swing bowling introduced by George Hirst, the little man who became my second father, and the South African googly bowlers.

Without the passage of time clouding my judgement and without deceiving myself, I believe that by 1939, when Hitler intervened, I had as many shots as Bradman, which is not for one moment to suggest I was as good. He was unique, with the quickest brain and feet I ever saw, and with perhaps the confidence and temperament every cricketer would wish to have. From 1938 to the war I made a lot of runs in Test cricket, including some in South Africa, my first tour, where the wickets were described as preposterously perfect. I did not manage a Test century, but I had five in other first-class matches. I took part in the last Test at Durban which lasted eight days without achieving a result. The eighth was rained off and there were two Sunday rest days. England, having made 654 for 5 towards the 696 needed to win, had to leave to catch the ship home. After that experience I became a convert to Test matches lasting no longer than four days!

Back home in 1939 I was praised for my 'variety of strokes' by Sir Pelham Warner, and, without boasting, I felt I could play them all. By coincidence, I scored five centuries on my second tour of South Africa in 1948–49 and, as in 1939, followed with twelve in the home season. Frankly, I would suggest to Don that it is most unlikely for anyone to score twelve centuries in a season without a measure of aggression. But it is true that I was brought up in a hard Yorkshire school; it was always drummed into me that my job as an opener was to take the shine off the ball and to stay at least until lunch. I was seldom encouraged to play the strokes I knew I could play, and, what's more, wanted to play.

Even after the war the Yorkshire tradition remained; there was scant sympathy for a batsman who had got himself dismissed by a stroke the old hands regarded as too adventurous. No excuses were accepted. I recall two occasions at Lord's where the pitch might be said to have behaved less impeccably than the crowd. There was the off-spinner bowled by Freddie Titmus from the pavilion end that pitched on my leg stump and 'went up the hill' to take my off stump, and a leg break from Jim Sims from the nursery end that landed on the off stump and struck the leg stump. On returning to the dressing room with some expectation of sympathy, I was met on both occasions by a voice demanding: 'Where were your bloody pads?'

I yield to no one in my admiration for the Don, but he had the considerable advantage of playing on pitches he could rely on, especially in his formative years, nor did he open the innings in fragile Test batting sides, a fact to weigh heavily on my shoulders. With customary perception Bradman acknowledges the mental fatigue involved in day-to-day professional cricket. All-the-year-round play becomes hard work; to maintain standards doubly so. Don played the comparatively small number of 338 first-class innings, and was in the fortunate position of being able to be selective in his tours. Indeed, his four tours were all to England. He spared himself much wear and tear, which is not to suggest that had he gone to the West Indies and South Africa he would not have been equally successful.

In contrast, I had 814 innings and, as a professional, I was obliged to accept all the invitations to go overseas, and in the course of eight years I scored 24,000 runs. The lot of the pro was hard. I remember Alec Bedser arriving for a Test in 1953 and asking to be excused net practice as he had bowled over thirty overs the previous day. Two days later I read in one newspaper how much fresher and more alive the Australians appeared as they took the field. Alec Bedser has argued with justification that Sydney Barnes was able to keep going as long as he did partly because he was not constantly engaged in county cricket.

As a generalization, my generation, I feel, played too much first-class cricket and, it is fair to say, it sometimes dulled the edge of our enthusiasm.

It is interesting to speculate what might have happened if the Don had been born English. Would he have been content to play as a pro? And if he had done so, would he had altered his methods? I think he was so exceptional that he would probably have played the same way . . . but for how long!

I soon discovered opinions and values can vary much in cricket. My innings at the Oval was seen through many pairs of eyes. Neville Cardus, though unstinted in his praise, declared I was not a brilliant player, which I took to be a reference to my supposed shortage of strokes. Yet on the same day, Wilfred Rhodes in the *Yorkshire Post* described me as 'a really beautiful stroke player'. Rhodes added that he was one of four on the ground who had seen R. E. Foster set up the previous Test record of 287 at Melbourne in 1903–4. The others were Sir Pelham Warner, Len Braund and Herbert Strudwick. R. E. Foster was no longer alive, but one of the first telegrams I opened was from his mother, then eighty-nine.

I was nevertheless told I could pack my bags for the 1940–41 MCC tour of Australia. It was just as well we could not look too far into the future. But, to press my claim that my war injury and subsequent responsibilities did have their effect, I quote from a South African source after MCC's tour there in 1938–39:

Those who had the opportunity of seeing one of the most delightful stroke players yet to have visited South Africa will look back with pleasant memories on the hours spent watching Hutton, the slightly built hero from Yorkshire.

Free from the watchful eye of selectors and his own crowd, Len Hutton took toll of the bowling whenever he went to the wicket with a feeling of abandon. This 22-year-old player from a county where they usually breed a batsman of a dour kind, with a world record in his pocket, was ever in quest of quick runs, and giving the spectators their money's worth. In fact if it were not for his own, shall I say, immaturity, Hutton would certainly have had many bigger totals to his credit out here.

In the future we are almost certain again to see Hutton on our grounds and then, unless something is done to assist the bowlers, records will go by the board.

In terms of figures I did better after the war than before. The prewar years included my start for Yorkshire, which obviously had periods when I was learning, to my cost! Irving Rosenwater, the noted statistician, provided me with the respective records as follows:

	Innings	Not out	Runs	Highest score	Average	100s
1934–39	271	33	11,658	364	48·98	36
1945–60	543	58	28,482	270*	58·72	93
	814	91	40,140	364	55.51	129

The figures include one first-class game in 1957 in the Old Trafford Centenary match (MCC *v.* Lancashire, scoring 76 and 25), and two in 1960 – 0 for Colonel L. C. Stevens's XI *v.* Cambridge University at Eastbourne; and 89 for MCC *v.* Ireland at Dublin, my final first-class innings.

It is an interesting fact that I never headed the first-class national batting averages, although, in all modesty, I am sure I could have done so if I had made it my prime objective. Such achievements did not unduly concern me, and in this respect I suppose I had a different approach from, say, Geoffrey Boycott.

2

Entering the Holy of Holies

Len Hutton, at the age of ten, if not earlier, was a cricketer, not just technically skilled, but with a firm ambition to play for Pudsey St Lawrence, Yorkshire and England. This aspiration was, if not in-born, built-in, and the wonder was not that the boy had this ambition, but that its absence would have been unthinkable.

A. A. Thompson in *Hutton and Washbrook*

When I was twelve years of age I was standing as close as I dared to Wilfred Rhodes during an evening charity match at Pudsey St Lawrence. Yorkshire were having a sticky time in their current match at Bradford and a spectator remarked that they could lose. 'We won't lose,' promised Wilfred, and they didn't. I never forgot that chance conversation, and it served as my personal philosophy in many a tight corner, particularly when I was captain of England. I always went for a win, but if it became impossible, I tried not to lose, and I never saw anything wrong in that outlook.

Once at Sheffield I had half an hour at the nets with Wilfred Rhodes. The all-too-brief encounter of opposite generations must have been an incongruous sight. Wilfred, a part of cricket history, took off his jacket, folded it carefully and placed it by the side netting. At the wicket, padded and gloved, the new and emerging batting champion — that is, if the pundits were to be believed — awaited with barely concealed expectation. The old man in the braces began to bowl with a classic, effortless and unforgotten rhythm, but after a few deliveries some of the misplaced confidence of youth took hold of me. Was this really the bowling that had captured 4187 wickets, I thought. It seemed easy enough; slow, a long time in the air; surely I would have time to go down the pitch and hit him on the full toss. True to the textbook, I duly advanced with eyes unwaveringly on the ball, head still and with my footwork precise and balanced. But, to my surprise, I could not get far enough, and I realized the ball was arriving at a different speed from the action indicated by the arm. So I altered my tactics to stay back and cut and pull. I was still obliged to go forward. The lesson I learned was that the truly great spinners drag the batsman forward. With Rhodes the ball was never there when you arrived. A God-given talent of arc and flight sparingly bestowed.

I was interested to hear Patsy Hendren say that Hedley Verity gave him more trouble than Rhodes, but they were different types, with Verity much faster than the orthodox left-arm spinner.

Clarrie Grimmett also bowled to me in his braces at Perth, and I was left to wonder at his masterly control of direction and length. He pitched leg and middle ball after ball, and told me that against the top batsmen like Hobbs, Sutcliffe and Hammond he concentrated on accuracy rather than spin. He and Bill O'Reilly must have been a marvellous partnership of guile, patience and Bill's drop of aggression.

I also had the experience of facing Sydney Barnes when I was in the Yorkshire Second XI and he was still playing for Staffordshire in his late fifties. I made enough runs to understand why many will have it that he was the greatest bowler of all time. Even then he cut and swung the ball and used the crease brilliantly. Before he stripped to play, he used so many bandages and elastic supports that he might have been a mobile Egyptian mummy, and when he retired in 1934, at the age of sixty-one, his wickets still cost only 11 runs apiece.

By all accounts Barnes had a fiery temperament and believed in his ability – and why not? After Jim Laker had taken all 10 in the 1956 Test with Australia, Sir Don Bradman and Alex Bannister, having done their pieces for the *Daily Mail*, saw Barnes in the Old Trafford car park.

'Well, what do you think of that?' they asked.

'No booger ever got all 10 when I was at th' other end' was the swift reply.

Cricket played an immensely important part in the lives of the communities in which I was raised. I saw my first county match between Yorkshire and Nottinghamshire at Bradford in 1927, and

I understood that George Gunn was something special as he took a beautiful half-century off Abe Waddington (who travelled around Australia with the team when we won the Ashes in 1954–55), Emmott Robinson and Wilfred Rhodes.

We were brought up to regard the local titans – from 'Long John' Tunnecliffe, a Britannia man and a staunch Methodist, to Herbert Sutcliffe – with the reverence that a pious Roman Catholic family has for the Pope. If I dreamed of playing for Pudsey St Lawrence, Yorkshire and England – though not necessarily in that order – it was a dream shared with every boy in Yorkshire old enough to hold a bat. I was never all that confident, but there were considerable advantages in being the youngest of a cricketing family living as near to the heartbeat of Yorkshire as Pudsey. I took to the game as naturally as a Sherpa to the mountains. The soul and passion of cricket must have been inside me, and in my young days with Yorkshire I loathed stumps being drawn at the close of play. I could not wait until the resumption of play the next morning. Sundays I could not abide. Alas, time took its toll and the enthusiasm died with the sheer drudgery of nonstop play and the constant pain in my arm, legs and wrist.

Many of the most blissful hours of my life were spent with Pudsey St Lawrence Second XI, going in at No. 8, with a bat too big for me. My tender young ears became attuned to the surprised remark as I went in to bat: 'What's this young booger doing 'ere?' After two seasons I was promoted to the first team. Fourteen years of age, and barely out of short pants. Though I had taken part in a little Sunday School League cricket, almost all of my boyhood was spent with older men. Thus, from the start it could be said that I had an adult approach to the game. At one stage my brothers, Edmond, an aggressive left-hander, George, one of my original opening partners, and Reginald were all in the same side. George was a tidy performer, and on one occasion during the first war when a number of county players were available he was the only local to hold his place.

I once made a speech in Yorkshire in which I said I had never feared Lindwall and Miller as much as I had feared Bill Hudson, the fast-bowling terror of the Pudsey of my schooldays. There was a grain of truth in it. I was never frightened of fast bowling as such, and I was only knocked out once when I completely lost sight of the ball at Johannesburg during MCC's 1938–39 tour. I woke up in hospital with no serious after-effects to learn that the ball had rolled onto my wicket! It goes without saying that I had a deep admiration for Lindwall and Miller, and my respect for Bill Hudson was that of a boy facing a giant of a 6-foot 3-inch, 16-stone 10-pound coal merchant able to hurl a cricket ball at him on a dangerous practice wicket. Standing up to Bill was a very useful start in conquering any dread of fast bowling.

My words prompted Derrick Boothroyd, a feature writer on the *Yorkshire Post*, to seek out Bill; the result was a delightful, if a little fanciful, vignette of Pudsey cricket life in his book *Nowt so Queer as Folk*.

'He were t'only one I could bowl to,' ruminated Bill. 'T'others wouldn't stand up to me – not even t'big 'uns. Mind you, I could chuck 'em down a bit in them days. I could throw the ball across the St Lawrence ground and twenty-four yards into the next field. And I'm not saying I couldn't lay 'em out. There were often a couple lying dead in t'pavilion when I'd been on.'

'And yet young Hutton stood up to you?'

'Aye, he did. And, think on, he were nobbut a lad of thirteen. A wonder, he was. He would hook ball into t'tennis ground off his chin. T'gardener would come next morning with half a dozen of 'em.'

'How did it all start?'

'Well, it were this way. Leonard was only a schoolboy and the first and second team players, including his brothers, considered him a damned nuisance. They used to let him field for 'em but Leonard wasn't satisfied with that. He were no darned good at fielding anyway. "Can't I have a bat?" he was always moaning. "No tha can't," they'd tell him. "We've got to get in our practice for Saturday."

'I reckon I took pity on him. Or maybe I wanted somebody to bowl at. I got old George – our groundsman until he was ninety – to put a special net up where I could bowl to him on his own. And when he'd finished I'd buy him a fish and a pennorth because he was never afraid of owt. Mind you, I did used to try and bowl on the off.'

'And then I suppose he got into the team?'

'Aye. It was about 1930. I had a bull-nosed Morris Cowley and because we were one short against East Bierley I went off to fetch him and he got 36. A good innings. But the best he ever played was his 115 against Bradford in the Priestley Cup. Far better than his 364 against Australia.'

There was also my highly unusual partnership with Edgar ('Little Ark') Oldroyd, who had just returned after yeoman service for

Yorkshire. There was a widely held belief that he was the best No. 3 never to have played for England. The mayor of Pudsey persuaded him to join St Lawrence as pro, but from the tales of the times he was none to keen to go in first with a 'slip of a lad'. But the mayor insisted: 'Slip of a lad or not, it's still t'Bradford League.' Edgar's defence on awkward pitches was notorious, and no doubt some of his technical expertise rubbed off on me. We must have presented a bizarre sight. The old pro with thirty-eight centuries for Yorkshire, and the shy fourteen-year-old who couldn't believe he was all that was being said about him.

If I had suffered from conceit, it would have been rapidly knocked out of me. There was little danger of a boy getting above his station in those days. Family life was the bedrock of society, and I had the best of backgrounds. Fulneck, where I was born, is a village on the southern slope of Pudsey, and was founded as a Moravian Protestant sect in the eighteenth century by a Count Zinzendorf, a wealthy foreigner, after a journey through the West Riding. All the property and schools are owned by the church, and my grandfather, a master builder, put up most of the buildings at the turn of the century, including the Pudsey Trinity Methodist church, and the house where I was born. Before moving south to Kingston, Surrey, for business reasons, I lived in a house which he built in 1875. Through him I have inherited an interest in buildings.

My two maiden aunts were schoolteachers and organized Gilbert and Sullivan shows for church funds and other charities. Gilbert and Sullivan became part of my boyhood, and I remained closely connected with village affairs until cricket became all-demanding. Despite my father's prowess, I think my cricket came from my grandmother's side of the family. Her brother, Seth Milner, took part in a number of notorious money matches that were a feature of the decade 1860–70.

Our family followed various trades, and they insisted that I tackled every job I undertook thoroughly and to the best of my ability – a sound precept for later life.

Regrettably, much of the interest and local rivalries have declined. The family car has undermined cricket to a large extent in the small towns and villages, and that goes some way to explain the wasting strength of Yorkshire. The rivalry between Pudsey St Lawrence and Pudsey Britannia stimulated enormous interest, as did the matches between the colliery teams. Every pit had its cricket team, and the players had a real standing in the community. Now there are few colliery teams, and some of the village clubs have disappeared. The internal combustion engine has changed the entire social fabric. Once upon a time the local cricket ground was the centre of relaxation, a place to go to, to pass the time pleasantly with friends, and it was not hard on the pocket. The 'goggle box' and the car have largely replaced the old cricket clubs as the symbols of relaxation.

For all the intense rivalries of the thirties, I think Australia's system led to an even sharper competitive edge, and their cricket was more purposefully organized. Bradman's ability remains beyond argument and comparison, but one basic difference between him and an English batsman like myself was that he was not satisfied with a century, or even a double-century. Six of his innings were over 300, thirty-seven over 200. While a century to him was but a landmark in an innings, I had to push myself hard to go beyond a century. When I first visited Australia I began to feel that Roses battles, fiercely competitive though they were, had nothing on matches between New South Wales and Victoria. Anything Victoria could do NSW could do better and vice versa. If Ponsford made a huge score, Don would cap it. The Sheffield Shield fixtures over four days were also geared to heavier scoring than the three-day English championship games. With Australia's ever increasing commercialization and emphasis on one-day cricket, the pattern is certain to change and it is possible they will face the same problems which have beset England in the last decade or so.

Yorkshire and Australia always had a healthy respect for each other. The county fixture was often described as the 'sixth' Test and the epic stories of bygone battles from the lips of Rhodes, Hirst, Sutcliffe and Co. stirred my imagination. As a sixteen-year-old, I followed Douglas Jardine's bodyline series with passionate interest. I could scarcely wait for the early edition of the *Yorkshire Post* to arrive with the long accounts of the Tests, and when Bill Bowes bowled Bradman for a duck at Melbourne in 1932–33 I was a-glow with delight until Christmas.

Facing Bill Bowes and Hedley Verity in the Winter Shed was my first big moment. Both became my staunch friends and I always insist that the two most intelligent fast bowlers of my time were Bowes and Ray Lindwall. To them fast bowling was an art form.

Harold Larwood, like Lindwall, had a glorious approach – like lethal poetry – to the wicket, and the day came when I played against Larwood. I was bowling my leg breaks when he came in to bat and he immediately gave a slip catch. As he passed me on his way back to the pavilion he stared at me without a trace of a smile and barked: 'I'll get you for that!' The words were spoken in such cold earnest they scared the living wits out of me. I was clearly meant to take the threat seriously and, sure enough, having struck his psychological blow, he bowled me for a duck, though, by then, he was on a short run.

In a later match I opened against Larwood and his old partner Bill Voce and I admitted to no small feeling of trepidation, particularly as no love was lost between Yorkshire and Nottinghamshire. To judge by their hostility with the new ball, Larwood and Voce were not unwilling subscribers to that mutual feeling. Voce gave me such a smack on my leg that I still wince at the memory. At their peak they must have been an awesome pair to deal with.

Senior players, I soon discovered, could be intimidating. Yorkshire went to Bristol when I was chasing 1000 runs before the end of May, and the first person I met on the ground was Tom Goddard, the off-spin bowler who was a rare handful on any wicket to give him the slightest help. Without wasting a word he declared flatly: 'Don't think you're going to get your 1000 on this wicket.' Tom, who turned the ball square at Bristol, was all too right.

In my Yorkshire Second XI days I was astonished to find that few of the team wanted to play in the championship side though many of the players would have comfortably held a place with most counties. The reason was George Macaulay, whose reputation as an off-spinner was matched by his caustic wit. In 1934 Test calls left vacancies and I was promoted. My delight was tempered by a dread of running foul of the fearsome Macaulay, but, acting on the advice of George Hirst to 'speak of people as you find them', I got on famously with him. His rapier-style wit appealed to me, but I had two close shaves.

As the junior member of the team playing at Southend I was given the job of collecting the baggage at the hotel and taking it to the station. Yorkshire were well beaten by Ken Farnes's bowling and, with time to spare, I duly went to the hotel, took the suitcases stacked in the foyer and put them in the guard's van. To my horror I saw Macaulay stalking down the platform carrying his bag and clearly looking for the offender who had left his case behind. Just as I was wondering how I could make my escape, I saw him upbraiding another player who, of course, was entirely blameless. By the time Macaulay found out his mistake he had simmered down, and I breathed again.

Cyril Turner and I were fielding at short leg to Macaulay at Lord's when 'Patsy' Hendren was batting. A simple catch was snicked between us. Cyril left it to me, and I left it to Cyril, and the ball dropped gently to the ground. The perfect misunderstanding. There was an ominous hush, and I was prepared for the worst. But instead of the expected fireworks, George looked at us, and roared: 'I'll get you two put in Madame Tussaud's!'

Arthur ('Ticker') Mitchell was famous in Yorkshire's ranks as a high-quality batsman, a superb close-to-the-wicket catcher and for a career-long record of never having uttered a word of praise to friend or foe alike. Even when a blinding catch was taken off his bowling he growled: 'Gerrup, you're making an exhibition of thiself.' To the detached outsider such remarks are funny, but to me he was something of an anti-hero. Mitchell's son was mischievously asked if he thought his father would have indulged in the modern practice of hugging and kissing after the fall of a wicket. 'He didn't even kiss my mother' was the reply.

In my early county days I was never allowed to field near the wicket, and I had an exceptionally exhausting day one hot August at the Oval. Before the boundary was brought in, the Oval was a vast expanse and the out-fielder had a hard time. All-run 5s were common at the Vauxhall end where there were a lot of bare patches left by the practice nets. In a dry spell the ground seemed as hard as a rock with areas as rough as a soccer goalmouth.

Surrey batted all day, and I ran, chased and made long returns to the wicket until my arm ached from shoulderblade to wrist. I was sweat-saturated, physically spent and satisfied that I had earned my pay. As I slumped on a bench to take off my boots and socks, Mitchell called me to show him one of my boots. Looking at the sole, he said sarcastically: 'What were wrong wi' thee today? Had tha got six inch nails in thi boots?'

After that I gave him a wide berth in the dressing room. He was too hard for me. Later I found myself standing next to him in the slips. For a time he did not deign to notice my presence and then I heard him say: 'What are you doing here? It took me ten years to get here . . . I don't know what this bluddy game is coming to!' I was eighteen at the time.

In my first Roses match I was batting with Mitchell at Old Trafford and, before I had got off the mark, I tried a square cut which
I missed by about an eighth of an inch. 'That's nae bluddy good,'
he shouted down the pitch. As the square cut was one of the few
shots I possessed at the time, I wondered whatever I was going to
do!

Another side to Mitchell was shown when Yorkshire visited
Oxford and Cambridge in early-season matches. Regrettably the
fixtures have gone by the board. A sad mistake. After play on the
delightful grounds – and a spring morning in the Parks or at Fenners
is a sheer delight – we would be invited to the various colleges, the
Hawks Club in Cambridge and Vincent's Club in Oxford. It was
stimulating merely to sit back and listen to the high-quality
conversation.

Mitchell, in an expansive mood, picked up a poker and proceeded
to demonstrate ways of coping with the new LBW law introduced
that season. If the students were as attentive at their lectures as they
were to the wise advice of the old Yorkshire pro, they must have
left university with good degrees. Having satisfied the eager theorists,
he told a story against himself which might explain why he could
be severe on newcomers to the county side. Yorkshire were at
Southampton and Wilfred Rhodes had bowled almost nonstop from
one end. By 6.15, fifteen minutes from the close of play, he had not
conceded a single boundary. Suddenly Lord Tennyson drove Wilfred
hard to cover where Mitchell let it go through his legs for 4. Wilfred
did not speak to Mitchell for two weeks!

My first day in the holy of holies (normally described as the
Yorkshire dressing room) was as twelfth man at Leicester. To share
the same space and be within the same walls as Sutcliffe, Bowes,
Verity, Mitchell and the rest was the thrill of my young life. My
eyes swept the room in disbelief that I was there. Almost to a man
they had played for England, at home and abroad. My eyes boggled
at the size of the pads they used. Sutcliffe even had three bats in his
bag. Had I been ordered to walk barefoot on broken glass I would
have instantly obeyed.

Imagine my astonishment when, during a stoppage for rain, a
character with a long scar down one side of his face and wearing a
cloth cap jauntily on the side of his head walked in with the familiar
air of meeting old friends.

'Show Len your card trick, Cookey' were the words which served as my introduction to this unlikely looking visitor. Whereupon I was initiated into the mysteries of the three-card trick, or Find the Lady. I was mesmerized, and I was soon to discover the reason why Cookey, who worked the trains and race tracks, had an ever open door to the Yorkshire dressing room.

On a previous visit to Leicester, Sir William Worsley, a former captain, and father of the Duchess of Kent, had his gold watch stolen. Alec Skelding, a Leicestershire fast bowler, poetry-writing umpire and a man of just renown, volunteered his assistance with the promise that his subtle local knowledge might be of value. 'I think I might know someone in a position to recover the missing watch,' he promised. The next day Cookey, who obviously enjoyed a range of contacts even beyond the command of Sir William, duly appeared at the ground with the said watch.

Cookey's reward was to be made an honorary, if unofficial, member of the dressing room, a privilege which many distinguished citizens in many walks of life in the north would have greatly coveted.

One evening after play, a group of players, accompanied by Cookey, were strolling back to the Stag and Pheasant where they were staying, when Arthur Mitchell, a dog lover, saw a woman walking an obvious pedigree. 'By heck, that's a beautiful dog,' he remarked. 'I wish I had him.'

'Would you really like him?' asked Cookey.

Without thinking of the possible consequences, Arthur said: 'Yes.'

Two hours later Cookey walked triumphantly into the hotel with the dog under his arm and presented it to an embarrassed Mitchell. And, believe me, Mitchell was seldom embarrassed. He spent the next two hours persuading Cookey to return the dog to its rightful owner.

Such lighthearted incidents, it has to be said, were far from typical of the discipline and thought that went into Yorkshire's cricket. Yorkshire were often champions because they were simply the best team, but, as in any field, a lot of hard work went into their success. There were exacting standards to strive for and maintain, and woe betide a younger player stepping out of line. The wisdom of Hirst and Rhodes and others had percolated down the generations almost as holy writ, commandments had to be obeyed and never questioned. I admit, however, some of the coaching and instruction was a little too much for me and affected my game.

At eighteen, one could hardly be expected to be able to sort out the difference between good and bad advice. All, I knew, was well intentioned, and I was a ready listener. In due course I came to understand that some of the advice was bad advice, and eventually that the best of all came from Brian Sellers, the captain. Sellers had a reputation for straight talking and his directness could burn the skin off the sensitive.

Yorkshire were at Worcester and I had reached the point when I was in desperate need of a morale-boosting innings. Sellers told me to go in and play my own game. I took him at his word, found my confidence in a long opening stand with Wilf Barber, and almost turned my maiden first-class century into a double. First in and last out, I made 196. Yorkshire's response was to rest me for the next half a dozen matches!

Confused though I might have been for a time, never a day went by without my learning something, and it was a mind-broadening exercise merely to listen to the senior players. Their knowledge of the game was profound, and I firmly believe it helped to have the captain change in a different room. I realize this opinion might be ridiculed in these days, but the separation gave the pros the freedom to talk and discuss tactics and players without hindrance. I am far from suggesting all the discussions implied criticism of the captain. On the contrary. But if the captain had been present, those views would have been bottled up or, if aired, provoked bad feeling. I do not think any real advantage is gained by the captain sharing the same room, any more than by a managing director sharing the same office. There is a lot to be said for the captain standing his distance from his team. It is not a question of snobbery, class divisions or any of that contentious area of debate, but merely commonsense. Unless a side is disciplined, it gets nowhere, and when I became captain of England I had to try to find a formula to compromise between the old and new styles. I knew I could not follow the old captains like 'Gubby' Allen, Douglas Jardine, Brian Sellers, Bev Lyon and Co., but I wanted to emulate the best of their methods. I had seen for myself the value of authority, and I tried to blend the old and new approaches. Whether I succeeded or not is for others to judge, but I will say one thing: a Test captain can have an unenviable task, and I reckon my West Indies adventure in 1953–54 sliced two years off my career. Later in 1954 Douglas Jardine sent me a cable of good wishes before the Brisbane Test and added: 'Your task is harder than mine was.' He understood what I was up against.

No one could have been more encouraging than Jardine. During the tour he wrote letters of support to me. They were especially important as I felt I had a kindred spirit at my side. He was able to appreciate my purpose, my ambition to win for England and the pressures on all sides. I looked upon him as a true friend and I always had a suspicion that there was an element at Lord's afraid that I planned to 'do a Jardine' with my fast bowlers in Australia. Nothing was farther from my thoughts.

At Yorkshire I felt in the course of time that I belonged to a fraternity sharing a special relationship. I was never more conscious of my privilege one dark day in Pindersfield Hospital, near Wakefield, when my future career hung in the balance.

I was still in bed after bone grafts from both legs to my broken arm. Sister told me I had a visitor and into the ward walked the tall, unmistakable, distinguished figure of Sir Stanley Jackson. Sir Stanley, with his proud record of service for state and cricket, was then seventy-two, and it could not have been easy for him to have made the round trip of 364 miles – a figure I can always remember! – by rail from London in the middle of the war.

It was hard for me to take in that the legendary 'Jackers' had come all that way to swop cricket yarns by my bedside. In his time he had been captain of Cambridge, Yorkshire and England, chairman of selectors and the scorer of a record five centuries in home Tests with Australia. As Governor of Bengal he had survived an assassination attempt and was a Member of Parliament from 1915 to 1926.

Early in his cricket career he came back from South Africa and promised to play at the Scarborough Festival. The town was plastered with posters announcing:

Gentlemen of England v. Players
Mr F. S. Jackson Will Certainly Play

The crowds flocked to see him hit a brilliant 134 in the first innings, and an equally impressive 42 in the second on a rain-damaged pitch.

His one regret, he told me, was not having a chance to tour Australia, but he had an exhaustive fund of stories about the fast bowlers he had met in home Tests. The names rang of history, ranging back to Frederick ('The Demon') Spofforth, born in Sydney of Yorkshire stock, through to Ernest Jones, who bowled the famous ball through W. G. Grace's beard ('Sorry, Doc, she slipped'), and Jack Gregory.

Spofforth, to quote his own words, 'developed the habit of bowling at all paces with an identical action' – an art perfected by Ray Lindwall. To my mind there is nothing more troublesome to the batsman than cleverly disguised pace variations.

Sir Stanley, with painful memories of two broken ribs when batting against him, nominated Jones as the fastest bowler he had ever seen. I wonder if he could have been faster than Frank Tyson for three Tests in 1954–55? I doubt it. There was some question of the legality of Jones's action, and in his native Adelaide he was no-balled for throwing. In one match in that fair city the wicketkeeper could not hold him and conceded 48 byes. The exasperated captain put himself as long stop and was knocked out trying to stop more byes.

If anyone should talk in disparaging terms to me of the old-style autocrats of cricket, I know one who did a lot for one depressed young cricketer with a single thoughtful gesture.

3

Aussie Bouncers – The Full Treatment

Ray Lindwall, Keith Miller and Bill Johnston, thoroughbreds all, fused their differing talents and characters into the most formidable bowling combination it was my lot to face and almost a generation of shell-shocked England batsmen can testify to their skill and belligerence. If I ever had the luxury of picking a side to face the proverbial Martian XI no time would be lost in naming Miller as my first choice. There was no department in the game in which he did not excel and leave the imprint of his exciting personality.

The author

First-class cricket would have ended in 1939 for me, had it not been for the skill, kindness and wonderful attention which I received from Mr R. Broomhead, the orthopaedic surgeon at Leeds, who treated me after my accident in an army gymnasium on 14 March 1941. I had been attempting a 'fly spring' when the mat slipped under me; my left arm was broken with complications and the ulna at the base of my left wrist was dislocated.

During the summer of 1941, after an operation on my left forearm known as open reduction, I returned to active service having spent approximately eight weeks in hospital. One day my commanding officer sent for me and explained that he had received a request for me to play in a Red Cross charity match at Sheffield. It was during this game that I first met Reg Simpson, who was to play many fine innings for Nottinghamshire and England years later. I made a century in the match, little realizing that it would be two years before I touched a cricket bat again.

Later that day I returned to barracks to spend a long, sleepless night with considerable pain in my arm. I reported sick the following

An early innings on Blackpool's sands at the age of eight. The bat may be too big and the cap set at a jaunty angle, but it is an interesting fact that I used the same grip throughout my career

One of my supreme moments. From the players' balcony at the Oval, I look down at a sea of happy faces celebrating the return of the Ashes after nineteen years. The Oval was always one of my happiest grounds

Where it all began. Pudsey St Lawrence ground, where as a schoolboy
I opened with the old Yorkshire pro Edgar Oldroyd and spent
many of my most cherished hours

And thirty years on when the eighteen players of the 1953
Ashes-winning series gathered for a dinner laid on by NatWest
during the World Cup won by India. How we talked our heads off!
Back row (left to right): Don Kenyon, Willie Watson, Fred Trueman,
Peter May, Roy Tattersall, Frank Tyson, Tony Lock, Reg Simpson,
Jim Laker, Tom Graveney, Brian Statham. Sitting: Godfrey Evans,
Bill Edrich, Freddie Brown, myself, Denis Compton, Alec Bedser,
Trevor Bailey

day, and later it was discovered that my arm had not healed. There followed two bone grafts and long periods in hospital. For two and a half years I was under Mr Broomhead's care, and I am convinced that, but for him, my first-class career would never have continued after the war.

When I resumed playing my left arm was almost two inches shorter than the right and never again was I to bat without some discomfort from my disablement. My wrist used to swell and the bone grafts from both legs to my arm often led to sore shins, particularly on the hard grounds overseas. It was a miracle that I was able to play first-class cricket again, knowing full well that a blow to the left forearm could put me out of business for good.

I had a grim time in Australia in 1946–47. Bouncers were ten a penny from Lindwall and Miller, and one or two other bowlers also liked to dish out the rough stuff. Just before the fourth Test in Adelaide in 1947, a retired test cricketer said to me: 'Len, they're trying to put you in hospital.' I knew full well what they were trying to do but managed to keep intact until the New South Wales game in Sydney just before the final Test. Ginty Lush, the NSW quick bowler, succeeded in putting me into the local hospital, but not for very long. However, it all came right in the end; I received no serious blows.

Over the years I have met many people in many countries. One lady whom I would like to meet again was the sister at the Military Hospital in York where I was taken after my initial accident. I was in considerable pain and she immediately gave me a large brandy. This was the best and most welcome drink in my life. It would be nice just to thank her again for her kindness which I have never forgotten.

The Victory series of 1945 against a side from the Royal Australian Air Force provided me with the confidence-boosting therapy every doctor would have prescribed. An average of 40 banished any lingering suspicions about my injured arm. The misery of those two bone-grafting operations, of eighteen months in hospital, and of my arm not being strong enough to hold my first-born son, Richard, was behind me. I played all the cricket I could get, including a return on Saturdays for Pudsey St Lawrence, which I captained in the second season. I linked up with Cyril Washbrook as an opening partner for the first time, and I was introduced to the many-sided talents of a Mosquito pilot – Keith Ross Miller.

Before the war and until he joined the RAAF in 1941, Miller was a fast-rising batting star for Victoria, and his development as a fast bowler during his service in England was noted with welcome surprise by the Australians. Not that they ought to have been too surprised as Miller, like Ray Lindwall, was a natural athlete and games player. There was one ball Miller bowled to Wally Hammond which left an uneasy suspicion with all the England Test players present that here was an adversary of the future to be reckoned with. The ball was just short of a length, too full to hook, and it whistled by Hammond's head. As a batsman, Miller averaged 60 in the series, and in another game for the Dominions – how dated that now sounds – he hit 185, including 124 in ninety minutes, and showed a partiality for driving into the upper tiers of the Lord's pavilion.

I always prided myself, given time, that I could work out methods to play most bowlers, but Miller was an exception, partly because half the time he himself did not know what he intended to do. He played instinctively, to enjoy himself, and he bowled according to his mood. Many's the time he would turn halfway to his mark and run in from a few strides without losing pace, but considerably disconcerting the batsman. You could never be sure what he was going to bowl – anything from a bouncer to a googly. At Sydney he once defeated me with a 'loosener' before taking the new ball, casually running in and producing a wicked back break, and I always believed there was a lot more to him than he allowed the public to see.

I am sure I speak for the majority of English players when I say they saw Miller as the natural successor to Lindsay Hassett as Australia's captain. Despite all the amusing stories about him – such as telling his fielders to 'scatter' or taking twelve players onto the field because he had forgotten to nominate his twelfth man – Miller was tactically as shrewd as any of the state captains I met in 1954–55 when he led New South Wales.

Miller and Bradman, distinct opposites in many ways, had an altercation on the field at Lord's in 1948 when Miller refused the new ball at the start of England's second innings. I was at the wicket and did not hear what was said, and I was surprised to be facing Johnston and not Miller. The story was that Miller was unfit and if it was his back, which was suspect after a pancake landing on an airfield near Kiel, Germany, he had my total sympathy for arthritis painfully ended my own career. Miller was pointedly omitted from Australia's next tour, to South Africa, but he was later big enough to go as a replacement.

It is easy to dismiss Miller as a playboy, and he was known to arrive at Lord's still wearing his dinner jacket. He once slipped off to Newmarket while the Aussies were playing Cambridge and returned to see Hassett leading his team onto the field. He was on the best of terms with everyone, from jockeys to the Mountbattens, and it was bad news if word went round the dressing room that Keith had been on the social round the night before. His cure for a hangover was to bowl flat out. But there was a very serious side to Keith, reflected in his love of classical music and his warm and generous personality; he was all too often in deadly earnest on the field. I often speculate what heights he might have achieved had he devoted himself entirely to bowling – every now and then he threw all his enthusiasm into his batting, for he once told me he preferred batting and batsmen were remembered before bowlers. I wonder, too, what they would have made of him in the prewar Yorkshire dressing room, or what he would have made of Macaulay and Mitchell!

The worst mistake a batsman could make against him was to hit him for 4. He accepted 1s, 2s and 3s, but boundaries were an indignity he did not cheerfully tolerate, and invariably the next ball would be an absolute fizzer. At Trent Bridge in 1948, he was trundling away with medium-pace off-breaks when I took two successive boundaries and 14 in the over. That was too much for Keith, but what else can a batsman do with the gift of half-volleys? I knew what to expect, and in eight balls I had five bouncers, one of which left the manufacturer's imprint on my left shoulder. Two others leaped at my throat just short of a length as if they had been bowled from no more than ten yards away with a tennis ball.

Generally, once I had a sight of the ball I did not fear being hit, but Miller was the exception. I never felt physically safe against him. Indeed, he was the only bowler I thought capable of getting me out with any of his various types of delivery. In Australia in 1954–55 when England threw off the depression of the Brisbane disaster, Miller was my secret dread. If there was one Australian bowler capable of rising to the challenge of Tyson and Statham and dashing my hopes, it was he. And he came within a touch of doing it. At Melbourne in the third Test he put everything into his bowling for ninety minutes before lunch though he wasn't fully fit, and he was thwarted only by Colin Cowdrey's youthful genius and nerve. At Adelaide, when England wanted a mere 94 to retain the Ashes, he scared me half to death with an unbelievable spell and a blinding catch. On a docile pitch he moved the ball around as if it were an English greentop.

Lindwall was a serious, thoughtful and supremely talented bowler, who did not need the type of challenge to bring out his best as sometimes was the case with Miller. Of the fraternity of fast bowlers able to bowl a bouncer, I would put Lindwall and Bowes apart as deep thinkers, paying the closest attention to detail, with the ability to probe and detect faults in the opposing batsmen. I was left in no doubt of what I was up against after my first meeting with Lindwall before the 1946–47 series began – not for showing me what he could do, but in the canny way he held himself back. I had been warned he had the deadliest bouncer in cricket but he did not show it until it suited him. Nor was I allowed a sight of his slower ball, the best of its type I ever encountered; Lindwall's tactic was to keep plugging away, hiding all his secrets and avoiding all temptation to gain a quick psychological advantage. He knew how to bide his time.

The genius of Lindwall was expressed in a variety of ways, not least in his cleverly disguised and devastating pace changes and in a bouncer delivered without any giveaways. Even Miller and the West Indian Wes Hall would telegraph their intentions in their run-up to bowl a bumper. Sir 'Plum' Warner once talked to me about Lindwall's 'shades of pace', an apt description. They were more than difficult to detect, and I cannot visualize any fast bowler improving on that area of Lindwall's craft. As would be expected, Lindwall made the maximum use of a new ball, making certain that his direction was right, pitching a full length to gain maximum use of the swing and forcing the batsman to offer a stroke. A high back-lift meant vulnerability to the well-pitched-up ball on the leg stump, and left-handers gave him no extra trouble as he was able to bring the ball back into them. Both Lindwall and Larwood had shoulders as broad as the bowmen of England and beautiful rhythmic runs to the wicket. When I saw Lindwall approaching I sensed the expectancy. A hush would descend on the ground and it was wonderful how the mind was concentrated.

By purists' standards his arm was low, a fact which, I think, helped him to move the ball away from the right-hander. No batsman could ever rest at ease and tell himself: 'I've got him!' He was particularly adept at laying traps for the unwary by bowling a few innocuous ones (by his standards), as if conceding second best, and just when the batsman was about to congratulate himself and visualize a big score, Lindwall, without apparent change of action, would produce one of his lightning specials. He had the capacity to strike at will.

I played in five series, three in Australia and two in England, against Lindwall and Miller, and possibly I took more stick from them than from any other of my contemporaries in any of the international sides, but I cannot recall a harsh or heated word being exchanged between us. They were hard, mighty hard, but they were totally fair and never tried to umpire me out. If a mistake was made they were genuinely upset and I cannot but compare their behaviour and attitudes — and those of Tyson, Statham and Bedser for that matter — with the boorish histrionics of the macho-type fast bowlers of the eighties. The same compliment can be passed to Johnston, their brilliant support. Lindwall and I seldom spoke to each other on the field as we were probably too engrossed in our tasks, and maybe we were not the chatting type. Once Lindwall drove me the fifteen minutes from the Sydney ground to the city centre and barely a word was spoken. A stranger might have been excused for thinking we were not on good terms, but that was far from the case. Since our playing days, we have extended our rivalry to the golf course if our paths meet, and we talk our heads off about old times!

Lindwall, Miller and Johnston, thoroughbreds all, fused their differing talents and characters into the most formidable combination it was my lot to face and almost a generation of shell-shocked England batsmen can testify to their skill and belligerence. The runs I made against them really counted, and my abilities and experience were stretched to the limit. I would look at Bradman conferring with Lindwall, Miller or Big Bill and wonder what they were hatching up, and I resolved if ever I became captain I would endeavour to implant the same curious doubts in the minds of my opponents. But when I attempted a similar psychological dodge I was accused of deliberate time wasting!

The effect of the unholy trio, as I saw them, on English batsmen was severe and significant, and greatly concerned me in my two series, at home and away, with Australia; our batting gained in confidence only after they broke up. And that is why I thought Peter

May inherited a better side in 1958–59 in Australia than the one I had led, but he ran headlong into a throwing and umpiring controversy and lost the series 4–0! The Australian approach often comes as a shock to English players, particularly if their cricket background is with one of the provincial counties where life is comparatively serene and unruffled. Suddenly to be transferred from, let us say, the greenery of Worcestershire, to play in front of a 60,000–80,000 crowd at Melbourne, or field in front of an impolite Hill at Sydney, is a nerve-wracking ordeal. Batting against Australia in a Test match in Australia brings unexpected pressures and demands, and it is an inescapable fact that they are after you from the word go. Something more than technique and the ability to bat is needed, as the Aussies set out with remorseless resolve to get on top. The old Roses matches before tense and partisan crowds were the ideal training ground and they bred players like Maurice Leyland, who went in against Australia determined not to wilt under pressure. Trevor Bailey was another. Some cope with the situation better than others.

Tom Graveney was the classic example of the talented English player who found it hard to adjust. A first glance could tell that he was a Test batsman, but he did not quite fulfil my hopes when he played under me, and I think his best cricket for England came in the second stage of his career when he was older and less susceptible to pressure.

In 1948 I was unfortunate to bat against Australia with the new ball which was available after only fifty-five overs. What went into the thinking of such a patently absurd experiment is difficult to imagine. There was no discernible point in its favour and it made spin bowling unfashionable. The farseeing at the time said it would kill spinners and though the experiment was hastily abandoned, it might have made its contribution, along with limited-over cricket, to the increase in pace bowling. Bradman, of course, was delighted to have a new ball after fifty-five overs and he could afford periods of defensive containment between the assaults of Lindwall and Miller.

Bill Johnston was a dual-purpose left-arm bowler, who started as a spinner and divided opinion in Victoria when he switched to the Bill Voce school of speed, swinging with his arm and developing the highly dangerous ball which goes the other way. English conditions were much to his liking and in 1948 he matched Lindwall with 27 Test wickets. At Bradford early in that tour Yorkshire had a tight struggle with the Australians and might have won but for a dropped catch. Johnston bowled both fast swing and slow spin and as I was in at one point for an hour for 5 runs, I knew exactly how good he was in both styles. Miller also bowled off-breaks during the innings, and a committee man expressed many local thoughts when he said to me: 'If only Keith Miller had been born a Yorkshireman.'

The most ferocious fast bowling I ever had to deal with was not, as might be guessed, against Lindwall and Miller, but against England's own Ken Farnes; what's more, the occasion was in the normally sedate atmosphere of a Gentlemen v. Players match at Lord's in 1938. Farnes had played in the first Test at Trent Bridge and he had been mauled by Stan McCabe. Farnes was inclined to be erratic, one day a Larwood, and another not much faster than Verity. I never saw worse fast bowling at Test level than by Farnes at Trent Bridge, and without detracting anything from McCabe's performance, it was little wonder that he ran riot. Wally Hammond, England's captain, took a lot of verbal punishment when McCabe scored 232 out of the 300 while he was at the wicket. Bradman told his players, some of whom were playing cards, to watch as they might not see stroke play like it again.

The next highest score was Bradman with 51 and, despite all his manoeuvring, Hammond could not keep McCabe away from the bowling when Australia were fighting to avoid the follow-on. At one point McCabe took 127 out of 148 in eighty minutes, and 72 out of 77 in the last-wicket stand with Fleetwood-Smith, which lasted only twenty-eight minutes.

As an exhibition of attacking stroke play it stirred the blood. McCabe destroyed Farnes, and it gave me an insight into a captain's dilemma when his prime bowler cannot respond. Hammond knew the best way to galvanize Farnes was to annoy him and, having been dropped by England, he was certainly annoyed. Gentlemen v. Players at Lord's was the ideal vehicle to demonstrate to Hammond and the selectors, then under the chairmanship of Sir Plum Warner, that he was still the fastest in the land. He made the point with considerable emphasis. *Wisden* and other contemporary accounts report that he bowled a length, which was not strictly accurate. I can vouch that he pitched just short of a length, and he had the height and pace to make the ball rear spitefully and alarmingly at head height. I find it impossible to think bodyline could have been more frightening and intimidating.

Bill Edrich and I opened for the Players with a few minutes to go

at the end of the first day, and in the one over Farnes bowled from
the pavilion end – long before there was a sightscreen – he had 2
wickets. Edrich, later to turn amateur – his eyes might have been
cast in the direction of the England captaincy after Hammond retired
– was struck in the face via his glove, attempting to fend off a truly
wicked flier. When he came to he was told he had been caught at
backward point. Bill spent the next day in bed and came back to
score 78 in the second innings.

Wicketkeeper Fred Price, an occasional opener for Middlesex, was
sent in as nightwatchman with no more enthuasism than if he had
been pressganged for Nelson's Navy, not without cause believing
his duty was only marginally less hazardous. In moments of crisis
Fred was apt to stutter, and after one delivery an explosion of sound
came from the other end which was generally taken to mean 'What
the hell's going on here?' He did not appear unduly dismayed when
he, too, was caught off a fast flier. The next morning Farnes
continued in the same vein, and on three occasions a stump landed
at the feet of Paul Gibb, the wicketkeeper, standing far back.

I felt I was at the wrong end of a shooting gallery. One ball flew
by my left arm, another by my right, and I reckon my half-century
represented runs as hard-earned as any in my career. He finished
with 8 for 43, a quite marvellous performance. In the midst of the
chaos Frank Woolley, captain of the Players and in his final season,
arrived at the wicket to a standing ovation. Reaching the crease, he
stood straight and erect, and with old-fashioned dignity raised his
cap in a charming and unforgettable gesture. He also batted with
appropriate dignity. Some years later, before MCC granted honorary
membership to distinguished old players, I saw him outside the
pavilion patiently waiting to be 'signed in'. Paul Gibb, of Cambridge,
Yorkshire and England, was obliged to resign his membership when
he became a professional with Essex according to the custom of the
day.

As I batted I often glanced in Hammond's direction at slip in the
hope of reading his thoughts. Had Farnes bowled anything like as
well for England at Trent Bridge as he did for the Gentlemen at
Lord's, the Test might have been a different story and Hammond
hailed as a winning captain. Sadly, Farnes was killed in a flying
accident early in the war.

Hammond's captaincy was not highly regarded in some quarters,
and, to some of his fellow players, he was inclined to be an aloof

and Olympian figure. I did not, however, number myself among his critics on either score. To me there could be no serious argument against his position as captain for he was comfortably the most talented player, with a wide experience. On the matter of his changing status from professional to amateur in order to take on the job, I had more sympathy for Hammond than for the prevailing system. He was not to blame for the way things were done in those days. By the late thirties the system was outrunning its course, but I felt Hammond was wrong to turn amateur for it didn't change him in any way. There would have been the same respect for him as for a pro captain.

I was thankful I did not have to face the same problem in 1952; frankly, on a matter of principle I could not see myself taking the same course as Hammond. It would not have been right. I was never under the slightest illusion that I was a temporary captain, keeping the seat warm until the right amateur came along, and it was widely reported that I was reappointed captain for Australia in 1954–55 by a single vote, though it was officially stated that the choice was unanimous. I do not know if there was any truth in the original version. I was never told and I never asked, preferring to let sleeping dogs lie; but, in fairness, I had a trying summer in 1954 with my health and the season was well advanced before I was declared fit for the tour. I had, however, told the selectors that I was prepared to go to Australia whether I was captain or not. I wanted to be as straight with the selectors and MCC as they had always been with me.

England's captaincy invariably creates a furore of public debate, and there cannot be many jobs exposed to so much criticism of either an informed or an ill-informed nature. Hammond came in for more than his fair share of criticism, but let's face it, his elderly team to Australia in 1946–47 did not stand a realistic chance. Only four of us, Jack Ikin, Alec Bedser, Denis Compton and Godfrey Evans were under thirty. England were pressed into a series long before there was a prospect of building a side so soon after the war and, as so often happens, the luck and the umpiring decisions went to the much stronger side. If Hammond had enjoyed Bradman's resources – perhaps if Miller had swopped sides – he would have won universal praise as a leader.

In assessing Hammond I freely admit to being one of his fervent admirers. We got on well together. He was friendly and approachable, and I soon discovered the stories about him in York-shire's dressing room were not exaggerations.

The one unfailing way for a cricketer to discover the true merit of another player is in the middle. Hammond had extraordinary ability. I fielded while he scored centuries at Bradford and Bristol which were nothing short of masterpieces, especially on the spin-taking pitch at Bristol. As a bowler he deceived me with a fractionally slower ball, which only a first-class bowler can produce. I also had the immense good fortune to be playing when he scored his historic 240 against Australia at Lord's in 1938. Quite unforgettable.

Hammond and Sutcliffe, as personalities, had much in common. Both were in total command of themselves, at once commanding respect and creating an aura of superiority in the sense that failure on their part did not seem at all likely! Though I had fifteen stands of a century or more with Herbert, I have to make the uneasy confession for a Yorkshireman that Hammond was the easiest partner I ever batted with. Batting with either, however, was an education, starting with calling so perfectly judged that it was auto-matically entrusted to them – no hurrying, no scurrying, no desperate changes of mind or hesitations. I had one recurring nightmare with Hammond. What if I ran the great man out? Fortunately my fears were never realized! From the non-striker's end Hammond's athleti-cism, balance and economy of movement were very apparent. Timing, positioning and footwork were perfectly coordinated and, bearing in mind that I watched Hobbs only briefly as a schoolboy, I never saw a finer English batsman than Hammond. A prince among cricketers.

If Hammond had a hard task as captain after the war, his successor, Norman Yardley, had even more daunting roles. Yardley followed the formidable Brian Sellers after the great prewar York-shire side had broken up. Even I felt a virtual stranger at times as Yorkshire attempted to rebuild. In the 1948 home series Yardley was pitted against Bradman, who was resolved to be the first touring captain to return home unbeaten. Yardley had no chance.

It was under Yardley's captaincy that I was dropped for the first and only time by England against Australia in 1948. While it is true I did not have a good second Test at Lord's, with scores of 20 and 13, I was not alone among England's batsmen. Denis Compton scored the only half-century. I heard the news that I had been left out over the radio. The selectors never offered me a reason or explained what was behind their decision. Had they done so it might have softened the blow.

Jim Kilburn had this to say in his book *Cricket Decade* (1959):

The decision caused a furious division of contemporary opinion, expressed in columns of letters to the newspapers and fierce arguments wherever cricket was discussed. Hutton himself remained discreetly outside the controversy. All the provocative questioning failed to produce a contentious line for the journalists. Twice, at least, Hutton could have burst into public protest against seeming injustice and been sure of a considerable measure of sympathy. This was one of them. The other was the announcement, before the team sailed, of Compton as vice-captain to F. R. Brown on the 1950–51 tour of Australia. A wrong word spoken in untrustworthy hearing, a hasty letter written and posted, could have been the end of Hutton's international career on either occasion. The temptation must have been enormous but Hutton held his peace. He never missed another Test match for which he was available, and he came to rank among the most successful of all England captains.

The one personal satisfaction I gained from the puzzling affair of the one-Test sacking was to hold fast to my resolve not to be drawn into a response and become involved in an argument I could not win. My telephone was red hot from newspapers, radio, and the sympathizers and the inquisitive. Even if I had broken my silence and allowed myself to be quoted, I could not have shed any light on the affair.

Privately I held the selectors – Group Captain A. J. Holmes, Johnny Clay, Walter Robins and skipper Yardley – to be wrong. That was all there was to it. Hard as I searched my mind for an answer, I came up with nothing, and I am still none the wiser. I have toyed with the idea that it might have been connected in some way with a request I made to Yorkshire for a one-match rest before the Lord's Test. Maybe that was my mistake, and it could have suggested that a surfeit of bumpers had broken my nerve or left me in the wrong frame of mind. All I wanted was to be physically right for the big match. Without wanting to make excuses, it was a fact of my life that my accident in 1941 left me with difficulties.

A highly placed official tried to console me with his belief that had the third Test been at Headingley, my home ground, and not Old Trafford, Washbrook would have been left out, but it was a thought which didn't appeal to me as Washbrook didn't deserve the axe any more than I did. George Emmett, a noted stroke-maker for Gloucestershire, took my place and found Lindwall too much for him, but had he succeeded, presumably I would have stayed out. When I returned for the fourth Test at Headingley, Washbrook and I put on 168 in the first innings and 129 in the second, which gave rise to another argument. Some said I had benefited from a rest from Test cricket and others that it proved I should never have been dropped!

The Lord's failure came during a consistent season of 2654 runs with an average of 64·73; a year later my aggregate of 3429 runs was more than any Yorkshire batsman in a season, beating Sutcliffe's 3326 in 1932. It included 1000 by 8 June, a record 1294 in June despite three successive ducks, and a further 1050 in August. I played in all four Tests against New Zealand, including 206 at the Oval – how I loved that ground! – but Washbrook was left out for a bowler. England had seven. Once, in a reminiscent mood, George Hirst was talking of the summer of 1906 when he scored 2385 runs and took 208 wickets. I asked him how he felt at the end of the season. 'Tired' was his simple reply. I knew what he meant by September 1949!

Denis Compton's promotion as vice-captain to Freddie Brown in Australia in 1950–51 did not surprise me. There was no way I could compete with him in the popularity stakes, and the debonair way he played his cricket clearly and deservedly attracted both the powers-that-be and the public. To Lord's he must have appeared to be a highly attractive prospect as a future Test captain leading England into a new and glittering era. Everyone warmed to his style and zest; he was a batting genius and as he was also a winter hero for Arsenal – he was never out of the sporting spotlight. I admired him greatly, particularly for the way he coped with the adulation which followed his triumphs in 1947. I never saw our situation as Compton v. Hutton, or in the light of North v. South with the honour of the vice-captaincy going to a privileged 'man of Lord's'. Rather, I thought it a reasonable assumption that the bluff captain looked for a personality as close to his own as he could find to be his first lieutenant. That man was more likely to be Compton than Hutton.

There was, however, one fatal flaw, and that was to shackle the free-ranging Compton personality and activities to the responsibilities of team management. The Comptons and Bothams of cricket have great and special gifts which should not be saddled with the cares of office. Denis and I started our Test careers in the same series with New Zealand in 1937 and we have been likened to the Cavalier and the Roundhead. I don't think he always appreciated the Yorkshire approach to cricket, and there has been a special edge to the rivalry between Yorkshire and Middlesex since a bitter match way back in the twenties. It doesn't count for much as far as I am concerned, and I always had the highest regard for Compton's ability. Oddly we did not have many big stands together, and I was saddened when his form fell apart in the 1950–51 series in Australia. His football injury had begun to trouble him, though, as sometimes happens, he scored heavily enough in the other first-class fixtures.

The very last thing I wanted was to leapfrog to the captaincy over the back of Compton's failures, but whether I liked it or not, it was a fact that his misfortunes cleared my path. I never deliberately sought the Test leadership, and when the appointment against India in 1952 was announced, it took time for it to sink in. Before the choice was made there was the customary speculation and, being a pragmatist and an old hand, I took predictions that I was the front-runner with a pinch of salt. When Norman Yardley, chairman of selectors, rang and invited me to captain England in the forthcoming home series with India, I accepted without hesitation, but the full implications did not hit me until later. Ten years were to pass before the distinction between amateur and professional was removed and all became cricketers; in the fifties the old system, with its good and bad points, had begun to creak in a rapidly changing society. Professional captains were emerging among the counties, with Tom Dollery (Warwickshire), Jim Langridge (Sussex) and Middlesex's odd and short-lived arrangement of a joint captaincy between Edrich (amateur) and Compton (pro). I always had an open mind on the issue, but with England it was imperative to have the best man for the job. If I was considered that man, so be it. I would do my best.

My appointment marked the end of long-established traditions and the beginning of a new era, no matter that it was in the nature of a stopgap operation. I was not naive enough to believe I would not come under the closest scrutiny, and maybe provoke a backlash from the inflexible traditionalists. I could see their point of view and, in the interests of England's Test side, I hoped they would see mine, for I was plainly better placed than any of the previous postwar captains to get results against the strongest opposition. The ice had been broken with a victory at Melbourne in 1951 and two young fast bowlers, Trueman and Statham, were coming through. Bedser was still unsurpassed and I had more than a passing interest in a fast bowler from Lancashire currently qualifying for Northamptonshire.

My introduction had been in a one-day match at Redcar. It meant nothing to me when a raw-boned lad with rather a cumbersome action charged in from an overlong run. In his first over he produced a full toss which thudded against my pads before I could use my bat in defence – and that hadn't happened to me for a long time with an English bowler.

Frank Tyson was his name, and that evening I wrote to Gubby Allen to tell him I had seen a genuine fast bowler. The name was noted, and in 1953 Freddie Brown was both captain of Northamptonshire and chairman of selectors. He had been to Australia with Jardine's side in 1932–33 and, after Tyson had appeared against the touring Indians in 1952 in a non-championship match, he declared he had not seen faster bowling since Larwood. Tyson was on the way. I could not have had more cheering news. A further advantage was that Tyson was able to escape the trumpetings of advance publicity. He was the ace that England was able to hold back.

4
England's First Professional Captain

For a long time Hutton would not allow his crown to rest easily on his head, though he ought to have known that no one was more fitted to wear it. He was not only England's greatest batsman but also England's most appropriate leader. Hutton's captaincy grew in authority though he always seemed to feel himself on trial, restricted by custom and consequences. He was persistently anxious not to tread on corns. He wanted his team to be all of his own frame of mind and then he would guarantee more victories than defeats. Victories were important to Hutton; he did not play in Test matches as a pastime.

J. M. Kilburn in *Cricket Decade* (1959)

It is an extraordinary fact, and must be scarcely credible to the modern generation of cricketers, that I had played in several matches at Lord's for Yorkshire before I first went into the pavilion. I took part in two matches during MCC's Anniversary Cricket Week in May 1937, scoring a century for North against South, which probably clinched my place for my maiden Test, and for the Rest against Gubby Allen's MCC Australian XI in 1936–37. Until then I had changed with the other professionals in their own separate quarters. The pros did not use the pavilion.

When I was ushered into the pavilion dressing rooms used by amateurs it was almost too much for me. I had never seen such spacious changing rooms nor experienced an atmosphere like it. I was entranced by this new world, and could hardly believe I was actually in the pavilion, and would enter the playing area via the Long Room and through the main gate. In the eighties my reaction must appear quaint to say the least, but, rightly or wrongly, when

I entered first-class cricket, there was a clear dividing line between amateur and pro and the habits and customs were part of the game.

At Lord's we pros had a room situated on the wing of the pavilion next to what is now the Warner Stand. The old press box was immediately above, and even the national paper writers had no access to the pavilion unless they were members. Test teams and official announcements were made through the news agencies.

The pros went onto the field by their own gate and joined the amateurs on the way to the wicket. We thought nothing of it for it was protocol, the accepted custom, and Lord's was steeped in tradition, and we respected tradition. The pros' room, now a plush members' bar, had hard, upright chairs, and by standing on tiptoe it was possible to watch the play – but only just. Oddly, some of the Middlesex players, including Patsy Hendren, shared the accommodation reserved for the visiting pros. Though a Yorkshireman, Thomas Lord, brought cricket to Lord's, Yorkshire teams regarded the place with a mixture of awe, fear and sometimes positive hatred.

In due course MCC were to alter a rule in order to make me an honorary life member while I was still playing. Yet when I took MCC, then responsible for England's overseas tours, to Australia in 1954–55, I was not a member, though my manager Geoffrey Howard and the scorer and baggage master George Duckworth were – George in an honorary capacity as a former player. On my first tours to South Africa and Australia, the amateurs sat apart in the ship's dining room, and as late as 1950 the Adelaide Club invited only amateurs and the MCC members of the visiting press corps to a reception.

Having spent my formative years absorbing such habits and customs, it was hardly surprising in the early days after my appointment as captain in 1952 that I should harbour some misgivings and reservations. Would Lord's, the citadel of tradition, accept me – the symbol of radical change? I always anticipated a minority opposition from the dyed-in-the-wool traditionalists and it duly came. A few scars remain, but I quickly discovered my main fears to be utterly groundless. Every MCC official gave his complete support and the secretary, Ronnie Aird, friendly and courteous, was always at my disposal, particularly before the team left for Australia in 1954–55. The same could be said of Harry Altham, chairman of what was then, in my opinion, an overlarge selection committee. Altham's devotion to cricket was complete, and though there were one or two positions I was not happy about, Tyson and Cowdrey were inspired selections and all came right in the end.

If the officials at Lord's were all that I could have hoped for, I also found the overwhelming majority of the rank-and-file MCC members were also well disposed towards me, which, after all, was not all that surprising as most of the occupants of the Long Room are either past or present cricketers, with the welfare of the game very much at heart.

There was, however, one important factor in my appointment which I had entirely overlooked – and that was that Lord's could conceivably have worried about me and what plots I might be hatching, particularly if I had a battery of fast bowlers at my disposal! It never occurred to me that the boot might be on the other foot, but it did not take me long to discover the spectre of bodyline still haunted the corridors of power. I accepted it was not unreasonable for MCC to fear the consequences of a determined and independent-minded captain achieving results by – shall we say – unconventional methods. I had already made clear my thoughts that England's prospects were not high without two authentic fast bowlers at least, and now England were in a position to send more than two. Curiously, while spinners like O'Reilly and Grimmett of Australia and Ramadhin and Valentine of the West Indies could be match-winners in England, spin bowlers never brought similar success to England overseas. The facts of history and my own playing experience led to the one conclusion that England's best hopes rested with pace, but MCC had no cause for concern. I never had any intentions of 'doing a Jardine' in any shape or form, and though I was always committed to a pace attack and orthodox tactics, bodyline – as I saw it, a one-off operation designed to combat Bradman – never remotely figured in my plans, which were outlined at press conferences aboard the *Orsova* and after MCC's arrival at Perth.

I cannot claim that I was totally indifferent to the various newspaper controversies at home and abroad, the few personal attacks, and the amateur *v.* pro issue which inevitably cropped up in the summer of 1954 in the wake of the unhappy West Indies tour. Anyone in the eye of an argument who says he is unscathed is probably deluding himself or has not understood the situation. A cricketer in the public eye soon learns the art of discrimination in his reading habits, and to suffer the fool gladly. If he believed every word he read he would alternately live in the clouds or in the pits, according to his latest performance; but I have never defeated an intense embarrassment enough to read lengthy articles or books in which I am the main subject. I confess I have not read one biography for that very reason, though I bought half a dozen copies which I signed as Christmas or birthday presents. I have happily read Sir Neville Cardus's cricket writing and other general works on the game, but I cannot bring myself to read about myself.

Yorkshire, in my time, were always accompanied by a sizeable press corps and it was said by outsiders that it was always possible to tell if Yorkshire were doing well by the chatter of typewriters! Northern writers of the calibre of Jim Kilburn, John Bapty and Frank Stainton, who were joined later by Bill Bowes, helped me to gain an invaluable insight into the ways of journalists when the national paper writers went on tour with MCC sides. The Yorkshire experiences taught me to realize that journalists have a job to do, and serve the particular needs of their newspaper. I did not always agree with what I read, but the majority were fair and sympathetic to my cause and, indeed, had called for my appointment.

Also I made a particular point of not becoming involved in stories unless I was directly approached. In the West Indies, strange as it may seem in these publicity-conscious days, I was officially barred from being quoted. When later I went into the press box for the London *Evening News* I saw even more clearly the two approaches of player and writer. Once, when I was captain, I was on the receiving end of a real blast from one writer and, somewhat to his consternation, I sat at his table at breakfast. In front of us were the strident headlines. I blandly observed: 'You must have a difficult job satisfying your editors.' He did not answer, and we left it at that.

The now familiar press conference was a rarity when I took over and I sometimes wondered how Jardine, Hammond, Sellers, Fender and other captains of their authoritative style would have reacted to some of the questions fired at me.

I bluntly told one aggressive radio questioner at Brisbane that England were about to play in a cricket match, not take part in warfare, and generally I devised a method to duck the loaded question as I evaded the bumper. It is difficult for me to explain just how I did it, and I cannot do better than to quote from Colin Cowdrey's book *MCC – The Autobiography of a Cricketer* (1976). Colin took a seat at the back during a conference given on board the *Orsova* before docking at Fremantle and attended by both

English and Australian journalists, most of the latter having travelled from the eastern states. Clearly it was important that as a professional captain I should make a good impression. It would have been bad for the side if I had been wrong-footed. This is how Colin – allowing himself poetic licence with my Yorkshire accent – saw my performance.

The Australian Press, I suspect, were expecting a lot of bravado, even bombast. They received the opposite. When they phrased a question to bring a head-on collision Hutton sat there, smiling slightly, turning the words over and over in his mind. Sometimes the pauses lasted fully thirty seconds and they became so long that twice at least Geoffrey Howard, the England team manager, glanced round to see if the captain had fallen asleep. When the answer came it would be shrewd, pointed and dryly witty. After about a dozen answers Hutton had them rolling in the gangways.

It was all underplayed. 'Noo, we 'avent got mooch bowling. Got a chap called Tyson but you won't 'ave 'eard of him because he's 'ardly ever played.

'Ah, yes, Lock and Laker. Aye, good boolers but we 'ad to leave them behind (no explanation). Batsmen? Well we 'avent got any batsmen, really. We've got these youngsters, May and Cowdrey, but we haven't got any batsmen.' Then wearily: 'What it comes to is that we're startin' all over again. We've a lot to learn from you.'

They asked him what he thought of Australia's new ball attack. Another long pause as he groped to try and remember their names. 'Oo, aye. Lindwall and that other fella.' Pause again. 'Don't think they like me very much. Didn't really know whether I ought to have coom back out 'ere again.'

Question: 'What do you think of Arthur Morris now?' Answer, after an immense silence: ''Ave they got any sightscreens yet down at the bottom end at Brisbane?' Long silence. 'Saw Arthur Morris make 196 once when the sightscreen had blown down.' Then he would lean forward, almost confidentially, to one of the reporters and say: 'Remember that, Bill, the day when the sightscreens blew down?' and then he would retreat into some extensive reverie of his own, while the entire Australian Press contingent sat transfixed by the performance in total, respectful silence.

It was a brilliant achievement. He took the wind out of their sails with almost every reply. He had the whole room poised, waiting for the next answer, and when the answer came it told them nothing at all. When the question was tough he glanced it neatly down to fine-leg and they actually applauded the way he did it.

Sadly, as Colin sat listening to the conference, a cable was being delivered at the team's hotel at Perth bearing the news that his father had died. Three weeks earlier I had met Colin's parents at the dockside at Tilbury and had chatted with them for twenty minutes or so. My last words to Colin's father were: 'I'll look after him' – a promise I tried to keep. I made a point of talking and playing deck games with him. Colin was naturally stunned by his bereavement, and I thought the best thing to do was to leave him in the privacy of his own room. At dinner I put my hand on his shoulder and told him I was sorry, which I felt to be a pitifully inadequate gesture, but from them on I made sure Colin was kept busy.

Colin was a late selection and was given the 'feeling' of the England dressing room as twelfth man for the Oval Test with Pakistan – not, as it turned out, an auspicious occasion. I had seen him play for Kent against Yorkshire, at Oxford and at the Scarborough Festival, where I had the best of reasons to remember him as he ran me out at 99 and I missed a fourth successive century. When he batted against Alec Bedser and Warwickshire's New Zealander Tom Pritchard, who was quite lively, I urged him to stand up higher and play straighter and not allow himself to be overawed by the quality of the bowling. His technique and match temperament were, however, highly impressive. At Oxford I had seen how straight was his bat and how much time he had for his shots, always the hallmark of class. He told me he was a 'total disciple' of my methods, which was flattering, but, more important, it was an assurance that he had studied technique and put a lot of thought into his play.

When his name came up for discussion he had a strong advocate in Gubby Allen, who vouched for his class. As I have always had a high regard for Allen's judgement, and he had seen far more of Cowdrey than I had, I was easily persuaded. Allen was completely vindicated, but it was still in the nature of a brave decision as Cowdrey had gone a little back on his 1953 form and had yet to score a championship century.

If Cowdrey was a risk, Tyson was a real shot in the dark – but it landed smack in the bull's eye. In total, Tyson's experience amounted to no more than a season and while there was no doubting his speed, he was erratic and his stamina had not really been put to the test. Incredibly, as it now seems, his native Lancashire let him go because they doubted his physique. On the memorable morning in the third Test at Melbourne after he and Statham had routed

Australia, Frank wrote in his diary: 'Perhaps the luckiest and certainly the happiest day of my life. I bowled Australia out before lunch.' The selectors might have added their footnote: 'Perhaps this was the luckiest selection of our lives.'

I had an open mind about taking him. My long-term plan of saving Trueman for Australia had been upset by Bedser's unavailability for the West Indies. Trueman went on a tour too early, and if his maiden tour had been to Australia and not to the touchy West Indian islands, I think it would have been better for him and better for English cricket. The Aussies wouldn't have taken the loquacious Freddie so seriously as did the West Indians and he would have been answered in kind, that's for sure. Australia might have knocked off some of Trueman's rough edges and found him a good bloke and a fierce competitor.

I have read that I never forgave Trueman for his abrasive conduct in the West Indies and, as a result, he never played under my captaincy again. This is untrue. The fact is he had my vote for Australia but the majority were against him. It is also a fact that his claims were given full and fair consideration, but with several candidates available the committee could be choosy.

Jim Laker's omission left me very unhappy, but it seemed there were too many long memories of his early failure against Australia, and of some heavy punishment when he conceded nine 6s over a short boundary in MCC's match at Lord's in 1948. Laker was expensive in the 1948 series, but his 9 wickets in 1953 were at 23 apiece. At the time it was standard English thinking that off-spinners were wrong for Australia, but a class bowler is a class bowler. When Laker did go to Australia and the home batsmen were thirsting for revenge for the indignities he had imposed on them in 1956, he gave the perfect answer with his immaculate line and length. But an off-spinner was sent with me – Jim McConnon, of Glamorgan, who had a big reputation as a close-in fielder and came on strongly in the second half of the season. McConnon was a good bowler but he wasn't a Laker, and in my opinion there was no justification for his selection, certainly not in front of Laker. Unfortunately, he was hit in the groin and finished up in hospital; later a broken bone caused him to return home early.

As Laker's fame spread in the fifties, Yorkshire began to regret that one of their own who had attended the prewar coaching sessions at Headingley had slipped through the net. At the age of sixteen,

Laker, a bank clerk at Bradford, had been No. 4 for Saltaire in the Bradford League. He bowled fast. During the war he developed off-spinning on the mat at Cairo after El Alamein and, while awaiting demob, he was billeted at Catford. His exploits for that club took him to the Oval and Yorkshire readily consented to Surrey's application for his registration.

In the fifties a Yorkshire committee man asked me who was the best off-spinner in the land. Naturally I replied: 'Jim Laker, the Yorkshireman.'

'When you go to the Oval, sound him out and see if he would like to come back to Yorkshire,' I was told.

I duly saw Jim, who could have played for Yorkshire in the following year, as a cricketer is always eligible for the county of his birth. Laker, however, domiciled in Surrey, was not interested. During the war Maurice Leyland invited Dennis Brookes to return from Northamptonshire, also without success. Brookes became captain and president of Northamptonshire, and was chairman of the local bench. Astonishingly Warwickshire turned down both Verity and Bowes! And, before them, Rhodes.

Laker's famous partner, Tony Lock, was another casualty of selection, but he had some trouble with his faster delivery which had been no-balled. My slow bowlers were Johnny Wardle and Bob Appleyard, whose unusual style of swing and spin put him into a high bracket.

Whatever the criticisms of the selection for Australia might have been, a lot of thought and care went into the discussions. On that score I was more satisfied than I had been over the selection for the West Indies tour of 1953–54. Not enough time was given for that selection. I regretted the haste. As a concession to the venerable Sir Pelham Warner, who first served as a selector in 1905, the final decisions were taken during the fifth Test with Australia at the Oval. England were engaged in a titanic struggle to gain the Ashes for the first time in nineteen years, and as far as I was concerned, the timing could not have been more inappropriate. I wanted to direct my whole attention and energies to the task of beating the Australians.

Sir Pelham, I suspect, was feeling his age, but I am sure he gave the most careful thought and care to the selection of the side. I also concede that he had seen more cricket in his long life than I was likely to do, and he knew more about the game. He was also a very powerful influence, and accustomed to getting his way, albeit in an unfailingly courteous manner. For all that, I would have preferred another time and place and longer deliberation. Having seen Ken Suttle, the Sussex left-hander, score one of his seven centuries that summer, Sir Pelham was very keen on his inclusion, but it didn't work out well.

When Sir Pelham gazed across the table at the young captain, who showed such an interest in fast bowlers, I wondered what thoughts were passing through his mind. Had he known that, like Jardine, my ancestors came from across the border, he might have been troubled. But he knew I was a true Yorkshireman from the county who never believed it unprincipled to play hard. Sir Pelham often gave me his gaze as if trying to read my mind, but kept his thoughts to himself.

Bedser's withdrawal from the side for the West Indies was a severe blow, but in view of his excessive workload for England and Surrey since 1946 – he was all but bowled to a standstill – there had to be understanding for Surrey's insistence on his taking a winter's rest. In two series alone in Australia he had bowled 459 eight-ball overs, and he had around 500 behind him when he went to Trent Bridge in 1953 – almost as many as bowlers complete in a season in these days. Yet he took 39 wickets in the series. One of the compliments I treasure was *Wisden*'s summing-up of the 1950–51 Australian tour: 'England possessed the best batsman in Hutton, the best bowler in Bedser and the better wicketkeeper in Evans.'

I had planned to give Alec as near to a holiday in the West Indies as possible, without too much involvement in the lesser matches played on pitches like a macadam road surface, and reserve him for the Test matches. Bedser's capacity for hard work and his zest for the game might have made him unwilling to accept the arrangement, but his support and down-to-earth commonsense would have been invaluable on the troubled tour. And, as I have said already, Trueman would not have been called up so soon. *Wisden* took me to task for not bringing 'my lively young colt' to heel sooner. Under normal conditions Trueman would have been on a tighter leash, but incident after incident tumbled from the clear blue Caribbean skies, and I had no time for the personal attention I had intended to give him. When Trueman started with Yorkshire I made it my business to sit alongside him in dressing rooms and at meal tables to try to protect him from the barbs of other players. In most ways he was likable and fiercely loyal. I had hoped to do a similar job in the

West Indies had it been necessary, but there was hardly time to look after myself let alone anyone else.

Yardley handled the young Trueman very well with a mixture of sympathetic understanding and forceful advice. Invariably he brought Trueman back to have a go at tail-enders.

One of the drawbacks of being a 'character' is that it attracts every type of publicity, good and bad, and Trueman becomes the source of every story making the rounds of the pavilion bars. Many of the tales are apocryphal, the invention of a wag somewhere down the line. An example was the 'Hey, Gunga Din, pass t'salt', alleged to have been made to an Indian diplomat at a reception. Not that Freddie can't be very funny with his impromptu remarks, like asking David Sheppard, who had just dropped a catch off him, to imagine it was Sunday and keep his hands together. Freddie's father, Alan, a Yorkshire miner, showed his humour one morning on early shift when he was being ribbed in the cage on the way to the coal face. Trueman junior was having a barren run at the time and the air was thick with observations like: 'Tha didn't tell us tha lad had turned slow bowler' and 'We thought lad was fast bowler.' No response was made until the cage slowed down in the last thirty yards of its descent. Alan looked round and asked: 'Did tha notice Queen when teams were presented t'other day at Lord's? Queen spoke to our Fred, moved on and came back. I'll tell tha what she said. She said: "I forgot to ask tha – 'ows tha father?" '

Trueman was upset that he didn't make the Australian tour, and when he missed another MCC side to South Africa in 1956–57, the announcement coincided with one of his best performances. Snatching his sweater from the umpire, he said to the world in general: 'Tell the selectors to put that in their pipes and smoke it!'

It must have been galling for Trueman to move aside, even temporarily, and it is an academic argument how far a captain should influence the selectors. As I considered myself a stopgap, I was at a disadvantage among selectors with amateur backgrounds and distinguished playing records. Consider my position at my first selection meetings in 1952 to choose the English side to play India. I looked around the table and there were three former England amateur Test captains. Norman Yardley was my current Yorkshire captain, Freddie Brown had recently been my Test captain in Australia, and Bob Wyatt was a prewar leader with immense experience. The fourth member was Leslie Ames, the first ex-professional to be appointed a selector. He was scoring runs and keeping wicket for England when I was a schoolboy. I felt rather like a head boy called to a meeting of house masters and, as there seemed to be no shortage of sense, I was mainly content to rely on their judgement.

Years later when I became a Test selector it was very apparent to me that Tony Greig, the captain, had no such inhibitions and reservations. I helped to make him captain after Mike Denness, poor fellow, put Australia in to bat and lost, and it did not take me long to realize I had made a mistake. I soon suspected that he regarded Alec Bedser, the chairman Charles Elliott, Ken Barrington and myself as surplus to his requirements.

His attitude suggested he was a veteran of many Test series with Australia and was a Test captain of vast experience. I would not deny Greig's attributes and the way he lifted the morale and spirit of the England dressing room, especially during the 1976–77 visit to India, but he did not have a monopoly of cricket wisdom and was a little too sure of himself for my comfort. All his enthusiasms were suddenly transferred to Kerry Packer's world series cricket and he was dumped from the captaincy.

Greig had every right to make his own choice and I doubt whether, as a South African, he had the same feeling of allegiance to English cricket which was second nature to my generation. I have heard this view derided, but loyalty to county and country was unquestioned in my time, and I sincerely hope it has not vanished for good.

One of the surprises of the Greig era was the recall of Brian Close at the age of forty-five to try to dampen the fire of the West Indies fast bowling in the 1976 home series. Unfortunately, a Test trial at Bristol coincided with an obligatory business meeting for me in Germany. Whilst the trial was taking place Close made scores of 88 and 40 off the West Indies at Taunton and some, apparently Greig among their number, took it as further evidence that he was the best player of fast bowling in the country. Greig had Barrington's support and the voting was 2–2. At the time – Bedser wisely made it his business to get the procedure changed – the captain and not the chairman had the casting vote. Close was in. I was more than a little surprised to find what had happened in my absence; having said that, it must be clear which way I would have voted. Having known Brian since he came into the Yorkshire side in his teens, I naturally had a high opinion of his determination and spirit, but, over the years, it has been consistently proved that these admirable qualities are not enough in the highest class. There have, it is true, been many examples of players brought back for specific tasks with the desired result, but I believe it is better to go for the younger man.

To his credit, Close battled valiantly and was not a failure in his three Tests, and I was saddened to see him and John Edrich the victims of a nonstop battering from the West Indies fast bowlers. Clive Lloyd, the captain, admitted 'our fellows got carried away' – a remark to make me wonder what captains and umpires are there for.

In 1953, to my regret, I failed to persuade the selectors to pick Cyril Washbrook as my opening batting partner. I was not a captain to tell the selectors: 'I must have so and so – or else!' I do not believe in that attitude but, to my mind, it was a mistake not to have granted my request. Without question he was the best Test opening partner I had. We had much in common. We had learned our cricket in similar northern surroundings. We gave each other confidence. No matter how experienced a batsman might be, he likes to have some assurance from his partner, and there were times when my partners were so overcome by the occasion that they were half out before they took guard.

Our record of eight century stands for England, including 359 at Johannesburg in 1948–49 and twenty of 50 or more, should have influenced the selectors. We had five other century stands, including two of over 200, in other matches. We batted as a pair, but Cyril did not seem too popular with the selectors when I pressed his claims. Unfortunately, he had failed in Australia in 1950–51, owing partly, I am sure, to the fact that he had other matters on his mind. In the late summer of 1950 he had accepted a directorship with a Manchester firm of sports outfitters – the kind of offer he could not refuse at that stage of his career. Almost immediately he was named by MCC for the Australian tour. He felt he could not accept, and withdrew. One or two newspapers whipped up synthetic indignation and claimed cricket should be his business, but Cyril had every right to look ahead to a future career.

In the end, after an upsetting controversy, MCC agreed he should fly out instead of travelling with the rest of the party by ship. Cyril never settled on the tour, and maybe the lesson to be learned was not to persuade a player to tour against his wishes. Whether the selectors held this episode against Cyril I do not know, and it was a fact that he and Denis Compton had failed in the Tests of that series. Ironically, three years later Gubby Allen fell back on Washbrook's experience to steady the boat and he played a crucial innings to turn the rubber against Australia. I gather Peter May, the captain, was reluctant to have him. Different selectors, different ideas!

I first saw Cyril in a Rosebuds match – Yorkshire Second XI v. Lancashire Second XI for the uninitiated – when he scored 202 not out. Alas for me, 202 more than my score. From that day on he was my ideal opening batsman; apart from his technique, I admired his composure. We became not only opening partners but firm friends, and in the course of time I was amused by my youthful belief that Lancastrians and Aussies were my natural cricket enemies!

The way Washbrook dealt with Cuan McCarthy at Johannesburg in 1948–49 was masterly. McCarthy wasn't a Lindwall or a Miller, but he was fast enough. Cyril excelled in the hook and cut, and he would have been even more dangerous but for the leg-before law change which obliged him to modify his back-foot technique.

Cyril Turner was a perceptive observer and it was partly on his advice that I converted Trevor Bailey into an opening batsman. I tried it out in the Edgbaston Test trial, the right time for an experiment, and the writers descended on me to ask if the selectors had known in advance of my intentions. The answer was a plain no. There were two reasons for the experiment: one, Trevor had the technical skill and nerve to stand up against the new ball and, with luck, give England a start; two, with his limited range of strokes there was little advantage to be gained in his being in the second half of the order.

Always in those days there was Wilfred Rhodes's contention in my mind that, to win in Australia, England needed to have a 25 per cent better side than the Australians. I feared that margin would be hard to achieve because some of the established batsmen had too much of Lindwall and Miller in their systems. There was a chance that Bailey might stiffen the batting. It was much needed.

Bailey had that measure of confidence, as distinct from conceit, which is essential at Test level. The Aussies never seem to lack it. They mature quicker, owing in large part to the conditions they enjoy in their formative years and to the competitive nature of their national character.

My years as captain and selector taught me one truth, and that is that no one, or no committee, is infallible. Mistakes are inevitable and, like umpires, the best selectors make the fewest mistakes. A captaincy blunder, the toss of a coin, a dropped catch, an umpiring decision and sheer unforeseeable bad luck can destroy hours of discussion and planning. Selectors need as much luck as players and umpires, and I cannot imagine a body of men more conscientious or fair-minded. Every method of selection has been tried at one time or another, from the small to the large committee, but I am opposed to the appointment of a soccer-style supremo for cricket. I dread to think of the consequences should that glib and superficially attractive idea be accepted. As one man cannot be in more than one place at a time, it would be an impossible assignment, with a heavy reliance on county managers, captains, officials and newspaper opinion. I cannot imagine a more difficult position.

In 1938 two county captains, Brian Sellers and Maurice Turnbull, of Glamorgan, were appointed selectors. As active players it was deemed they were able to study form at close hand, and be in constant touch with player opinion. The odd result was that Sellers did not see a single hour of the Test series, and Turnbull was present only at the start of the first Test at Trent Bridge. A selector needs to be in close touch with the side he has helped to choose. Also, as Sir Pelham Warner, chairman in 1938, remarked: 'Playing cricketers on a selection committee are prone not to appreciate fully their own county men. Far from favouring them, the reverse is the case.' It is probably just as true today.

The best guarantee of expert selection, in my view, can be expected from a small committee of former Test players with experience of overseas tours, and with an ability to work in close cooperation with a give-and-take captain. The 1954 committee for the Australian tour was far too big. The more members there are, the more the conflicting ideas about players fill the air. The one basic inescapable truth is that the most able panel can only select from the talent available. In recent years the mass importation of overseas players and the structure of the domestic competitions have greatly reduced the number of players of genuine class.

A supremo is no answer; nor am I able to accept the position of the county manager. If I understood the exact nature of his duties perhaps I would be more sympathetic. If the job is to concentrate on organizing cricket within the county, coaching the young, recruiting and having contact with leagues, clubs and schools, I should be 100 per cent behind such an appointment. My confusion starts with his position in relation to the county side, and where he stands with his captain. As the captain has to be in sole charge – any other system is unworkable – I find it hard to place the manager's responsibilities. It is like having two captains on the bridge of a ship. If I had been captain of Yorkshire, a distinction never to come my way, I do not think I could have accepted a manager by my side, no matter how well intentioned he might have been, or how close a friend. A Test captain would be in precisely the same situation with a supremo.

The growth of the county manager suggests a lack of confidence in the modern captain, a loss of authority and, to some extent, a failure of the system. Today's captains lack the independence of the old-style amateur, who could stand up to his county committee. The mind boggles at the thought of Brian Sellers, Percy Fender and captains of that ilk being told they had to have a manager to help run their side.

Captains are judged on results and, as a consequence, history can lie. There have been bad captains carried by good teams, and good captains let down by bad teams. The supreme test is for a captain to make the best of his resources, and be astute enough to turn a moderate side into a winning one. When I was sometimes accused of being defensive, I thought how easy it was to sit in judgement and not have to take the consequences of mistakes, or even of ill luck. Responsibility can be a millstone around a captain's neck.

At Sydney in 1954 I had to make the most painful decision of my captaincy and drop Alec Bedser, who had carried England's attack brilliantly for so many campaigns. I realize now I should have handled such a delicate matter differently.

After the unmitigated disaster of Brisbane, when England's bowling was obliterated by Australia, the tour committee discussed the almost unheard-of possibility of Alec having to go for the second Test. The ultimate decision, however, was mine and mine alone, and I can assure Alec that the prospect was upsetting to me. Not only was he a truly great bowler, but we had been through fire and high water together for many years. We spent happy hours discussing tactics. (On and off the field he was the ideal team match.)

I hoped against hope that Alec might come to me and say: 'Look, I'm not 100 per cent fit, and don't consider me until I am.' But Alec was the type of fighter who would drag himself onto the field to do his bit. His fitness was the prime concern of both the tour committee and myself. I had noticed on the ship that he was not his usual self, and within a day of his arrival in Perth he went down with shingles, a painful and debilitating illness. A doctor told me that it would take weeks for him to be right again, but he was so keen to get back, and I was so keen to have him back, that he played in three matches before the first Test and bowled well enough to make the Test team. I wish the doctor had been more decisive and flatly told me he was not to play for a defined period. Alec could have gone away and rested until he was fit.

Another doubt had crept into my mind. George Duckworth, the scorer, drew my attention to the number of no-balls Alec bowled, which suggested he was untypically straining to get to the wicket. Also, although he was still a fine catcher in gully positions, he was rather slow in the field. I figured if he was rested at Sydney he would be refreshed and come back for the third match at Melbourne, but by then events had overtaken me and I certainly couldn't split the spearhead attack of Tyson and Statham.

In mitigation, I had a lot of things on my mind before I pinned up the team sheets, minus the name of Alec Bedser, in the dressing rooms at Sydney and Melbourne, but I wish now I had talked with him and said: 'Sorry, old mate, but you'll have to move over in the interests of the side. I know you'll be upset, but I'd like you to know that I'm upset too. I hate to have to do it.'

I thought I knew Alec almost as well as his brother Eric, but I didn't realize how sensitive was his nature – and I mean that in the kindest possible way. Alec, who would bowl his heart out for England, was as keyed up emotionally before he opened the bowling as any batsman waiting to go in on a big occasion. I have gone to Alec before the first ball and asked him about his field and he was so tense that he could hardly speak. This amiable giant of a man, with a lion's strength, could experience the emotions of a sensitive artist. In an over or so he would be fine, but I suppose that sensitivity helped to make him the bowler he was, and the man he is.

I wonder if the course of history would have changed if Alec had missed Brisbane and started at Sydney. Conceivably Tyson and not Bedser might have been missed out!

A cricketer's life is full of ups and downs, and it was of great regret to me that Alec was edged out. Cricket can be cruel, as I quickly learned. When George Hirst, after long hours of patient coaching and advice, recommended me for Yorkshire Second XI, he told me in his fatherly way: 'Well, lad, it's up to you now. I can't help you when you're out there. You're on your own, and you've got to do it yourself.'

I was out for a duck. I felt miserable for myself; miserable for George. To make it worse I collected another duck in the next match. More misery for myself; more misery on behalf of George.

Years later, when I was tipped for my first Test, I could hardly bear the strain of waiting. England's team to play New Zealand in 1937 was to be announced on a Sunday, on the one o'clock news bulletin. I went for a walk, leaving my mother with pad and pencil and instructions to write the names down carefully. When I returned I had only to look in her eyes to know I was in. 'That's grand,' I said rather lamely. 'Yes, it's grand,' she said – a brief exchange of words to hide one of the sweetest moments of a career which took in seventy-nine Tests. I celebrated with 271 not out against Derbyshire, an innings which was nothing less than indulgent self-gratification.

Then, for no logical reason, the fiddle went out of tune at Lord's. I was a little tired physically, and pent up mentally, but I was bloated with runs. I missed the comforting familiarity of the pros' dressing room, and familiar faces of Yorkshire players. When I got to the wicket there was a lot of movement of the ball under cloud cover and I could not get away from that very fine bowler, Jack Cowie. The first run would not come, and the worst happened. In the second innings I improved. I scored 1!

After my duck I went to a cinema on the Sunday to try to escape from my depression, and I had hardly sat down than I was watching myself on a newsreel being dismissed! In my embarrassment I looked to my left and to my right to see if I was being recognized. Then I saw the funny side of it and laughed. I had no excuses, but it took me several seasons to get used to the slope at Lord's.

Between the first and second Tests Yorkshire went to Cardiff and in the course of the game the dressing rooms were entered and pilfered. My wallet containing a fair sum of money – around £60 – disappeared, and I thought it about time my luck changed. It did, with a maiden Test century at Old Trafford. I felt much closer to home, among my own sort of people, a familiar dressing room and on one of my favourite grounds. The cloth caps and raincoats of the north were the homely and comforting inspiration I needed. I liked the wit and humour of the place. Once, as I was going out to bat in a Roses match at Old Trafford, a broad Lancashire accent said: 'Think on, lad. Don't be so long out there t'day.' Two weeks later I passed the same man on my way out for England against South Africa. On this occasion he gave me a grin and said: 'Now it's all reet t'day. Tha can stay as long as tha likes.'

Bramall Lane, now, alas, surrendered to football, was the ground for lively wit. The Sheffield spectator had no equal anywhere in the world, and it was a treat to field near the boundary and listen to the comments. One handed down in the Yorkshire dressing room involved George Macaulay, and there is a moral to it.

Don Bradman had been batting only a short time and, as usual, looked to be in ominous form. Macaulay, who had been known to quail batsmen with a glare and a mutter, asked for the ball and in a loud voice declared: 'Let me 'ave a go at this booger.' His first over produced the considered achievement of a maiden to Bradman, but in the next he was hit for five boundaries, and a further 16 runs in his third over. As silently he took his sweater, a voice with the strength of a loudhailer came from the crowd: 'Tha should have kept tha bloody mouth shut, George.'

One of the strangest observations made to me was by Sir Hugh Foot, brother of Michael, and then Governor of Jamaica. At a reception at Kingston given to MCC in 1953–54 we got into a discussion about the selection of teams and he said: 'No batsman with blue eyes should ever be chosen for a tour of the West Indies.' I was too polite to ask why, and wondered whether he had noticed my blue eyes. The majority of the MCC batsmen had blue eyes, and I trust he did not check his theory with the averages at the end of the series!

5
Ashes Crown the Year

He is a quiet man, Hutton; a fighter, but a fighter by hanging on rather than by the great gesture. He is shrewd, too, counting his advantages and using them, never building on hopes but eking out his gains to the best purpose. Good attacking captains have not been scarce. Good defensive captains are fewer because defence is apt to look dull, to be unpopular and unspectacular . . . it has been a great season for him. Hutton is a man battered by cricket, pale, with a not unattractive broken nose, that sadly foreshortened arm and a physique which is frail for one who may bat a day or more. Throughout this series, he spoke little and when he spoke, he spoke sense. It may be that he made mistakes, but he did not make the mistake which mattered – that of losing a match.

John Arlott in *Test Match Diary 1953*

My nose was broken in a curious accident at Old Trafford. My heart was all but broken when Australia snatched victory by scoring 404 in 344 minutes at Headingley in 1948. And the pallor, mentioned above might have been the Pudsey air or the result of reading the morning's newspapers! The injury came in a Yorkshire Second XI match in 1933. A ball had passed wide of the leg stump and, as there was an unusually long delay, I turned round to see what had happened. As I did so Bill Farrimond, the wicketkeeper, who spent a large slice of his career as a reserve but went on MCC tours to South Africa and the West Indies, threw the ball back to the bowler. Unfortunately for me, I was hit smack on the nose from only a few inches away and I had to undergo an operation in 1935, which, I am sure, cost me my form that season.

As for the opinion that I was a defensive captain, I always insist that I defended when it was necessary and attacked when I had the chance. I could give chapter and verse on defensive measures used by other captains which passed unnoticed, and I was often inclined to think some of my critics lived in ivory towers and were insensitive to the fact that the public, particularly in 1953, were longing for a measure of revenge against Australia. When I took over, there had been a humiliating defeat in the home series with the West Indies in 1950. England would not have recovered the Ashes in 1953 without two exceptional rearguard actions at Lord's and Headingley which proved the mettle of the side. Test matches are tests of strength and pride, and I doubt if there would have been general acclaim if England had sacrificed their chances by imprudent attack. I was always very conscious of my double responsibility as No. 1 batsman and captain. In cricket, generalities tend to take root and I think it absurd to blame me as preoccupied with defence.

Attack is a splendid tactic if there is the batting or bowling to sustain it and a captain has a side one or two classes better, as Bradman had in two postwar series. Frank Worrell could afford aggressive batting when he led his attractive side in Australia in 1960–61 because, as he said, he could gamble on at least two of his batsmen coming off. I have read that I set a bad example by playing spin from the crease, but I can assure my critics that I would have given much to have gone down the pitch to attack. Yet I doubt if the ground, or the press box, would have rung with sympathetic understanding if I had missed a straight ball and been stumped by a yard or two. If England's batting had been less fragile and less dependent on a few batsmen, I could have had a different approach. Theory is cheap, and I doubt whether it was properly understood that the twin spinners of 1950, Ramadhin and Valentine, especially in English conditions, were not long in the air, were not easy to get at and, considering they had virtually no previous experience, they bowled to their fields with remarkable consistency. Their captains, John Goddard and Jeff Stollmeyer, did a lot for them and Stollmeyer in particular developed field setting to a fine art. He was so meticulous that I would stand at the wicket wondering how much longer he would take; but he got it right in the end and made it very hard to find scoring lanes. While it is true that Miller did a demolition job when Ramadhin went to Australia, English and Australian conditions are different, the Australians were forewarned of a threat and England did not have a Miller.

Ramadhin and Valentine were outstanding bowlers, but they still needed help and support. Stollmeyer not only handled them judiciously but, in general, was as shrewd a captain as I came across. I expected he would show all the perceptive qualities of a cricket student, be able accurately to sum up the opposition, assess players and be tactically aware, but I confess I was surprised by the high order of those qualities. I also quickly discovered that his position was no sinecure, and he had difficulties to match my own on that volatile tour. In my book, Stollmeyer deserves a high ranking among postwar Test captains.

Starting with Vijay Hazare of India, I was singularly fortunate to have friendly and cooperative opposite numbers as captains. Hazare, an accomplished batsman and a former pro with Rawtenstall and Royton, had a side which became disjointed and demolished by Trueman's speed. They couldn't cope with Bedser. I wouldn't have wanted to change places with Hazare. I also called all the shots when England went to New Zealand in 1955 and dismissed Geoff Rabone's team for a record low score of 26. The New Zealand players made it into a joke and wore a special tie with a motif of the figure: 26. Significantly, I was not accused of being defensive when my bowlers pulverized India and New Zealand!

Hassett, Australia's captain in 1953, was an old rival dating back to 1938. I never heard an angry word spoken to or about the impish little man with a keen sense of humour and fair play. In fact I doubt whether it would have been possible to have crossed swords with him; his sportsmanship and understanding greatly contributed to the excellent relations between the sides in the Coronation series. As the invincible Bradman's successor, and at a time of rebuilding for Australia, he had no easy task, with the novel experience for an Australian captain (of the time) of being put under pressure. His years of captaincy at many levels came to his aid. In contrast, before I captained England in 1952, my captaincy experience had been restricted to a season with Pudsey St Lawrence towards the end of the war, and odd matches here and there. Lindsay was as much a friend as an opponent. Everyone in the game had a lot of time for him, and I was no exception.

Ian Johnson was not everyone's choice in Australia for the captaincy for our tour there in 1954–55, particularly as Miller was available. Johnson was a toughie behind his wide and ready smile. He was the hardest and least flexible of the Test captains I met as

England's leader, and with him I had my only instance of dissension. Alan Davidson was bowling left arm over the wicket during the 1955 Adelaide Test and was creating a rough patch with his follow-through. Davidson had long spikes, and the marks on the pitch were not only a clear breach of the regulations, but could have been exploited by an off-break bowler.

I drew an umpire's attention to the matter, but no action was taken. Later I again complained; again I was ignored. Alan continued with his follow-through, and the third time I mentioned it, Johnson, fielding at mid-off, cottoned on and told the umpire in no uncertain language not to take any notice. The umpire duly obliged and, though I was singularly unimpressed, I allowed the situation to stand and got on with my innings. I never willingly got involved in incidents or disagreements, partly because it is not in my nature, partly because it is unprofessional, and partly as a concession to the ethics of the game. I was, however, privately annoyed that an umpire should allow such a malpractice to continue.

Modern umpires are rightly strict about bowlers running down the pitch, and at Adelaide I would have been within my rights to have insisted on the laws being observed.

At the end of the over Miller passed between Johnson and myself and waggishly admonished us with the words: 'Now, now, children, no quarrelling.'

The 1952 series with India was a successful rehearsal for the coming battle for the Ashes, though I still felt the batting lacked real authority and, above all, confidence. There was good reason for gratification at the strength of the bowling and, indeed, India's inability to cope with Trueman and Bedser scarcely put the new captain's tactical skills to the test. If it had not rained at the Oval the result would have been a clean sweep. India could not conceal a terror against speed, and it seemed that Trueman had only to run in as fast as he could to spread panic. In the first match, fittingly at Headingley for both Trueman and myself, India lost 4 wickets without a run at the start of their second innings – 3 to Trueman and 1 to Bedser.

There was nothing in the wicket to account for the debacle, and I turned to the players and said: 'Take a good look at the board for you'll never see another like it in a Test.' Except for the figure 4 against the fall of wickets there were noughts everywhere. Australia were close with the first three out for 0 at Brisbane in 1950, but that was on a treacherous wicket. India at Headingley had five out for 26 and the final total was 165. By the eighties India, with a new generation of cricketers, won the Prudential Cup and showed that the old traditional fear of fast bowling had long since disappeared.

India hastily recruited Vinoo Mankad for the second Test at Lord's. He had been playing for Haslingden in the Lancashire League, and at the time I could not understand what one of the world's leading all-rounders – I would have put him in the first five – was doing in Saturday afternoon cricket when his country toured England. England won comfortably by 8 wickets, but Mankad played England on his own. As opening batsman he aggregated 256 runs, including a then record of 184 in the second innings, and bowled, in all, 97 overs with his left-arm spin.

Godfrey Evans almost scored 100 runs before lunch on the third morning and when I commiserated with him on getting so close to such a distinction he laughed and said: 'Oh, those sorts of records are only for the real batsmen.'

On the fourth evening England were left to get 77 to win and clearly there were many in the crowd hoping for a heady stampede to complete victory. But the pitch was beginning to wear and, believe me, Mankad, who came on after one over with a ball rubbed in the dust to remove the shine, and the off-spinner Ghulam Ahmed needed a lot of watching. I was not out of form, having made 150 in the first innings, and when Simpson was run out at 8 I saw no point in taking risks. Wisden described it as a 'pathetic display but with the weather stable Hutton was satisfied to let the match drift into the fifth day'. On another page of the same edition the editor complained: 'In our uncertain climate Hutton took an unnecessary risk in waiting until the fifth day for victory.' Of course, I wasn't 'satisfied' to let the match go into a fifth day, but neither writer seemed to understand how well the Indian spinners bowled. Often I read criticism of the run rate when by rights praise should have gone to the bowlers. If Peter May and I had been able to apply the knockout blow there and then, we would have done so with the utmost relish and earned ourselves a day off!

A lot of the critics dismissed the Old Trafford Test as a bad joke after India were routed for totals of 58 and 82 inside a day, Trueman taking 8 for 31 in the first innings and Bedser 5 for 27 in the second. India, admittedly, cut a pitiful figure, and one of the bowlers said it was the first time he had bowled at stumps without a batsman in his range of vision. There was a tendency to retreat in the direction of square leg, and one batsman ran in, hardly took time to take guard, and ran out again. I never saw anything like it at Test level, but it was a heartening fact that England had a fast bowler to demoralize opponents.

Tony Lock was also introduced against India, and actually took a catch the first time he handled the ball for England. An aggressive player, he was an immense asset to every side he played for, never giving up and fighting to the last ditch. As a close fielder he was peerless, outstandingly brave, and he had the ideal temperament.

The Australians had the bowlers to deal out shocks. A classic example was the way in which they cut the West Indies down to size in 1951-52 in another of those rubbers described as 'for the championship of the world'. Australia won four of the five Tests, the averages of the three Ws ranged from 53·70 to 14·50, and Sonny Ramadhin left the field in tears at Melbourne. His wickets cost 49·64 each.

There is one vital aspect of the 1953 series against Australia which is invariably overlooked – and that was the excellent spirit and determination in the English ranks. Without it England would never have won, and survived the difficult Lord's and Headingley Tests to go to the Oval all square. There were so many dramas and changes of fortune in that wonderful summer that I must have gone through every emotion known to man. There was the severe disappointment at Trent Bridge where I am convinced Bedser's 14 wickets would have taken England to victory but for rain; the overwhelming sense of relief at Lord's when Watson and Bailey staged their epic resistance after all sensible hope had been abandoned – I was so tense I could not bear to watch half the time; the ebb and flow at Old Trafford with Australia's sensational collapse to 31 for 8 in the last unbelievable hour (some of the London journalists, having written off the match as a draw, left early, only to hear the stupefying news at Crewe Station that Australia were 31 for 6); the strain and anguish of another desperate rearguard action at Headingley (I counter-attacked by opening with Tony Lock in the hope of exploiting spin at the end where Alan Davidson had turned one or two); and, finally, the glorious, unforgettable moment of victory at the Oval. It took some time for the fact to sink in that the Ashes were back after nineteen long years.

I lost all five tosses, and it is far from the truth that I was relieved not to have to make the decision at the Oval. On the contrary, I badly wanted to bat first as I suspected the pitch would eventually take spin – as indeed it did. There was not much in it in the first innings, and my chief concern was that Australia would not score too many runs in their second knock and leave England with a large target on a turning wicket. All 9 Australian wickets to fall to bowlers were shared by Lock (5 for 45) and Laker – De Courcy was run out – and England were left to get 132. By now there was real turn, but fortunately not too fast, and, equally fortunately, Australia's attack was not as well balanced as England's. Hassett used spin at one end and alternated with Lindwall and Miller at the other. I was annoyed to be run out, but when their form was most needed Denis Compton and Bill Edrich found it so well that they looked as if they could have gone on to centuries.

England's players could almost sense the swell of popular senti-ment, and after waiting so long for a victory over Australia it was an excusable emotion. There have been better Test sides to tour England, but few can have been so warmly regarded or, in Lindsay Hassett, have had a captain of more chivalry and fight.

My personal feelings could be imagined. Bedser, Evans, Compton, Edrich and I had been on the receiving end since 1946. We had started with the maulings by Bradman's vastly superior sides and, Edrich apart, had also suffered a 4–1 beating in 1950–51.

I had a lasting regret that Cyril Washbrook was not there to savour the moment. Nor Watson (in the north we called him Billy rather than Willie as his father, Billy, was a well-known Bradford footballer). If he and Bailey had not batted from 12.30 until 5.40 at Lord's on the last day, Australia would have gone one ahead and, in all likelihood, it would have stayed that way. It was Watson's maiden Test against Australia and, while it is true the pitch became progressively slower, the demands on him and Trevor were abnormal. Their discipline and concentration had to be verging on the inhuman. At tea one of the players looked at Billy and voiced all our thoughts: 'I'm lost in admiration. He's batted all this time knowing that if he makes one mistake, just one tiny error of judge-ment, we have had it. And he's still at it.'

In such moments superstition is apt to take over and throughout the partnership Freddie Brown sat in a chair not daring to move lest it turn England's luck! All I could do in the intervals was to encour-age them to stick it out, just as Hedley Verity had done with me in

1938. Then, if I had got out on my way to Bradman's record, it would have been disappointing and unlikely to have affected the result. Here it was so different, and when the last ball had been bowled and England had escaped I began to believe in miracles. To save the match after three being out for 12 – we were set the impossible task of 343 to win – and Compton at 73 in a full day's play was truly remarkable, and I think the last day seemed the longest ever.

One of my big disappointments of the rubber was to have been bowled second ball by Lindwall on my own home ground at Heading-ley after Hassett (said to have feared Bedser on a greenish pitch) had put England in. The start was delayed for twenty minutes, and Lindwall opened at the football stand end where there was no screen in those days. I never saw the ball which yorked me. Not to my surprise, I read that I made a rather crude jab with my bat some distance from my pad.

There were two other occasions when, for no accountable reason, I lost sight of the ball. The first was at Johannesburg in 1938 when H. Q. Davies hit and felled me. Leslie Ames later told me that he did not see his first ball either. Fortunately it passed by his head six to eight inches away. The second experience was at Lord's in the 1950 Test with the West Indies when, in the second innings, Valentine was bowling from the nursery end. According to general opinion, the ball came 'up the hill', which I accept as accurate for the simple reason that I cannot argue otherwise. By all accounts it was a good ball which might have bowled me had I seen it all the way. But it is, believe me, a blank and hopeless feeling when you lose sight of the ball completely and poke out a dead bat in sheer desperation.

I have always maintained the necessity of effective sightscreens. Against a dark background, or poor screens, there is a real fear, particularly at the start of an innings, of losing the ball in flight. I never once had the problem in Australia's clear light. They also have good screens.

Another incident etched in my mind was going for a vital catch in the Oval Test of 1953. Trueman was bowling from the pavilion end and Neil Harvey, going for a hook, just failed to middle it properly and it went in the air. I set off running backwards towards deepish square leg with a thousand thoughts rushing through my head. After what seemed to be an age I took the catch at shoulder height, and I felt the peace of relief. Apart from the fact that it was Trueman's first Australian wicket, I felt that if we kept our heads we were on the way.

A lot was made of the fact that Australia's scoring rate throughout the series was faster than England's. As far as I was concerned, that was an interesting rather than a vital statistic, which would not have been seized upon had the result gone the other way. I am certain the public would not have enjoyed the reverse position, and I believe the English can be oversensitive in such matters. Not so much was made of England's casualty rate. The injury bogey was not laid to rest until the Oval. I also recognize Australia were handicapped by Bill Johnston's injury. He would have been hard to handle at Old Trafford and Headingley.

England's patchy batting, in truth, did not leave me with scope to attack, and, considering everything, I was personally happy to bat as freely as I did. Compton was tormented by his knee injury and was not the Denis of old, Graveney lacked consistency, and from Edrich, second in the averages with 39·00, the figure went down to Simpson with 13·50. I was the only batsman on either side to exceed an average of 50 and, all in all, it was not a vintage series for batsmen. Hassett had to go in first and was Australia's most successful batsman with 36·50. Bradman would not have thought much of that!

If Trueman, on National Service, had been playing regularly for Yorkshire and therefore for England, he would have been invaluable. Without him I had to use Bedser to the best possible advantage, including keeping him reasonably fresh for the arrival of the new ball. A Bedser–Trueman partnership throughout the five matches would have been ideal, and when they came together at the Oval they shared 7 of the first-innings wickets. Bedser, as always, carried his enormous burden superbly, and by gaining a mastery over Morris and his fellow left-hander, Harvey, he must have demolished most of Hassett's batting plans.

I don't know if the Aussies planned to try to knock Bedser down at the first hurdle, but I was very surprised to see Graeme Hole in the first over of the first Test attempt to drive him in the most cavalier of fashions. He was bowled, and Alec was treated with the respect he deserved from then on. I depended on Bedser for penetration, for accuracy in the holding operations, and for the bulk of the wickets. Just how much rested on the most overworked bowler in the land was shown by the fact that his four main supports, Bailey, Lock, Laker and Wardle, took 38 wickets between them – one fewer than Bedser.

May, having been put out temporarily by Lindwall, had to postpone his greater glories, and too many of the batsmen did not come off for a variety of reasons.

At the end, when it was all over, the pinpricking criticisms of my supposed caution from predictable quarters did not seem to be too important. I felt like the general who had survived some early reverses to win the last all-important battle, the one to count. When I saw the crowds, happy and cheering, massed in front of the pavilion at the Oval, I knew the struggle had been worthwhile. The chaos in the dressing room after the match was madly happy. I didn't know where the people came from; I saw people I had never seen before or since, and in the middle of the scrum were the friendly Aussies. There was such confusion that I never saw Miller throwing the champagne empties at the dressing-room clock, though others assured me he did. All around was glorious bedlam, though one Aussie told me he could not face going home after losing.

There was nowhere to sit down, kit was strewn everywhere, a bat here, a shirt there. I found my pads on the other side of the room, and I never did recover some of my shirts.

It was mid-evening before I was allowed to leave. I arrived at Pudsey at 1 a.m. having been driven home by a friend along the A1 – and that's how I felt, A1. The Oval was always a favourite ground for me and for many other Yorkshiremen. I thought of that long, long innings in 1938 and of Hedley Verity – how he would have relished the moment in his quiet way – of my hundredth first-class century on the ground, the fearful whipping England had endured against Australia in 1948 when I was last out for 30 out of 52 to a breathtaking catch down the leg side by Don Tallon. After that England debacle, I had gone to field at deep square leg by the new scoreboard and had turned to the crowd and asked: 'Are there any fast bowlers among you?' Now England had fast bowlers and the Ashes.

I thought, too, of George Hirst, who had done so much for me, and Wilfred Rhodes, England's last pair, who had gathered the last 15 runs to beat Australia in singles. Some have it that the famous story of 'we'll get 'em in singles' is a romantic myth. George, however, once assured me: 'When Wilfred came in, I said to him: "Now

Wilfred, there's no need to bustle. We'll get 'em in singles," and we did.'

There was the matchless partnership on a sticky wicket between Jack Hobbs and Herbert Sutcliffe in 1926 when England regained the Ashes after a long run of defeats after the first war. If I could be granted one wish from a good cricketing fairy, I would be tempted to ask to see a rerun of that famous stand. Rhodes, who played in the match at the age of forty-eight, used to talk about it with a faraway look in his eyes.

I also thought of Cyril Turner, my closest companion from 1933 to 1939. No young player could have had a better friend. He freely passed on his intimate knowledge of the game, his valuable views on cricket and cricketers – including the Yorkshire team – and, a clean-living man himself, he was like a second father to me. He always called Brian Sellers 'Crackerjack' and when Yorkshire played at Lord's or at the Oval our routine was a meal of steak and chips followed by a visit to the Palladium or the old Holborn Empire. We saw most of the great prewar performers. I recall those days with nostalgia and gratitude for my friendships. The old system in which a senior player looked after a junior was excellent, and I could not have had a better guide and philosopher. Sometimes we were joined by Horace Fisher, a fitness fanatic and left-arm bowler who spent most of his time in the leagues. Yet he contrived to gain the most coveted Yorkshire cap without serving the customary three years. No one quite knew how he did it.

So ended one of my most unforgettable days. As George Hirst had said all those years ago – there was no need to bustle. We got there in the end.

6

Caribbean Cauldron

To set out the origins and assess the responsibilities for the tension which marred so much of MCC's tour of the West Indies in the early months of 1954 is anything but simple. Certainly the early insistence of so many people that the 'cricket championship of the world' was at stake did nothing to ease the situation. Nor did the constant emphasis upon victory which the MCC players found to be stressed by English residents in the West Indies. A certain amount of tension was thus created before a ball had been bowled. This quickly became heightened through crowds, whose intense noise, coupled with almost ceaseless torrid heat, provided a background in which tempers too easily became frayed. At times some crowds were demonstrative and twice they became menacing. Convinced by the happenings on the field that the general standard of umpiring in the West Indies was not adequate for Test cricket, the touring team felt that the crowd atmosphere made the work of the men in the middle even harder than it should have been. The MCC players sympathised with the umpires threatened with physical violence, as marred the First and Third Tests. When, as the West Indies players admitted, the majority of disputed decisions, usually at moments of match crisis, went against MCC, they wondered how in the circumstances any umpire could remain completely calm and controlled.

To a man the MCC team recognised their responsibilities as ambassadors of sport but, being human, the less phlegmatic did not always hide their annoyance and displeasure. In some instances only someone with the forbearance of the most highly trained diplomat could have been expected to preserve absolute sangfroid. Dramatic gestures of disappointment and untactful remarks, however understandable some of them were in the heat of the moment, caused resentment among West Indies officials, umpires and others. No doubt some of the 'incid-

ents' were exaggerated, but to deny their existence . . . would be only
a disservice to the future welfare of the game.

Wisden Cricketers' Almanack, 1955

The West Indies tour of 1954 left me physically and mentally
drained, and I am in no doubt that my playing career was foreshortened maybe by two years as a result. In the following summer
I was fit only to play in two of the four Tests with Pakistan, in
twenty-two first-class matches, and it was a close call that I was
well enough to go to Australia.

For a variety of reasons, mostly beyond my understanding, cricket
was caught up in the maelstrom of Caribbean politics and other
emotive matters. An overheated crowd reaction to Test matches
which were unwisely regarded as for the unofficial championship of
the world erupted with a riot, and off the field there was a riot of
another variety – words and rumours. The MCC players were
sucked into an impossible vortex and being cricketers and not trained
diplomats, they reacted in different ways. MCC had hardly set foot
in Jamaica than some of the white community, who seemed to be
slowly adjusting to the winds of change, were drilling it into the
players how important it was for them to win. The so-called world
championship tag was a nuisance. Stories as unfettered as the trade
winds swept the islands – often fanned by ill-informed press
comment – and finally an incident was manufactured in which I
was alleged to have insulted Mr Alex Bustamente, Jamaica's Chief
Minister. The charge was so baseless that it was incredible it was
ever made, and I cannot believe any touring captain anywhere has
been obliged to endure such a blatant discourtesy. I was so shocked
by the scene in the dressing room caused by uninvited officials, who
burst in like the Gestapo, that I could not concentrate and lost my
wicket as soon as my innings was resumed. Fortunately, by then,
England were in a good position.

MCC were condemned and defended with equal passion, and
doubtless mistakes were made by both sides. I have in mind batsmen
staying at the wicket after they were fairly and squarely out, and
verbal outbursts at umpiring decisions. But it is a sad reflection on
the decline in standards that the incidents, regrettable though they
were, were mild compared with kicking down of stumps, players
attacking each other and bat throwing and other examples of bad
behaviour in the seventies and eighties. It can also be stressed that

England were blameless in the Georgetown riot – a crowd distur-
bance now unfortunately more common in some parts of the world
– and in the threats made to an umpire at Jamaica. There were
occasions when I wondered what the 'strong' leaders of the past,
like Jardine and Sellers, would have done had they been in my
situation. I do not accept that a different and stricter style of leadership would have automatically avoided trouble.

A theory was advanced that some West Indian elements felt
slighted at having to play host to the first touring professional
captain. In the eighties such a view appears to be absurdly irrational,
but little was rational during the tour and maybe there was something in the contention. The time was at the fag-end of colonial days,
and there were some in the communities who had obviously been
well sheltered from social changes. One of the English correspond-
ents was asked not to type because the occupants of the adjoining
room were changing for dinner, and it now seems singularly strange
in post-Worrell–Sobers–Lloyd days that I should have once been
taken aside by a prominent official and told that West Indies cricket
would be doomed if ever a black captain was appointed.

Charles Palmer, the tour player–manager, was also a sitting target
for critics. He was charged with being 'too conciliatory', which
meant he tried everything in his power to defuse the situation with
calm reasoning. Both Charles and I were in a no-win position, and
as I shared his burden and understood his problems I know that no
manager could have tried harder, been more diplomatic, or done his
onerous job better. When the brakes fail and a car careers down
hill, the driver cannot be blamed. Charles was in the driving seat in
an uncontrollable position. One official at Kingston did not
exchange a single word with him throughout two visits to Jamaica,
and well might it be asked how is it possible not to be on friendly
terms with such a likable man. Charles's many years of service in
the game at county and national level were properly rewarded when
he became president of MCC.

In retrospect it is all too clear how ill-starred the omens for the
tour were. Even before MCC went for a three weeks' tuning-up in
Bermuda there was a local squabble over the choice of the grounds.
Not that it mattered much as it rained most of the time. The absence
of Bedser threw Trueman into an adventure for which he was not
properly prepared. On the eve of our departure Viscount Monckton
(then Sir Walter) lectured us on the political pitfalls which might be

ahead – excellent as far as it went, but it did not tell us how sensitive the situation could be. The West Indies consist of a group of widely scattered islands with separate customs and cultures, even currencies, and every attempt to form a collective political federation has failed. The genius of Sir Frank Worrell was his ability to bring the fragmented islands together. Cricket perhaps is the one unifying force, but in the fifties inter-island jealousies often emerged. One example was that each island provided the umpires for its Test match. The inevitable result was that the standards varied widely.

Large-scale betting and cheap rum stoked up crowd excitement, and the noise in the middle of the ground was frequently so loud that I had to shout my instructions to fielders.

Having made two previous visits with Yorkshire to Jamaica, in 1936 under the managership of George Hirst, and as a reinforcement to Gubby Allen's injury-stricken team in 1947–48, I knew how hospitable the West Indies were to visiting cricketers. Without wanting to be ungrateful or unsociable, however, I did not want my players to be committed to a round of functions, and for the young players in particular to have potent drinks thrust on them. In a sense my argument was a compliment to the West Indies, whose cricket standards were the admiration of the world. For the first time England had sent the strongest available side (albeit chosen in too much of a hurry!) and it needed to be on top form to hold the brilliant West Indies, who had recently thrashed us on our own grounds. There is nothing more tiring than standing around having to indulge in small talk with strangers, who either pump the players dry with cricket talk or find it hard to discover a common ground of polite chitchat. Often the same people were at every function. Accordingly, I asked Lord's to try to keep the social engagements to an acceptable number without giving offence.

My plea in this direction was never intended as an antisocial gesture, or as a rebuff to generous hosts, but purely in the best interests of the side. For some reason the story circulated that I had ordered MCC players not to fraternize with the opposition. That was quite untrue and I was surprised to read in Jeff Stollmeyer's book *Everything Under the Sun** that the 'truth leaked out through other members of the England team that Len had asked his players not to mix with their West Indian counterparts'.

* Stanley Paul, 1983.

Hearsay evidence is never accepted in law, and I can only conclude that someone either misunderstood me or got hold of the wrong end of the stick, though I can't think why. Relationships between the players were better and more easily achieved than with some officials, a minority of the press, and hotheads in the public. In some instances there was an anti-British sentiment, and once rumours started it was no more possible to stop them than nail jelly to a wall. Events became so bizarre that one of the English journalists told me he worried every night because the stories he had dispatched to London were hardly credible and he was bound to be accused of wild exaggeration.

Twice the manager and I had to deal with complaints from white people about the behaviour of MCC players, and while we were deeply concerned and did out best, we could not abandon our many duties to sift out conflicting evidence and perhaps apportion blame. An English visitor to Barbados alleged that two of the team had offended her in a hotel lift. She identified them as Trueman and Lock. I told them to meet her the following morning and, if they were in the wrong, to apologize. The meeting began with a threat to report the pair to Lord's and she proceeded with an open throttle to give them a piece of her mind. When she had gone I said to Trueman: 'I thought you took that pretty well.'

He retorted: 'So did I, considering it wasn't us!'

Actually we all finished on the best of terms, and she insisted on giving the whole team a champagne party.

The manager and I were also called out before breakfast one morning at Bridgetown to deal with a demand that Graveney be sent home because it was said he had been rude at a function the previous night. Graveney insisted that he had been defending the name of his team-mates after some remarks had been made about them. No action was taken, but it was all very wearing, very unnecessary, and I had to admit it put me off my stride.

There was no shortage of advice to us. Advice is easy, and I never pictured myself with a bat in one hand and big stick in the other. The manager, a former schoolmaster, was like a Dutch uncle, and I was desperately trying to marshal my playing resources after two defeats in the opening two Tests.

The most embarrassing incident on the field was in the fourth Test at Port-of-Spain when J. K. Holt was caught at slip by Graveney off Compton off the last ball before a lunch interval. The dismissal

ck 'The Master' Hobbs, whose ability to
ore runs on every type of wicket earned him
e title of England's greatest ever batsman.
dolized him and was awestruck when we
st met

Hedley Verity, the great England and
Yorkshire slow left-arm bowler, and a close
personal friend, who did so much to help me
through my marathon record innings of 364

ith my favourite partner Cyril Washbrook
ing greeted by a Test crowd at Headingley
owing the fervour Yorkshire reserve for one
their own

Our illustrious predecessors, Jack Hobbs and
Herbert Sutcliffe, my mentor, open for
England at the Oval in 1930

George Hirst, another of Yorkshire's immortals, became a second father to me when I was sent to be coached by him. I'm glad to say that he lived to share my major achievements.

Big Bill Bowes, fast bowler and deep student of the game. I owed much to his wise teachings

Wilfred Rhodes, still bowling in 1930, had no peer as an all-rounder and cricket sage. Another who set me on the right road by example and advice

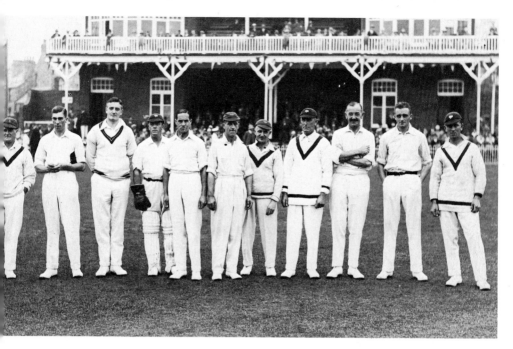

The palmy prewar days when Yorkshire carried all before them.
Top: the 1926 side at Scarborough. Left to right: R. Kilner, A. Mitchell,
T. A. Jacques, A. Dolphin, H. Sutcliffe, P. Holmes. E. Robinson,
W. Rhodes, A. W. Lupton (captain), G. G. Macaulay, M. Leyland.
Below: 1937, also at Scarborough. Left to right: H. Verity, W. Bowes,
N. Yardley, B. Sellers (captain), H. Sutcliffe, F. Smailes, W. Barber,
A. Wood, M. Leyland, C. Turner, myself. Ellis Robinson, a regular,
was not playing in the match

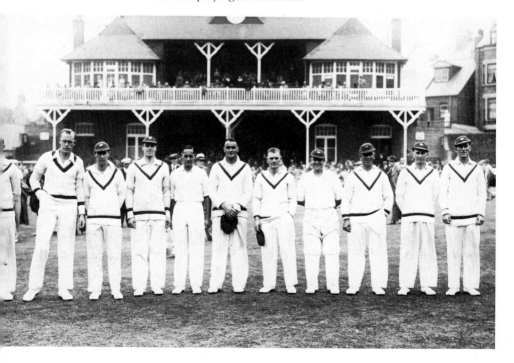

Top left: A nostalgic reminder of my world record. Hedley Verity is the wicketkeeper as I bat on the Bognor Regis beach on the Sunday of the Oval Test in 1938. *Top right*: Don Bradman, the finest of all batsmen, and my inspiration as I watched him score 309 in a day at Headingley in 1930. Eight years later I was to break his record

The scene in the middle as the sporting Aussies congratulate me on passing Don's record. Bill Brown shakes my hand while umpire Frank Chester and Joe Hardstaff watch from the other wicket. In mid-wicket, Don, who has just seen his score of 334 overtaken, steps aside from the celebrations to consult bowler Fleetwood-Smith

George Headley, the first and perhaps the best of the distinguished
line of black West Indies batsmen. He scored so many runs that
his followers called Bradman the 'white Headley'

The scoring chart of my innings of 364. The wicket on the left is at the
pavilion end of the Oval

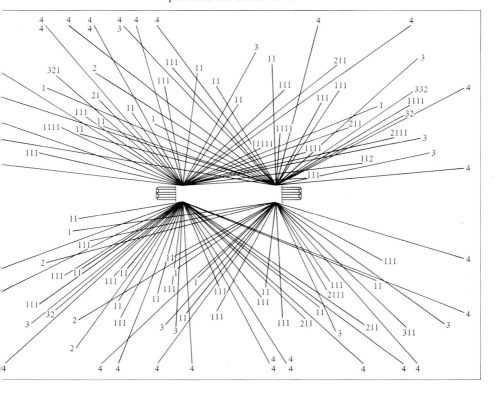

Not such happy moments. *Above*: Bowled by Australian off-spinner
Ian Johnson in the summer of 1948. *Below*: My cap was knocked
off by Ray Lindwall in the final Test at the Oval in 1953. Fortunately
it dropped beyond the stumps to the disappointment of the eager
Aussies

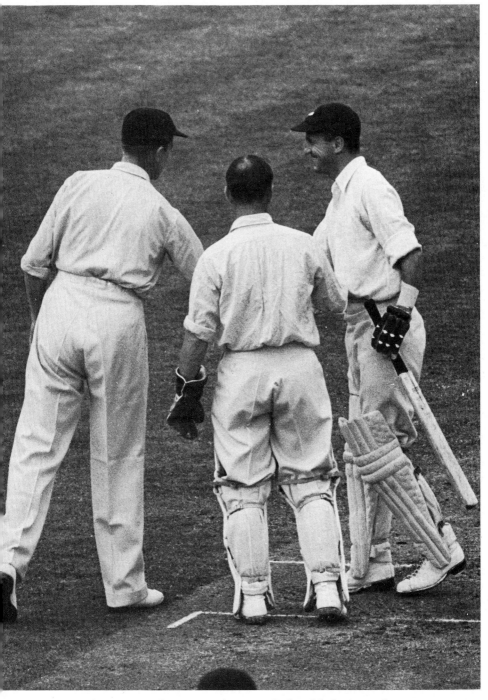

Another occasion for congratulations. The handshake comes from
Jim Laker, supported by Arthur McIntyre, to mark my hundredth
first-class century at the Oval – where else? – in 1951

The finish of a drive against the Indian spinner Vinoo Mankad, who
had a remarkable all-round Test at Lord's in 1952, the year I was
appointed as England's first ever professional captain

in the eyes of the fielders could not have been more straightforward. A googly was misread and went off the edge of the bat at waist height direct to slip. To our surprise Holt stayed at the wicket waiting for a decision. Compton appealed without apparent success. I was staggered and Compton stupefied when Ellis Achong refused to uphold the appeal – an appeal which should never have been necessary. Graveney, who was nearest the members' pavilion, threw the ball down in disgust with some observation out of my hearing and stalked off to a round of booing.

There were three parts to a totally unnecessary incident for which MCC, at least locally, took total blame. The batsman shouldn't have stayed – he had every right to do so if he was in any doubt, but how he could have been in doubt escaped me; the umpire shouldn't have made such a whopping mistake; and Graveney shouldn't have lost his temper.

Taken in isolation the incident was bad, but in the broader context of what had gone before Graveney's explosion was more understandable. The local papers had a field day and, as captain, I took the brunt of the blame, especially from the pen of an expatriate Yorkshireman.

Wisden calculated the ratio of umpiring mistakes was seven or eight to two in favour of the West Indies, and at the end of the tour Charles Palmer, trying to be honest and constructive in the interests of the game, made a statement in which he said: 'By analysis we consider that mistakes have been more against them than for MCC, and I repeat this does not imply dishonesty.' I associated myself with the comment. Since those days umpiring in Test matches has come under fire from various captains and managers to a degree unknown in my era. Television and the playback has made the lot of the umpire even harder, and it seems to me that it is incredible that a game which has become so professionalized still relies, to a large extent, on amateur officials, some of whom have never played above club level. I am not suggesting all umpires must necessarily be former first-class players; but it does help and is one of the important reasons why English professional umpires are in a class of their own. Nearly all are former county players.

It did not need a crystal ball to foresee one of the emotive issues could be the use of bumpers. Trueman was immediately 'Mr Bumper Man' in a calypso and every bouncer produced excited approval or disapproval according to which side was bowling. The West Indies had one authentic fast bowler in Frank King and England had

Trueman, Statham, Moss and Bailey. Before the team left – incident-ally the first MCC party to go by air from England – bumpers were a topic of discussion at Lord's and Stollmeyer approached the manager on the same subject. Not because England would have been considerably disadvantaged but because a no-bumpers pact was impracticable, I felt it was a matter for the umpires. If they con-sidered bumpers were being overdone, they had the authority to step in. I did not think either Stollmeyer or myself could go back to our bowlers and say: 'You've got to cut out bouncers.' They were not banished by law and if there was a bumper-happy bowler in the series, it was King. He must have averaged three an over.

Except for the fourth Test on the mat at Port-of-Spain, bumpers were not used to excess. In these days their use is restricted, and perhaps not before time, as they were getting out of control. I understand the reason for the use of helmets, though I doubt if I would have worn one. I found the more protection and equipment I carried the more encumbered I felt. After the war I experimented with a protection on my left arm, but after a while I discarded it as it hampered me. Too much gear slows a batsman down and in excessive heat it is as uncomfortable as a hair shirt. Some modern batsmen are so padded up that they might have stepped off an American football field. Helmets tend to make batsmen anonymous lookalikes, and surely there is no need for them against medium-pace bowlers. Even allowing for nonstop pace bowling and changes for the worst in wickets, I cannot picture Hobbs, Sutcliffe, Hammond, Leyland, Woolley and Co. in helmets, and Gary Sobers didn't do too badly without even a thigh pad. The best protection is still to be found in footwork, keeping the head still and eyes on the ball, and judgement and nerve.

From England's viewpoint the West Indies tour could be divided into two parts, the first of which produced two miserable defeats at Jamaica and Barbados with morale sinking low. Unquestionably the West Indies were the better side, with England far below their potential, but having said that, there were two crucial leg-before decisions, one of which went against myself in the first Test, and the other against Compton in the second. Possibly they affected the results but equally England should never have been in a position to lose two matches on two decisions. The matches should have been safe by then, and the truth was England did not reach their potential until the third Test. It takes time to acclimatize to the light, pace and so on, and even Frankie Worrell, then at Manchester University, assured me it took him several weeks to resettle when he returned home. The boat was badly rocked by the petty off-the-field incidents, and the threat of Ramadhin and Valentine was still to be removed.

The first Test defeat was both a surprise and a bitter blow to my hopes. To be honest, the possibility of losing at Sabina Park had not seriously occurred to me, as I did not think either side was likely to be dismissed twice on a pitch which was as hard as concrete. Stollmeyer has since told me that he had similar thoughts. I thought the bat would be in such command that my problem might be to keep my bowlers in good heart; if I played a spinner like Laker or Wardle, one of the stroke-makers like Weekes or Walcott might put him out of business for the tour. When I had played for Yorkshire in Jamaica before the war just about one innings apiece was completed inside five days and I thought something of that order might happen in the Test. In a sense the match was to be a holding operation.

A lot of words were spilled over my alleged 'fixation' for pace when I omitted Laker, but I did not read one critic who tumbled to the real reason. Unfortunately for England, the course of the match did not go according to plan, and Stollmeyer must have been immensely gratified, not to say relieved, by the unexpected bonus of a victory. Stollmeyer banked his reputation on two decisions. The first was the inclusion of George Headley, which brought him into disagreement with Sir Errol dos Santos, then president of the Board, and howls of indignation from the other islands, and the second was not to enforce the follow-on. Headley was forty-four years old and had been playing in the Birmingham League. A public subscription brought him back to Jamaica to be available against MCC and when he was selected the *Trinidad Guardian* thundered on the front page: 'Even charity can find no justification for the inclusion of the aged Headley.'

In four preliminary innings against MCC George scored 1, 12, 5 and 53 not out, thanks to two missed chances off successive balls, and Stollmeyer took the last as evidence of his ability to shore up an innings. There had been wild talk of digging up the pitch, or boycotting the match, if he did not play. Whether such threats were to be taken seriously I have no way of knowing, but George's selection was indicative of Stollmeyer's thinking that he might be hard-pressed. Headley rightly had a devoted following. No one admired him more than I did, as I fielded at Lord's in 1939 when he scored faultless centuries in both innings on a losing side. For years he *was* the West Indies batting and he has to be mentioned in the same breath as Bradman (the 'white Headley' according to Jamaicans), Hammond and Hobbs. Clarrie Grimmett described him as the 'greatest on-side batsman ever'.

I had mixed feelings about giving him one off the mark as a little gesture to one of cricket's master batsmen who had never failed in a series between 1929 and 1939 and, as a scorer, was second only to Bradman – but I decided to do so. I trust he accepted it in the spirit in which it was intended – as a salute and not out of sympathy. He made 16 and 1, having his stumps spreadeagled in the second innings by Lock's fast ball which, not surprisingly, he did not see. A faster ball from an alleged slow bowler would be hard to imagine. Subsequently Lock was no-balled for throwing to add to the problems.

One of the turning points was a stand by Gerry Gomez and the wicketkeeper Cliff McWatt which added 60 astounding runs off the new ball. Until then England had done reasonably well, and it was one of those infuriating occasions for a captain, bowlers and fielders when the batsmen fling the bat at everything within reach, 4s are sprayed in every direction and catches go down – five in this instance. The captain cannot believe the batsmen's luck can hold, and it becomes impossible to set a field. The noise and pandemonium were more like a frenzied football cup tie than a cricket match and excitement rose to such a pitch that a 4 was signalled when Compton – though hampered by a peanut vendor – fielded the ball yards inside the boundary.

England still looked capable of avoiding defeat when Watson, who made 116, and I put on 130 for the first wicket in the second innings. I was halfway to a century when I was given out leg before playing forward to Gomez. Gerry was always a fair appealer but when a batsman has played as long as I had he has a fair idea when he is out, and I was surprised not to be given the benefit of the doubt. But there it was. After May and Graveney there was an unseemly collapse, England were defeated and Stollmeyer was vindicated. His decision not to enforce the follow-on – partly because his spinners had sore fingers – caused an eruption of anger among the home crowd and 150 extra police were sent to the ground. The next morning four women entered, dressed in severe unrelieved black, explaining: 'We are in mourning for West Indies cricket killed by Jeff Stollmeyer.' By mid-afternoon presumably they slipped out for a change of outfit. Stollmeyer was justified, but there was a chilling little example of the fanaticism of West Indies cricket when his plane – and MCC's – was searched for bombs before taking off for Barbados.

Troubles never come singly and the second Test also ended disastrously. Ramadhin had still not been dealt with and that exciting moment I had known at the Oval only months before now seemed light years away. In the pre-Test game with Barbados, thrillingly won by MCC by 1 wicket, I had played with a chill on the liver and batted at No. 8, fortunately with some success. A few days earlier a report had been sent to a London newspaper that I was to be flown home for an operation for the removal of kidney stones. Where the story originated, or why no effort was made to check with me or the manager, I do not know. Normally the answer to an invention of that kind is to ignore it, to carry on playing and allow the lie to die a natural death. The manager, however, had to take calls from other newspapers checking the facts, and my concern was to get a message to my wife Dorothy that I was not on my way back bound for the operating table.

While that little bit of nonsense was being sorted out, Lock's faster delivery was again no-balled, and he was now a marked bowler. I had to tell him not to bowl that ball unless he had my permission, which, in view of what had happened, was unlikely.

News also filtered through that 50 per cent of letter writers to the *Evening Standard* did not think Denis Compton was worth his place in the Test team, a view with which I profoundly disagreed, and was an unhelpful contribution to a struggling team. Denis gave the most appropriate of answers with 93 in the second innings of the Test before being given out to a googly from Jeff Stollmeyer, a decision which surprised the players in a position to judge. By general consent Denis was unlucky to have to go.

After the game Denis went for one of his periodical checkups on his knee, and after looking at the plates, the doctor told him: 'You can't play cricket with this knee.'

'But I do,' answered Denis.

'Then you'll have to take a month's rest.'

'Sorry, but I'm playing in two days' time.'

There was always a fear that Denis might succumb to the pain of his knee and not last out the series. Yet he always came back and those who were inclined to regard him as a bit of a glamour boy did not know that he could be as tough as any. He had to be to continue playing with his handicap.

Nothing went right in the Test. There were the much unwanted problems off the field and, as rumour spread unchecked, I could not do much else than drop anchor and hope to ride out the storm.

Even in the darkest periods I was still stubbornly confident that the West Indies bowling could be handled as long as a complex over Ramadhin and Valentine did not develop and, by the end of the series, the widely held belief that the 'Calypso Twins' were dependent on each other was exposed as a fallacy. While Ramadhin finished with 23 wickets, 15 more than the next wicket-takers Atkinson and King, Valentine faded and died as a threat to England.

I was often tempted to think that someone on high slipped Ramadhin and Valentine and the Australian Jack Iverson into the international scene in a mischievous moment. Lindwall, Miller, Hammond, whom I saw bowl leg breaks and googlies in the manner born in South Africa, and other great cricketers looked the part from head to toe. They were athletic, as graceful as ballerinas and with a presence to command deference. Yet Iverson was big, raw-boned and clumsy; Ramadhin, a friendless orphan raised in a Canadian Mission School in a Trinidad village, was so slight of frame that his captain John Goddard joked that he couldn't put him on if a breeze was blowing; and Valentine, bespectacled, awkward-looking in his movements, had such an air of innocence that he might have come along to help put the nets up for the big-time players.

When I first saw Ramadhin and Valentine, neither yet twenty and with combined first-class experience of two matches by Ramadhin, I thought the West Indies had taken an outrageous gamble. While I had vaguely heard of Iverson before going to Australia, Valentine and Ramadhin came out of the blue. I shudder to think what Messrs Rhodes and Hirst, the arch-perfectionists, would have made of Valentine's open-chested action. He was nothing like the classical slow left-arm spinners of the Rhodes, Verity and Charlie Parker mould. Valentine gave the ball little or no air, but he spun it appreciably, was direct, offered little respite because he was so accurate and could bowl for lengthy spells.

Bowling methods fascinated me, and I always tried to test the intelligence of a bowler. The more nous he had, the more difficult he was to bat against. I also had respect for the accurate bowler able to turn the ball an inch or two, or just enough to beat the bat. Australia's Fleetwood-Smith could spin the ball like a top and had flight, but he was never certain where the ball would drop. The best bowlers have a natural gift for the essential basics of length and direction, plus something extra which is often difficult to define. Most batsmen play from the bowler's action. Batsmen did to their cost against O'Reilly and Ramadhin, and Rhodes had a deceptively quick arm action. The ball appeared to be released at a different pace from his hand than the turn of his arm indicated. Ramadhin was not dissimilar.

Ramadhin, with his sleeves rolled down and buttoned at the wrist, was difficult to spot, especially against a dark background, and it was much easier to pick his leg break or leg cutter in the clearer light of the West Indies or Australia. He quickly gained a reputation as a 'mystery' bowler, but actually 95 per cent of his deliveries were off-breaks and, in my opinion, his standard ball, the off-break, had the suspicion of a jerk or a throw. The speed of his arm action was confusing but, from the close range of a non-striker, I thought there was a jerk. His leg break or cutter was usually given more air and would have passed the closest scrutiny. He spun the ball a lot, and even when his secrets had been uncovered he was still an extraordinary bowler. Until Peter May and Colin Cowdrey had their record stand of 411 at Edgbaston in 1957 he was never really conquered by English batsmen. When MCC went to Georgetown in 1954 I noticed a variation of the three-card trick played outside the ground. Instead of 'finding the lady', punters were invited to find Ramadhin. They had my sympathy.

Iverson devised a freakish method of using his thumb and middle finger like the trigger of a gun. Early on in the 1950–51 tour he suddenly turned a ball a good twelve inches on a typically hard Sydney pitch. I couldn't have been more surprised. It took England three Tests to fathom. Ninety-five per cent were googlies, but by then the series belonged to Australia. Iverson's strange grip was perfected with a table tennis ball in a YMCA tent in Port Moresby during the war and there was a thirteen-year gap in his career. He introduced variations to produce the leg break, off-break and top spinner and when he was not taking wickets – 21 in the series at only 15·23 each – he attacked the leg stump with five defenders that side of the wicket. And I was the captain accused of being defensive!

Iverson left the international scene as abruptly as he had entered it, and England can be considered a little unlucky that they should meet him in his crowded hour of glory.

Jim Laker was pre-eminent with spin, flight and control, plus the ability to defend, and I would like to see more strive for the accuracy and subtle pace changes shown by Derek Underwood. The Valentines and Underwoods are hard to attack. Of the two, Valentine spun the ball more and on three occasions in 1950 he dismissed me when I felt set. Ramadhin and Valentine richly deserve their special niche in Test history, but one of the significant reasons for England's comeback in 1954 was the virtual fade-out of Valentine after the first innings of the Second Test.

There was a chorus to a calypso which ran:

> Lennie Hutton that English skipper
> He's known throughout the world as a real good cricketer
> His determination with the MCC
> Is to lead them always to victory.

After two defeats the words had a mocking ring, but the last two lines remained apt. I was still lying awake in the tropical nights wondering how the tide could be turned. I never thought the cause was irretrievably lost.

7
Final Triumph

The West Indies spectators are great gamblers on the game. It's the sort of crowd where I should have thought a racing man like Keith Miller would find himself very much at home. The crowd at Georgetown was expectant, excited, ready to burst out into applause and jubilation at a century partnership. Then Cliff McWatt, a local hero, was hopelessly and utterly run out. A thousand bets had been lost. Someone yelled disapproval and threw a bottle on to the pitch; then someone else and someone else. Packing cases were added to the bottles. Soon it seemed that everyone was throwing bottles and they came on to the field in thousands. The mood of the crowd developed quickly into a kind of frenzy and it spread like a bush fire. An official came on to the ground to ask Hutton to take his team off. Len never had a greater moment than when he replied: 'No. I want a couple of wickets before the close of play to-night.' He was cool, nerveless, quite unconcerned about the demonstrating crowds which surrounded him in angry thousands. He was superbly defiant. It was, if you like, the saying of the century. It was characteristic Len.

Denis Compton in *End of an Innings* (1958)

Two down and three to go – and one on the Trinidad mat which was not expected to provide an outright result – meant England had to win the third Test to have a chance of squaring the rubber. On the face of it England were scuppered but, as Wilfred Rhodes had said all those years before at Pudsey, there was no such thing as a hopeless cause. I read a boast in a local paper that the West Indies had at least two teams capable of beating England but, despite the position, I could sense a far more united side, maybe drawn together by the constant criticism and a sense that many were 'agin us'. There were small but important developments, like Graveney emerging as a slip fielder, a new position for him, and, unbeknown to me at the time, a small dinner party arranged by senior players including Compton and Bailey, pledged to rally to my support.

In the match with Guyana (then known as British Guiana) it was all too clear that the two umpires were not of the required standard for the Test for which they had been nominated. I had no alternative but to object, and to ask for two senior umpires to be flown from either Jamaica or Barbados. While the local Board upheld my complaint they flatly refused to have 'outside' replacements as they called them. I had again entered sensitive local territory.

Stollmeyer, who had seen the British Guiana match, gave me his support and a meeting was held to thrash out the problem. Berkeley Gaskin, a former Test bowler, husband of a cabinet minister and later a touring manager, was invited to attend, but when it was suggested he should umpire he was through the door in less time than it takes to say 'Not out!' I have never seen anyone disappear so quickly. Clearly he knew a thing or two about local conditions!

After a long discussion the Board recommended a retired Chinese umpire named 'Wing' Gillette and 'Badge' Menzies, the Indian groundsman at the Bourda ground staging the Test. Menzies accepted on the condition that he continued to supervise the preparation of the Test pitch. The result was that he started work at seven in the morning and carried on until play started. After umpiring all day he returned to his ground duties at close of play. Often during the intervals he was to be seen helping with the rolling and patching, and re-marking the creases.

As MCC beat British Guiana by an innings and 99 runs, with Watson and Graveney sharing a partnership of 402 – it wouldn't have ended there if they had not thrown their wickets away to give others an innings – I was able to form my views on the umpiring from a position of strength. Some years later Bobby Simpson's Australians ran into a similar problem at Georgetown and Gerry Gomez, then a Test selector and radio commentator, took over and, as would be expected, did a first-class job. At stumps he sprinted over to the commentary box, and it could not be said that he lacked a close-up of the play. In a Test at Manchester just after the war, R. C. Robertson Glasgow was put behind a post in the press box which slotted out his view of one end of the pitch. So he reported only what he saw at the other end!

The defeat of British Guiana completed a hat-trick of victories over Colony sides, as they were then called, a fact to strengthen my belief that England were at last a match for the West Indies and, if only we could concentrate on the cricket without political interference, there was still a chance of saving the series. Before arriving in Georgetown I had been warned by home sources that Guiana, on the South America mainland, was a political hotbed and visiting cricketers, particularly from England, were natural targets for demonstrations and political intrigues. There was nothing I could do about it, only hope for the best and try to concentrate the team's thoughts on winning the match. It was not easy to keep young men happy in Georgetown in those days. Modern players would have been shocked by the hotel accommodation, and if it hadn't been for the kindness of some of the residents it would have been even more difficult. One evening at a cinema there was an amusing, and perhaps revealing, insight into local tastes with a film based on the life of Joe Louis, the American boxing champion. The story had linking newsreel films of his actual fights and when they were shown almost the entire audience leaped to its feet cheering and gripped with excitement.

Two real strokes of luck came England's way in the Test. Presumably to accommodate Bob Christiani, the local hero who had made 55 and 82 in the Colony fixture, the West Indies dropped fast bowler King. Christiani was undoubtedly a fine player with a good Test record, but his inclusion upset the balance of the side. I wryly guessed what would have been said of me had England been two ahead and packed their side with batting, but the pitch was probably faster than in any of the other four matches and it was a costly error.

Then England won the toss, and I was never more determined, as W. G. Grace used to say, 'to take what the gods offered'. England made 435, and my contribution was 169. At one stage Valentine bowled to me with seven fielders on the off-side, and the only response I could make was to hit against the spin and miss the two fielders on the leg-side. I felt confident enough to attack even good length deliveries with this method, and the innings was one I look back on with pride.

Then followed as fine a spell of fast bowling by Brian Statham as it was ever my good fortune to see. Indeed, England were also indebted to Bailey for another magnificent performance in the final Test. Two great bowlers. Statham was so accurate that I never saw him properly collared anywhere in the world, and he often set up wickets for his partners, because he was so accurate.

On the notable occasion at Georgetown he began by dismissing Worrell, opening in place of the injured J. K. Holt, with a perfect late out-swinger. Stollmeyer went to a ball which both Evans and I put in the same class as Bedser's famous delivery to Bradman in 1947 at Adelaide.

Brian was always a grand lad. None was easier to skipper. He accepted the worst of fate's jests with whimsical humour, and he was so honest that he admitted his delivery to Stollmeyer was part accident; I would add part genius, too. As he was about to release the ball he felt his fingers move across the seam. The effect was devastating. An in-swinger, pitching on the leg stump, became a fast leg cutter and hit the top of the off stump. The perfect delivery. Understandably Jeff said he did not see the ball once it had pitched.

A calculated risk was taken with Walcott, next in. I knew his natural instinct would be to counter-attack, and consequently I wanted to force him onto his back foot. Compton and Bailey were stationed as joint silly mid-offs, no place for the faint-hearted at the best of times and calling for extra nerve with Clyde, a magnificent and powerful striker of the ball, at dangerously short range. I thought there might be the chance of an error if a drive was attempted against a fast full-length ball early in his innings – and Clyde would want to be rid of the threat of two attacking fielders so close to the bat. Sure enough, he opened his mighty shoulders and bisected the intrepid pair with a typically blistering drive. Statham kept his head, and again pitched the ball well up. Again Walcott went to drive, but was fractionally late and had his stumps spreadeagled. Class bowling indeed.

At lunch there was a tropical downpour, but the next day wickets fell until McWatt and Holt, needing a runner, shared an eighth wicket stand. Excitement was at fever pitch. The noise was deafening, but going for the hundredth run of the partnership McWatt was hopelessly short and Badge Menzies's decision against him from square leg was a formality.

Suddenly, to my surprise, I saw Menzies running full pelt in the direction of the pavilion. Until that moment I had not seen the bottles, boxes and other missiles falling in the area recently occupied by the fast-disappearing umpire.

My first reaction was to yell to Watson, fielding on the boundary nearest to the pavilion, to stop him. I realized that if Menzies went off it would be for good, and possibly the match and the series would come to an untimely end. I didn't think my voice could carry over the bedlam, but Watson successfully interpreted my anxious semaphore and stopped Menzies. Billy said that when he came to a halt Menzies was shaking with fright. I raced across to assure him that there was nothing to fear and we would look after him. He appeared singularly unconvinced and replied: 'But I have to live here, Mr Hutton!'

Frankly it never occurred to me, or the team, to leave the field and after ten minutes or so Mr W. S. Jones, president of the local Board, came to me and suggested going off. 'The scene is becoming ugly,' he said. I figured it would become uglier still if we went and play was abandoned for the day or, worse still, if a rumour spread that the game would be scrubbed out. I told Mr Jones: 'These people are not going to get us off. That may be their idea but, if so, they are wrong. I want a wicket or two before the close.'

Ramadhin, one of the batsmen, overheard my remark and announced, as if he meant it: 'Well, you can have mine for a start.' When the game restarted, concentration lost, he was bowled by Laker's first straight ball.

Afterwards I was told that a church leader had, a week earlier, warned both the Guiana Board and the editor of the local newspaper *Argosy* that he had picked up information of trouble being organized for the Test. If it was an organized demonstration, all I can say is that it was brilliantly timed. The far more likely cause was a combustion of rum, betting and acute disappointment at a wicket falling one run short of a century partnership. I was desperately sorry for the officials who watched the riot with tears streaming down their cheeks.

The locals took precautions to the end. In the last over umpire Gillette asked Evans to bring in the bails and ball as he did not wish to stay. The moment the last ball was bowled he and Menzies fled as fast as their legs could take them while the fielders strolled off with studied nonchalance. At the pavilion officials and English residents formed a protective wall, and behind them were the ranks of the riot police armed with tear gas and truncheons.

That evening the team dined on a British ship docked conveniently by; when we returned to the hotel no one seemed to want to know us. The Governor contacted me to ask if I wanted troops as a protection but, with the manager's agreement, I declined as I thought it might exacerbate the situation. A four-man guard was posted outside Menzies's house inside the cricket ground. The Test was a terrifying ordeal for him but, despite all the pressures on him, he made only one umpiring mistake as far as could be seen.

All came right in the end. England were given a warm ovation inside the ground and outside a sizable group chanted 'Hutton the Victor'. Lord's cabled their congragulations both to the team and for my own contribution as a 'fine example in difficult circumstances'. That cable, the friendly farewell, the result and the uplifted team spirit amply atoned for the sleepless nights worrying under my mosquito net. I knew England were now a formidable team, but always at the back of my mind was a niggling fear I might be involved in another rumpus before the end of the tour. That fear was to be realized.

As anticipated, the fourth Test was a high-scoring draw. The mat was the winner. Trueman and King had a bit of a bumper war, Laker was hit in the eye by a bouncer – fortunately with no lasting effect – and furious words were spilled over the Graveney ball-throwing episode.

The West Indies made 681 for 8 declared, with Weekes scoring 206, Worrell 167 and Walcott 124, and Statham was injured. England replied with 537, with May scoring 135 and Compton 133.

Lovely Queen's Park, with its backcloth of mountains, has long since abandoned the mat for natural grass, but in the course of the Test I learned a little about the mat. On one of my morning inspections it was found that a wet patch on a length at one end had not dried out. The clay and sand base under the mat was damp and Stollmeyer and the home officials were sportingly concerned that if the base was exposed to the sun too long it would overbake and produce a 'flier'. Play started over forty minutes late, during which time the crowd sat patiently – further proof of the unpredictability of the crowds in the West Indies.

I am sure that if it had been left to the players, without emotions being stoked up by too many words and too many rumours, the tour would have been infinitely more pleasant. Unfortunately the atmosphere when MCC returned to Jamaica was frigid. A friend of the MCC manager was ordered from the pavilion when Charles Palmer tried to sign him in, and the complimentary tickets I had passed to friends were torn up in front of Compton whom I had asked to look after them while I was attending to routine captaincy business.

The blow-up I had dreaded came when I returned to the pavilion for a tea interval during the Test. I had batted all day, and nine hours in all, to reach 205, and my thoughts ware naturally concentrated on a cup of tea, a change of my sweat-caked clothing and the luxury of putting my feet up for a few precious minutes. At Sabina Park the players go through an aisle of members in the pavilion before turning for the dressing rooms, and as I passed through, head down, I would not have recognized my wife had she been there. To the shouts of 'Well done' I replied with 'Thank you'. Someone briefly touched my arm. I have no idea who it was, but if a cricketer stopped every time he was touched on the arm he would never get on or off the field.

No sooner was I in the dressing room when the door was flung open and an official was ranting at Charles Palmer saying 'This is the crowning insult' and a lot more besides. I was told I had insulted Mr Alex Bustamente, Jamaica's Chief Minister, by not stopping to acknowledge his personal congratulations as I left the field. I was never more flabbergasted in my life. For one thing I did not know what the man was talking about; for another I could not believe anyone could burst into the privacy of a dressing room during the course of a match and proceed to make wild accusations. Moreover, I resented the use of the words 'crowning insult' as if to suggest there had been others.

Though it might appear to most cricketers to have been a singularly inappropriate time for a conversation, naturally I would have stopped and shown every courtesy to Mr Bustamente had I known he was there and wanted a word with me. Some West Indian friends of mine, with a better knowledge of local affairs, have suggested that as a photographer was present it could have been a put-up job. Whether the presence of a photographer provided such evidence or who might have been behind it I do not know. Frankly I was too sick to care, but when I had a drink that evening with Mr Bustamente he assured me he had not felt slighted and said he understood I had not recognized him among the crowd.

The bit, however, was between my teeth and there was no let-up. At the end of the day a local reporter went to Mr Bustamente and declared: 'You have been insulted. Will you make a statement?' The Chief Minister replied: 'No, I have not been insulted. Hutton's a fine young fellow and we have talked together and had a drink together. I repeat, I have not been insulted.' Normally one would think that would have been the end of the matter, but the story was prominently front-paged the next morning and described as an 'unpleasant incident'. Mr Bustamente's statement was nowhere to be seen, and a letter I sent, once again stressing the fact that never for one moment was there any intention to offend him, was discovered on page 8. Another letter, from an English journalist who was present when Mr Bustamente made his statement, which sought to clarify the facts and put the miserable affair into perspective went unpublished. The final paragraph read: 'As a suitable parallel I would not dare to ask Mr Churchill for a considered statement for publication about an incident in which he was involved and then, substituting my own account, ignore the Prime Minister's statement.'

Unfortunately I was in such a mental whirl after the rumpus, and not knowing how the trumped-up incident might end, I could not hope to concentrate when my innings was resumed, and I did not add to my score. Clearly no blame could be attached personally to the Chief Minister but the score line in *Wisden* might have read:

Hutton b Bustamente 205

It was one of my better innings and due credit was given, but I was surprised to find Jeff Stollmeyer in *Everything Under the Sun* write:

Hutton took Bailey in with him rather than Watson, the other regular opener. I mention this because Hutton refused more than one single to third man so that, as it appeared to us, Bailey, in effect, would have to face up to the hostility of King. Our other opening bowler, Gomez, was only medium pace and Atkinson only a bit quicker. While I don't think that Bailey particularly enjoyed this tactic, it paid dividends because it was Hutton's innings, following on England's fine bowling, that put the match beyond our reach.

I cannot believe that Jeffrey intended to insinuate that I ducked away from King, or that he is not aware of the time-honoured practice of batsmen in a partnership taking a bowler each in the interests of the side. Any inference that I particularly disliked King is plainly ridiculous as I probably had more practice against the really quick stuff than any batsmen in Test cricket. As Jeff can testify from personal experience, it took some nerve to stand up to Lindwall, Miller and Johnston, and I never shirked fast bowling.

King dismissed me once during the series, and that was to the only ball in the entire match which behaved abnormally on the Trinidad mat. To the English team King bowled more bumpers than good-length balls, and Bailey knew how to deal with bouncers. To refresh my memory I spoke to Trevor and he laughed at the suggestion that he did not 'particularly enjoy' taking King. 'I wasn't worried,' he said. 'For a little while it made good tactical sense, and in any case you were hitting 2s and 4s at the other end. Every leading batsman in the world with the interests of the team uppermost would have done exactly the same.'

The most extraordinary feature of Bailey's inspired bowling in the first West Indies innings, which got us on the victory path, was that everything was wrong for him. On the day before the Test I had looked at the pitch with the groundsman, who said that the side batting first ought to make 700. Looking at the strip, rolled and rolled again until it shone under the Caribbean sun, I was inclined to agree; I thought England's only chance was to win the toss, aim for 400 plus, and hope by some miracle to bowl the West Indies out twice. My feelings can be imagined when I lost the toss . . . and the miracle occurred with the opposition routed for an unbelievable 139 by Bailey, who had 7 for 34 in the sixteen best overs he ever bowled. Bailey rates this as his best performance and no one would venture to disagree. There was a little bit of moisture in the pitch left over from the watering, but the interesting fact is that the cross-breeze actually did not favour him, nor presumably had Statham been fit and played – an injury problem which entailed the inclusion of three spinners – would he have opened with Trueman.

As Trueman was the faster bowler Bailey had to bowl against the wind (it is also a thought that if Bedser had been there Bailey would have started at the other end!) and the cross-wind was also in the wrong direction for Bailey's out-swingers. Trueman, of course, also bowled the out-swinger so, in theory, he had all the advantages. 'When I started I would have gladly settled for, say, 3 for 100,' says Trevor. One gropes for an alternative phrase to the old cliché about cricket's glorious uncertainties, but surely the time-honoured words fit the case and, once again, Bailey was shown to be one of the most capable and intelligent cricketers of our times. He was every captain's ideal: responsive, perceptive, guaranteed to be a tactical move ahead of his shrewdest opponent, and never overawed or intimidated. Unlike too many English players, he was able to play to the maximum of his ability on the big occasions. Ask him to attack with the new ball and he would stretch the skill of any batsmen because of his complete mastery of the basics; ask him to bowl tight and he would do precisely that; ask him to open the batting to blunt the attack for the stroke-makers and he would be there fighting every inch of the way; ask him to field close or away from the bat and he'd be equally proficient. A fine all-rounder, and his service to England cannot be overestimated. Trevor was my vice-captain in the West Indies, but he lost his place as the heir apparent when he published some articles on the tour before the permitted time which, in those days, was two years. Now the presses are hot with player–writers as the last ball is bowled. It was a real pity Bailey dropped out in this way for he would have been a strong leader with many ideas.

A seventeen-year-old, making his Test debut, scored 14 not out and 26 from the No. 9 position with such skill and aplomb that a rapid rise in the order was fully forecast. Little did I imagine, however, that I was playing against a batsman who was eventually to break my Test record score. The young man, taking Valentine's place as an orthodox slow left-arm spinner, took 4 for 75, including Bailey with his second ball, a faster delivery. I made a mental note that he would be very useful in English conditions. I wasn't to know he could also bowl fast in the Alan Davidson mould, bowl Chinamen and googlies in the Jack Walsh fashion, and would become one of the finest West Indies batsmen. Garfield St Aubrun Sobers had arrived.

Walcott scored 50 in the first innings and 116 in the second as a forceful reminder of his greatness, but England coasted home by 9 wickets and shared the rubber. Two victories were compensation for a painful tour. Had it been my first series as captain I doubt if I would have had the heart and wish to continue. *Wisden* referred to my 'thankless' task and added: 'Instead of finding a friendly cricketing atmosphere Hutton and his fellow players were subjected to the deep impact of deep political and racial feeling – an experience all of them wish to forget. A few of the team did not hide their innermost feelings, with the result that they came under criticism. Although his own behaviour was blameless, small wonder all this petty wrangling caused a breakdown in Hutton's health.'

Manager Charles Palmer issued a farewell statement in which he said:

From a cricket point of view England go back with a better record than any previous touring side from England. We are naturally pleased about this, particularly when we remember that our efforts in the early stages were not very encouraging, and we are, of course, pleased that we attained that cohesion which enabled us to square the series of Test matches.

Both sides have played excellent cricket in hard-fought games. It was a great pity that some of the Test matches were so tense and after such battles it is perhaps a blessing that the Test match honours are divided.

The series has been marred by many incidents – often magnified out of all proportion by too many people – and these unfortunately produced a growing acrimony which everyone on every side must regret. It is comforting that the last Test match, while played keenly, was an exhilarating performance which did much to create more amicable relations. I feel that at times general feelings about the cricket got out of proportion. I do urge everyone in the West Indies to try to keep cricket as a game and to prevent extraneous influences from spoiling its essential character.

The umpiring has been the centre of much controversy. I wish to deny any allegations that we have assumed dishonesty. We have said that the standard of umpiring at times has not been good. . . . To the many people who have been kind to us in the West Indies we offer our sincere thanks.

Not being a human punchbag able to absorb blows without hurt, I have to admit I left the sunshine and palm trees of the West Indies with some relief. The alleged incident with the Chief Minister was the straw to break my back – not so much the actual charge, which was bad enough, but the words of the official who took it for granted that I, or the team, had been consistently guilty of misdemeanours. If I am permitted one satisfaction, it was in my refusal to be sidetracked from my duty to lead England to the best of my ability and to score as many runs as I could for England. My average for the Tests was 96·71; Denis Compton was next with 49·71, a marvellous achievement in view of his handicap. As an indication of the price I paid in health, stress and loss of form, I point to my subsequent Test record: v. Pakistan (two Tests) average 6·33; v. Australia 24·44 (compared with 52·12 in 1946–47 and 88·83 in 1950–51); v. New Zealand 22·33.

I was not passed fit for Australia until mid-July 1954. The season in many ways was a virtual write-off for me, culminating in the historic victory by Pakistan at the Oval when I returned as captain. A. H. Kardar's side had some outstanding players, like the 'little master', Hanif Mohammad, who was the very devil to get out if he put his mind to staying at the crease, Fazal Mahmood, a Bedser-type medium-fast bowler, and Imtiaz Ahmed, a wicketkeeper with a liking for tall scores with the bat. There were also a few light-weights in a side which, by real standards, was as green as the caps they wore. Up to the Oval, little in the three previous Tests had seriously suggested Pakistan were capable of holding England, then flush with bowlers of quality. England took the second Test by an innings after the first had been ruined by rain, and the weather saved them from overwhelming defeat at Manchester.

The Oval Test stands out as a classic example of the folly of underrating the opposition. To give some players chosen for the Australian tour Test match experience, Bedser and Bailey were left out, and as it happened they were sorely missed. The conditions would have been exactly right for Bedser and, instead, they presented Fazal Mahmood with a heaven-sent opportunity he was far too good a bowler to miss. His match aggregate of 12 for 99 was the major reason for a 24-run victory which shook international cricket. The excuse that England were not at full strength did not stand up for I would expect players bound for Australia to be Test material against all standards of opposition.

Pakistan created a record for first-time visitors by sharing the series, and they did so with their top batsman, Hanif Mohammad, averaging only 22·62, and with the highest innings in the four Tests of 69 by Maqsood Ahmed. Six England bastmen had better averages. The whole of London's Pakistan community seemed to jam into their dressing room, and I have rarely seen such emotion displayed on a cricket ground. Since those early days Pakistan have developed into a powerful side with many splendid batsmen and bowlers, but on that August morning I felt rather like the captain of Manchester United after losing a home cup-tie to a non-League club.

My Test scores were 0, 14 and 5 and it was one of the four defeats against eleven victories in my twenty-three Tests as captain. A season not to look back on with too much pride, and I appreciated how Johnny Warr must have felt on his first visit to Sheffield. His contribution to Middlesex's cause was minimal. He did nothing as a bowler and in the field the ball seemed to make a special point of never going anywhere near him. At the end of another over in which he had not taken an active part, a voice boomed: 'What hast tha coom t'Sheffield for, lad – t'buy penknife?'

8

Tyson Is a Knockout

Much of the credit for the English success deservedly went to the fast bowlers Tyson and Statham. Statham is a very fine bowler, deserving of more luck than he generally enjoyed in Australia. Like Doug Wright on previous tours he was often responsible for the softening-up process against Test batsmen without gaining the reward. Tyson and others owed much to Statham. Tyson became the man of the hour, a tough fellow well fitted by his strength, endurance and zest for work to fill the hero's role. I have referred to Tyson and Statham as the greatest fast-bowling combination of my experience. Together and individually they did great things. . . . Tyson's success was based on the intelligence to develop and use natural ability with the result that his progress was uncommonly rapid. It must have surprised everyone. Bowlers do come forward more rapidly than batsmen, but not usually at that rate.

E. M. Wellings in *The Ashes Retained*

I trust I will not be accused of a flight of fancy unbecoming a pragmatic old Yorkshire cricketer, but the meteoric rise of Frank ('Typhoon') Tyson can be traced from the time he bowled at Sydney in 1954 with a bump the size of an egg on the back of his head. The previous day he had turned his back on a bumper from Lindwall and took a fearful crack. We watched horrified as he went down like felled timber and lay inert and still. There was a hush around the ground, and it took quite a time to get him onto his feet and back to the dressing room, where he was stretched out on the massage table, surrounded by medics and anxious team-mates.

When he came out of his concussed state I swear there was a new light in his eyes as if a spark had been kindled deep down inside him. I am not given to fanciful imagination, and the fact is that when he resumed bowling the next day he was a yard, maybe a yard and a half, faster than before. I have often wondered how much that bouncer contributed to Tyson's, and England's, spectacular triumphs at Sydney, Melbourne and Adelaide. Of course, a front-rank batsman would never turn away from a bouncer, and Frank's experience was so limited up to then that I doubt if he had been on the receiving end of many short-pitched balls.

Be that as it may, the blow seemed to trigger off something, perhaps a new willpower, a fresh determination, perhaps even a desire to get his own back. But whatever the cause, a Tyson emerged who, for three Tests, must have been as fast as any bowler in the history of cricket. I can't believe anyone has been faster.

His pace at Sydney on that decisive and extraordinary day was nothing short of frightening. After one ball Evans and the slips exchanged significant glances and moved back several paces. I never saw Evans so far back, and I'm told exactly the same retreat was made when Frank bowled his first over for Northamptonshire under Freddie Brown. Soon the English fielders were saying: 'If we can get Ray to nut Frank again there'll be no holding him.' I could hardly suppress my delight.

There was a wind at Tyson's back – but he was just as fast in the arid, airless Melbourne Stadium during a heat wave and at Adelaide, also in soaring temperatures. Tyson took 6 wickets for 85 in the second innings at Sydney, with a match aggregate of 10, and a Test which had begun with England losing 8 wickets for 88 after being put in was dramatically won. England's first innings produced only 154 and an Australian journalist in a taxi back to the city declared that after Brisbane and now this the series would be a major flop. Australia didn't do all that better on the mottled pitch and they were pushed back by Bailey. May's century, Cowdrey's half-century and the bonus of 46 from the last pair, Appleyard and Statham, left Australia needing 223. Harvey scored a brilliant 92 not out, and while he threatened to win the game, it was a tremendous temptation not to overbowl Tyson. The more desperate the situation became for Australia, the more devastating was Harvey. He was one of the heroes of an epic. May was another, and Tyson delivered the final knockout with savage efficiency; but, to me, there was an unsung hero who was forgotten by all but the most discerning critics. When it was touch and go and vital to hold fast at one end while Tyson attacked at the other, Statham bowled flat out into the wind without relief for 85 minutes, and provided the type of service to earn a captain's eternal gratitude.

Tyson, the man of the hour, proved in one illuminating minute that he had a cricket brain as well as enormous physical strength and endurance. When Lindwall came in to bat, Tyson was bowling. A flashpoint situation. Everyone on the ground, probably including Lindwall, expected Tyson to finger the bump on his head and let fly a retaliatory bumper. Instead Frank slipped in the perfect spot-on yorker which utterly deceived and bowled Lindwall. Tyson's transformation from the expensive failure of the first Test to the exacting match-winner of the second bordered on the miraculous.

At Brisbane it was blindingly obvious that unless he cut his run-up by at least three or four yards he would soon be on his knees, a spent and useless force. My problem was to change virtually overnight the habits he had formed over the years from Manchester schooldays, Durham University and Northamptonshire without putting at risk his rhythm, speed and accuracy – not that Frank had been all that accurate until then. Tyson was put under a crash course and Alf Gover, the highly rated coach touring with the press corps, was recruited to help. Tyson had spent a winter felling trees to strengthen his back muscles and having some faults eradicated at Gover's Indoor School. Fortunately Tyson willingly cooperated and adapted to a shortened run with surprising ease. The results exceeded our expectations, and after he was streamlined he had lost none of his pace and gained in accuracy. Frank and I had an excellent rapport, and the natural understanding of fellow northerners counted for much.

Until we met on the ship I had not seen much of him, but my first impressions were of a conscientious and intelligent man – he took his BA degree on returning from Australia. From the day the *Orsova* left Tilbury he pounded the decks before breakfast, even in the torrid heat of the Red Sea. Often, walking back to his bowling mark, he recited Wordsworth to concentrate his mind. I make no claims to being a literary man, but I dredged up from my misspent schooldays enough to quote a line from the same poet when I tossed the ball to him to open the bowling in a Test: 'Frank,' I said, 'England hath need of thee!'

I accept blame for the disaster of the first Test at Brisbane, where so many English hopes have been dashed since 1946. I misread the pitch, and that was all there was to it. Basically I was perhaps wrong to plan too far in advance, but that is normally accepted as a good fault, if fault it be. In putting Australia in first, I was trying to seize the initiative, which could not have been a bad objective. No previous England captain in Australia had taken a similar gamble, but pitches and circumstances change over the years, and on the evidence of the wickets and the tactics of the state captains in the run-up to Brisbane, including the Queensland match on the Test ground, it was a feasible tactic for a side banking on a pace attack. Generally the pitches were grassier and probably had less rolling than on my two previous visits to Australia, and in MCC's game with Queensland the ball moved and lifted in the early stages in a manner which encouraged me to believe Bedser, Statham, Bailey and Tyson could strike effectively. Ken Archer, Queensland's captain, put MCC in, and I thought the Test strip looked much the same. But it had dried out and proved to be slower and, by the end, crumbled a little, with a tendency for the ball to keep low.

Putting the opposition in had been the fashion in the MCC matches up to the Test with reasonable success, and it was not illogical to suppose, with the general conditions prevailing at the time, that an advantage could be gained in the first Test by batting second. At Perth, MCC beat both Western Australia and a Combined XI by conceding the first innings. Western Australia, not as strong then as they have been in recent years, were out for 103, and the Combined XI, including Harvey and Hole, made only 86, of which the local batsman John Rutherford at No. 1 scored 39. The conditions were not all that different as MCC made the rounds of the eastern states. At Sydney Miller sent MCC in and the first four were out for 38 before Cowdrey and I retrieved the position with centuries. Cowdrey made a second in the next innings and thus took a century in both innings in Australia off an attack including Crawford, Miller, Davidson and Benaud, before he had scored a championship 100 at home.

At Brisbane, MCC, again put in, had three bundled out for 18 and were rescued by Simpson and Compton, who both made centuries. And, it might be added, Arthur Morris, Australia's acting captain in the second Test at Sydney, also put England in – and lost the match. The scale of England's catastrophe at Brisbane was humiliating and for a time it was difficult to keep it in perspective and understand that one Test had gone and not the entire series. The unkindest comment was that I had been sold a gold brick by the state of the pitch in the state match, but it is easy to sit in judgement afterwards. England also sowed the seeds of their own destruction by dropping catch after catch in the worst exhibition of out-cricket I was obliged to endure in my term of office.

On reflection, I realize my original mistake was to proceed with my plan when Evans dropped out around breakfast time on the morning of the Test with a touch of sunstroke. There and then I should have emptied my mind of any thought of putting Australia in if I won the toss. Also, it would have been far wiser to have delayed Bedser's return though, as always, he was keen to play and I was keen to have him leading the attack. Actually I did not have much option but to put the emphasis on speed as the form of Appleyard and Wardle had been spasmodic at that point of the tour, and poor McConnon was in hospital with a groin injury.

I intend no reflection on Keith Andrew when I say I should have shied away from my intentions when Evans was pronounced unfit. It was almost like a warning from fate not to go ahead. If Keith had not been considered one of the two best wicketkeepers in England he would not have been in the party, but the fact was that he had not played in a Test before and Evans was an old hand whose presence was as valuable as his tremendous verve and skill. Over the years he had formed a superb partnership with Bedser, who insisted on his wicketkeeper standing up. They had an almost telepathic understanding, and one of my most vivid and abiding memories of the England side is of Evans taking the new ball swinging down the leg side. To understand Evans's contribution to a Test match it was necessary to be alongside him on the field and in the dressing room.

It is a cliché to describe a player as being able to rise to the big occasion. Godfrey went further, enjoying every moment and being the fulcrum of inspiration. The only time I saw him really downcast was after the Headingley defeat in 1948, but I imagine he cheered up more Test cricketers than any known player, and the tougher the crisis the better he was. At Adelaide, when England had to get 94 to win and Miller caused as many heart-flutterings as a fox in a hen roost, Evans went in to bat grinning all over his face and immediately bet Compton, his partner, a fiver that he would make the winning run. He did.

Put an England cap on Godfrey's head, fill the ground, and he became supercharged with energy, a dynamic force. On a day when nerves were as taut as a bow string, the extrovert, ebullient Evans positively bubbled with an infectious enthusiasm which was worth runs and wickets to England. Test matches were his theatre, and he was so often in the centre spotlight. They said in Kent that it was sometimes a different Evans in the county championship. I understand because I often felt a reaction after a Test. A Test takes a lot out of a player. I don't care how long he has been at that level or how many Tests he has played in. To return to the county scene can cause a natural reaction rather like a winding-down process, or a music-hall artiste going straight from the bright lights of the London Palladium to a provincial booking.

Unfortunately on that unlucky morning at Brisbane, Morris was missed off a difficult chance on the leg side at the wicket from Bedser before he had made the first of his 153 runs. There is always a temptation to think Evans would have taken the catch; I saw him take so many catches which it would be an exaggeration to describe as half-chances. Evans might or might not have caught Morris, but it would be manifestly unfair to imply that England's mis fortunes stemmed from that moment. Unfortunately it was the first of a dozen or so – I soon lost count – catches to be missed, and when I watched the unbelievable when Bailey at long leg missed Morris with a chance he would take ninety-nine times out of a hundred, I began to feel there was a curse on the side. The fielding was catastrophic and, to cap it all, Compton ran into the wooden palings on the boundary on the first morning and broke a bone in the back of his left hand. At No. 11 he made two token visits to the crease, scoring 2 not out and 0. His injury alone would have been enough to cope with in one Test. After Australia had won by an innings and 154 runs with a day to spare, I was comforted by an observation from Jack Fingleton who wrote: 'Australia had more luck than they are entitled to expect for a whole series.' Generally it was not a good time for a defeated captain to read the newspapers.

Inevitably my captaincy was called into question, which is one way of putting it, but I was not too badly shaken in my belief that England had the fast bowling to win the series. On the face of it that might appear an act of faith as the four main bowlers had each conceded well over 100 runs, Bedser was still having the after-effects of shingles and Tyson's run-up was in the process of being reduced. However, England could not possibly field as badly again and, having played in the states, I saw no talent outside the regular nucleus of internationals to cause me concern. The only course open to me was not to allow the side to remain deflated and to digest the lessons of defeat. I believed rock bottom had been reached, and there is some perverted consolation in having an idea that the bad luck arrives in one fell swoop.

There was another occasion in Australia when I felt I would rather be somewhere else. Walter Lindrum, the great Australian billiards player, invited several of my 1954–55 team to his home, and, after dinner, we went to the table. As I rather fancied myself I took on the champion, who suggested a game of 250 up. I broke and made what I thought was the perfect shot with red in baulk. Walter, however, went to the table and I did not have to play another shot! Half the England party was present and were not slow in recommending that I stick to cricket.

During the Queensland match I had a long chat with the Governor General, Field Marshal Sir William Slim. I mentioned that Field Marshal Lord Montgomery was another distinguished soldier who enjoyed watching cricket. Sir William chuckled and replied: 'If Monty tells you how to win a battle, listen carefully, but if he tells you how to win a cricket match, well, that's a different matter.' Later, at Canberra, the federal capital, MCC had a charity match against Sir Robert Menzies's Prime Minister's XI. The Governor General and the Prime Minister were in conversation when there was a loud thunderclap. Sir William raised his eyebrows and said: 'Sounds as if the Typhoon's bowling.'

Sir Robert yielded to no one as a true cricket lover, and I was given an interesting sidelight into Australia as a country where Jack is considered as good as his master when I once shared a hotel lift with him at Melbourne. He got out at the second floor and turned to say good night. The lift attendant, totally unimpressed by the presence of an eminent world statesman, responded with a cheery 'Good night, Bob'.

Wisden's description of the occasion as a 'gay charity match' would raise some comment in the eighties, and I hardly need add the gaiety referred to the 6s and 4s. The MCC captain temporarily revived his long-neglected leg-break bowling by taking 3 of the last 4 wickets to fall in eleven balls. There was no danger of him taking his bowling seriously, but I was a little perturbed that a whole week between Tests was occupied in the type of affair which did not permit serious match practice. The other occasion was a two-day game against a Queensland Country XI at Rockhampton, a town on the tropic of Capricorn, and providing a ground and atmosphere all of its own. Rodeos were staged on the ground and the game was billed as a 'mighty International contest'. The show ground was no doubt ideal for bucking broncos and the play was accompanied by racing commentaries and fishing prospects on the radio. The local president had a habit of following me everywhere – I am sure he meant well – and I was surprised to find myself alone at the crease. The pitch had been nurtured in the Botanical Gardens and transported almost blade by blade, but it did not last and after the first day I agreed to having it repaired. As the game by then was of little consequence, I suggested it be played to a finish with a little extra time added. MCC won in the time added on, and I came in for some severe criticism as a result. But all serious pretensions had disappeared when the pitch was doctored and I figured the game might as well have a definite conclusion. The local captain was with me but, frankly, I wasn't deeply concerned whether MCC won or drew.

Brisbane is a thriving and hospitable city but, having fallen flat on my own banana skin by misreading the pitch and participating in my third debacle in that fair city, my enthusiasm for the Wollongabba ground began to dwindle. It is strange how often England have been dogged by misfortune at Brisbane since the war, and my own experiences were extended by the teams led by May and Denness. In 1946 England had to use a pitch which literally had been a lake the day before with the stumps floating on the surface. Hailstones as big as golf balls pierced the roofs of cars parked around the ground. Miraculously play resumed on time the next morning and Miller's first ball, on a half-volley length, took Washbrook's cap off. Miller was unmanageable in the first innings and Toshack, shown by Bradman where to pitch the ball, was equally devastating in the second.

Hammond played an innings of unimaginable skill by standing aside to avoid the length ball and driving the overpitched; he made 32, which was worth more than a double century against weak bowling. Edrich took the flying deliveries on his body and came in looking as if he had gone ten rounds with Muhammad Ali. To cap everything, there was the second storm when the Don Bradman catch was disallowed.

Four years later in the 1950–51 tour, Bedser and Bailey dismissed

Australia for 228 on a good pitch despite an occasional variation of bounce. England's expectations were high until the hope-chilling drum of rain on corrugated iron roofs was heard after dinner. The rain continued throughout Saturday and Sunday, and with 228 in the bank Australia were rich. The previous week the pitch had also taken five inches of rain.

Before the match Freddie Brown had asked me if I objected moving down to No. 4 or 5 in a bid to strengthen the middle-order batting. I agreed if he considered it to be in the best interests of the side, but the theory was turned upside down by the conditions. In fairness to the skipper, it might have worked on a normal pitch. Originally I was due in at No. 4 and I was held back to No. 6 in the rather extravagant hope of the wicket improving. I was 8 not out when Brown declared at 68 for 7. Australia, who had three out before a run was on the board, answered by closing at 32 for 7, leaving England to get 193 to win and seventy minutes' batting that evening. By the close the contest was virtually won and lost. Again the plan was to keep me back, together with Compton, but Simpson was yorked first ball by Lindwall and 3 wickets vanished in the last ten minutes, one to a run-out going for a fourth when the ball was already on its way to Tallon the wicketkeeper. I shudder to think what some of the old Yorkshire professors would have thought of that and some of the risky shots which went in the air without going to hand.

I started at No. 8. The next morning Evans and Compton, at No. 9, disappeared in two balls by Johnston. Brown was out at 77, and I was 23 when I was joined by No. 11 Doug Wright. By the time he was out I had gone to 62, but any satisfaction I might have had with my own performance disappeared with the nature of the defeat. All the same, it was one of my best innings and I think it would have been better if I had gone in first. There were scathing criticisms. 'We squandered our greatest asset,' declared E. M. Wellings, who added: 'It is impossible to say what would have happened if Hutton had opened with Washbrook in the second innings. It is possible to say that that should have been the order because it would have offered England the best chance of winning. The alteration was a surprise to Washbrook and it is interesting to note that he was disconcerted by the loss of his usual partner and not a little dismayed.'

Captaincy decisions are not too difficult made sitting in the stand without the responsibility of taking the consequences. The same applies to selection, and I have often tempted to wonder if extreme critics would be prepared to put their theories into practice if the opportunity arose. On this occasion Brown's classic blunder was to lose the toss. Had England batted first and totalled 200 or so, that would have been enough. Such is the luck of the game.

Before Washbrook and I resumed our opening partnership for the last three Tests I batted at No. 4 at Melbourne where, unfortunately, I was the victim of the worst decision I suffered in Test cricket and was out for 12 just before lunch. I was given out caught at the wicket after the ball had lobbed up from my pads. In the second innings I top-scored with 40, but I think my natural position was No. 1. Generally speaking I am in favour of a settled order, and shuffling around all too often fails to correct the original weakness and creates a second.

Actually it was not the first time my position in the Test order was discussed. Because of the number of bouncers I was getting in Australia in 1946–47 (and I do not suggest I was alone in the firing line), Hammond and manager Rupert Howard asked me if I would prefer to go in lower down. As I did not think I would escape the barrage of bouncers I declined the offer, saying I would rather go in first. Hammond replied; 'I think you're right. No matter where you go in you'll still get 'em.'

The Oval in 1950 was the one occasion when I would have appreciated a change in the order for the second innings – and I am sure it would have been of advantage to England. I carried my bat for 202 out of a total of 344 on a drying pitch splendidly used by Ramadhin, Valentine and the West Indies captain John Goddard, who was able to make his off-break lift and turn a lot in the conditions. England failed by 10 runs to save the follow-on and I went in for a second time a very tired man indeed. In the ten minutes between the innings I had hoped skipper Freddie Brown might ask me if I wanted a break, but he did not do so and I did not think it was my place to make the suggestion. When I went out again I soon had a ball from Goddard which turned and lifted and I was caught at short leg by Christiani for 2. Had I not had such a brute of a ball so quickly I might well have settled in again, and England avoided the indignity of being bowled out by Valentine for 103.

Melbourne was a kinder ground to England than Brisbane in 1954, but I went there for the crucial Test with the father and mother of a cold and fretting about Bedser. I could not see any way of having him back as Tyson's 10 wickets at Sydney had cemented his position and he was far and away the fastest bowler on either side. Australia, by now, feared him and his partnership with Statham.

Tour captaincy can be a lonely and responsible job. You have your manager – and I was singularly fortunate with Charles Palmer and Geoffrey Howard – and a tour selection committee. I had Bailey and May as vice-captains. Again I was lucky. But, in the end, the major problems end with the captain and it is dead easy to be wrong for the best of reasons. There were no better moments in my career than when I saw my long-term strategy to use fast bowlers as the spearhead of my thrust produce my hoped-for results. When Tyson and Statham as a two-man team swept England to a historic victory at Melbourne, there was a sublime satisfaction for I knew, figuratively speaking, I had my hand on the Ashes.

In not much over an hour Australia were cracked like the shell of an egg under two hammer blows. They had begun the final innings needing 240, about par for the match, and were 79 for 2 at the close on the Saturday. Almost without exception the critics nominated Appleyard as the bowler most likely to use a pitch which had rapidly declined after two days – that is, if England were to win. To many it seemed wide open. There was mild surprise when I opened with Tyson and Statham as it was my experience of a wearing Australian wicket that fast bowlers are likely to get more out of it than spinners. Appleyard didn't even get on, and once Harvey, the danger man, had gone to a wonder catch by Evans off Tyson, I did not have to contemplate making a bowling change. I felt like a jockey riding a runaway Derby winner.

Between them Tyson and Statham bowled only 12·3 overs and 8 Australian wickets went for 36 runs. Tyson had 6 for 16 and 7 for 27 in all, and Statham 2 for 19, but I would never dare to separate the performances. Though Tyson had the most spectacular return, it would not have been possible without Statham's support, a fact which Bradman noted when we had a chat in the old Windsor Hotel afterwards. Looking at Statham enjoying a beer in the lounge, the Don nodded towards him and said: 'I hope the man gets the credit he deserves.' If Tyson's speed was terrifying, Statham's accuracy was faultless. In speed he suffered only by comparison. Their styles complemented each other perfectly, and there was no escape for

Australia's batsmen. Down at the docks in the South Wharf a liner ran up a nautical flag signal to read: 'Tyson'. My mind went back to the selection committee for the tour and the debates over his selection!

Rightly Tyson was the hero of the hour, but I trust the deeds of the two young batsmen May and Cowdrey will never be overlooked in assessing England's triumphs at Sydney and Melbourne. Without their quite brilliant batting a base would not have been set up for Tyson's dramatic assaults. When the senior batsmen struggled and lost in the second Test, May scored 104 in the second innings, and 91 in the third Test when the next highest contribution was my 42. Amid the wreckage caused by Miller on the first morning of the third Test, Cowdrey scored 102 out of a final total of 191. Just to emphasize the debt owed to these two young men I show the relevant stages of the innings:

England (second innings, second Test, Sydney)

Hutton c Benaud b Johnston	28
Bailey c Langley b Archer	6
May b Lindwall	104
Graveney c Langley b Johnston	0
Cowdrey c Archer b Benaud	54
Edrich b Archer	29

England (first innings, third Test, Melbourne)

Hutton c Hole b Miller	12
Edrich c Lindwall b Miller	4
May c Benaud b Lindwall	0
Cowdrey b Johnston	102
Compton c Harvey b Miller	4
Bailey c Maddocks b Johnston	30

England (second innings, third Test, Melbourne)

Hutton lbw b Archer	42
Edrich b Johnston	13
May b Johnston	91
Cowdrey b Benaud	7
Compton c Maddocks b Archer	23
Bailey not out	24

I doubt if either played better again, at least in a single innings, despite the many centuries they scored, because they could not have had more testing conditions; the bowling, especially from Lindwall and Miller, was of the highest calibre; and there could not have been a more testing examination of nerve and match temperament. May, of course, had some Tests behind him both at home and in the West Indies, but Cowdrey was a beginner. Melbourne was only his third Test, but he was astonishingly mature as he fended off the rising deliveries of Miller and Lindwall and drove majestically or clipped the ball off his legs with exquisite timing. May's driving off Lindwall at Sydney was nothing short of masterly, and it gave me intense joy to see young English batsmen make runs and make them so positively. Colin became something of an enigma, because, despite his many successes, it seemed he could not always accept just how talented he was.

Colin sometimes seems to have been puzzled by me to judge from his book *MCC*, quoting the occasion during one of our partnerships when I said to him: 'Hard work, isn't it – and you're not even getting paid for it.' Well, that was only my little bit of banter aimed at easing the tension, an off-the-cuff quip which was hardly significant. I also apparently surprised Compton during our stand against Australia at Lord's in 1953. 'There must be better jobs than this,' I said, a reference to the hard work batting against Lindwall, Miller and Co. Possibly at that precise moment the words may have come from the heart. Unfortunately Denis and I did not have too many big stands together or he might have become more accustomed to our droll Yorkshire humour.

Usually if I did something out of the ordinary or made casual quips, it was for a purpose. There was the occasion I sent out two bananas to Colin in the middle of a Test. He was playing a very important innings with Compton at Adelaide when the crowd began to get on their backs. The pitch was slow, Australia had a defensive field, Compton was rather out of touch, and, it had to be remembered, Colin was still relatively inexperienced. A lot rested on Cowdrey and, to my alarm, he started to play one or two reckless shots unbecoming the crucial situation. I wasn't sure whether Colin's 'rush of blood' was caused by the barracking, or the approach of lunch, and as it was imperative for him to stay, I figured I'd have to make my instructions clear. I told Vic Wilson, the twelfth man, to put two bananas from a fruit bowl in the dressing room in his pocket, go to the wicket, hand the bananas to our much prized young batsman with the instruction to calm down. I figured a touch of unorthodoxy would make a bigger impact than sending Wilson out with the customary and unsubtle pretext of changing a bat.

To the surprise of all, Wilson in flannels and blazer walked calmly to the middle and, under the curious gaze of fielders and umpires, produced and offered two bananas to Colin. 'What the hell are these for?' he demanded.

Wilson replied: 'Well, after seeing a couple of wild shots from you just now, the skipper thought you might be hungry. It rather suggests he is keen for you to stay out here batting and wants you to get your head down.'

The little ploy succeeded: Colin settled in again and scored 79 valuable runs.

I was not the only one to provide bizarre moments. At Melbourne, Compton, returning from hospital after an X-ray, was refused re-admission to the ground and had to jump the turnstile to rejoin the team. At Adelaide, Wardle and Graveney, also in blazers and flannels, stepped five yards outside the main gate and though the groundsman saw them go out he wouldn't let them come back without producing tickets.

Australia were spared one of the most embarrassing situations in the history of Test cricket by England's 1954–55 victory at Melbourne. The Sunday, the rest day, was as hot a day as ever I experienced. The city was scorched by a northerly wind blowing directly from the hinterland deserts. Fires raged throughout Victoria, and the temperature at Melbourne was 105°, falling only to 97° at midnight. The pitch, which had fast deteriorated from the second day, was parched with cracks when I last saw it on the Saturday evening.

When the England players arrived on the Monday morning, their curiosity was attracted by a change of colour in the pitch, and on trooping to the middle found that there was enough moisture in parts to rise above the welts of their shoes. The *Age*, a respected Melbourne newspaper, carried a front-page story unequivocally stating that the pitch had been under sprinklers and rolled which, it goes without saying, was a clear and serious violation of the regulations. An immediate official inquiry was conducted and it was emphatically denied that the pitch, or any part of the ground, had been watered since the start of the match. Neither Geoffrey Howard nor I was given a copy of the statement; nor was a single player from either side invited to give evidence at the inquiry. No explanation was offered to MCC for the appearance of the moisture and the disappearance of the cracks.

As I saw it, short of a frank admission that a mistake had been made, there was not much the authorities could do about a *fait accompli*. Nor was there anything I could do, and I wasn't prepared to be put off the job at hand – to take the last 8 Australian wickets. Had it been acknowledged that an inexperienced groundsman had made a mistake, we would not have been vastly entertained by the various efforts to explain the phenomenon.

A water diviner was unearthed to express the opinion that a subterranean tributary of the River Yarra must run under the ground and the abnormal heat had drawn water to the surface. Presumably it ran directly below the middle of the ground. No explanation was offered to cover the obvious question: why it had not happened in previous heatwaves, of which Melbourne had no shortage during mid-summer.

Two leading civil engineers with a string of letters after their names contributed to the arguments in an erudite letter from Melbourne University to the Victoria Cricket Association, claiming that the 'sweating' was a natural phenomenon. The reasons given were far above the understanding of us simple cricketers, and I am sure the groundsman shared my mirth years later when it was admitted that the pitch had indeed been watered. So was solved the alleged mystery of the self-watering wicket!

England's superiority was so firmly established after Melbourne that I knew the Ashes were for the taking, provided the team kept on the boil and there were no injuries to key bowlers. Statham, for one, needed no encouragement. At Mount Gambia against a South Australian Country XI he took 6 wickets, all bowled, without conceding a run and finished with 6 for 3. An opening batsman who had survived the opening spell looked on at the devastation at the other end and carried his bat. Handsome victories were achieved over Tasmania and South Australia – the latter taking the heaviest defeat imposed by MCC for forty-three years.

Much has been written of my despairing remark that Miller 'has done us' when four were out for 49 and Compton, next in, was sitting next to me in the final stages of the fourth Test in Adelaide. The words slipped out in a moment of panic, and we all had a good laugh about it after Compton had gone in, scored 34 not out and taken England to a 5-wicket victory – and England had won in

Australia for the first time since the bodyline series in 1932–33. There was such tension at the time that I think I could be allowed my little indiscretion as, until the winning run came, I went through every possible human emotion from despair to elation. Sydney was touch and go, Melbourne a struggle until the final morning, and here we were, on the brink of achieving all our highest hopes, and suddenly there was a crisis.

Ninety-four runs should have been a formality, but the scene was made for Miller and I knew it. In twenty balls he disposed of Edrich, myself and Cowdrey and superbly caught May in the covers. He made the ball do extraordinary things, even an old ball. It would have been less of a strain had I been batting, but I am not the best of watchers if there is a personal involvement. Miller, I have to admit, gave me some dreadful moments of pure anguish at Adelaide. There were times when I couldn't watch and, in due course, I suffered as a spectator when my son Richard played for Cambridge in the university match at Lord's, for Yorkshire and for England. The torment of a proud parent is indescribable. I am not a good watcher and, furthermore, bad county or Test cricket does not appeal to me.

Once again it was a burst from Tyson and Statham – not a single bouncer between them in the match! – which swung the fourth Test after an even first innings, but I also had trump cards in Bailey and Appleyard, who was twice the bowler from Christmas onwards. Both were invaluable when it was necessary to use the two main strike bowlers in short spells in the stifling heat. A tip from Gubby Allen, who was fortunately present, could not have been more opportune. In the first innings Statham was almost crippled by his boots which skinned his toes and caused bleeding. He was in considerable discomfort and, for once, did not take a wicket. I told Gubby of Brian's problem and he said: 'I had exactly the same difficulty when I bowled in Australia. I cut a hole in the toecap and found it worked.' I passed on the conversation and Gubby's advice was taken with very successful results.

There was an incident during Harvey's first innings which led me to get a quite undeserved reputation as the captain who deliberately slowed over rates down. Tyson was bowling to Harvey and was responding, perhaps unconsciously, to the tempo of the batting. Harvey had that impact on bowlers. He tended to make them quicken up their over rates and, in my opinion, that was one of the reasons why he did so well. Neil, one of the great left-handers, looked particularly dangerous and after each dashing stroke Tyson was marching back as if he could not wait to bowl the next ball. From my position at mid-on I went across to Tyson and told him: 'Ease up, Frank, take your time. You're doing exactly what he wants you to do.'

I strongly refute any suggestion that with cold-blooded deliberation I put a restraint on the over rate as a tactical policy. It is also a fact that fast bowlers must take time to bowl their overs and, as far as my memory goes back, that has been accepted in the game. Also, Tyson and Statham deserved all the help I could give them in field placings. Now and again I had a chat with one of them, a ploy I copied from the master tactician himself, Bradman. I was not as deliberate as Stollmeyer over field placings, and the tempo of play in 1954–55 could not have been bad as the first four Tests all ended with more than a day to spare. Between them, Appleyard and Wardle, the spinners, completed 149 overs against 294 by Tyson and Statham and seventy-three by Bailey. The matches were far too tense and dramatic for serious complaints of the tempo to be entertained and I believe it is manifestly unfair and wrong to link my series in Australia with the deliberate slowing-down tactic employed in later years.

My personal disappointment was not to get a century in my last tour of Australia, but scoring was generally low, with only two centuries from Australia, both in the first match at Brisbane by Morris and Harvey, and three by England – May, Cowdrey and Graveney. Incredibly, not a single century was scored against MCC, either by Australian or New Zealand batsmen after Brisbane, and I had four different partners, Simpson, Bailey, Edrich and Graveney in the Tests, with a top stand of 60 with Edrich at Adelaide. I might have gone on to a century but for an astonishing catch by Davidson. I hooked a long hop right in the middle of the bat, but Alan, at forward short leg, half-turned his back and shot out his hands in an instinctive gesture of self-protection. Somehow the ball stuck in those massive fists and 'The Claw' had made another miraculous catch. At Sydney he also caught me so superbly that I forgot my disappointment in admiration.

Only bad weather cost England a final triumph in the last Test at Sydney. New South Wales had its worst flooding for fifty years and pictures of a man clinging to a church spire as the waters swirled around him put the loss of a Test match into perspective. Graveney

hit the form I had always hoped he might produce and four successive boundaries off Miller, who applauded each stroke, took him to
his only century against Australia. The stroke play of Graveney and
May was memorable, and Australia followed on, this time falling
to Wardle. The game lasted only thirteen hours yet Australia lost
16 wickets, as if to emphasize the decline in their batting standards.
My last act in a Test match with Australia was to bowl the last over
and bowl Benaud. In 1939 I took 44 wickets with my leg breaks
and googlies, and my ambition began to stretch to doing the double
of 1000 runs and 100 wickets. The war and my injury, however,
put an end to my hope of becoming an all-rounder.

For the first and only time I heard Bradman, chairman of selectors,
booed by an Australian crowd when he went out to examine the
pitch, and I wondered whether the barrackers actually believed bad
selection had brought about Australia's defeat in the series. With
the same captain and players Australia went to the West Indies, won
three of the five Tests and remained unbeaten. But, as *Wisden* said,
England won on merit.

England rounded off the tour with a 100 per cent record in New
Zealand, who had slumped from the vintage year of 1949 when
they held England to four draws in three-day Tests. Now given five
days, New Zealand lost at Dunedin and Auckland inside three days,
and in the second match were dismissed for a record low total of
26. I don't know what the wickets were like at Port Elizabeth and
Edgbaston when South Africa went out for 30 in the previous low
record, but the Auckland pitch took a little spin at variable heights,
though not at any unusual pace. Usually a batting calamity is
brought about by one bowler – George Lohmann had 8 for 7 at
Port Elizabeth – or a pair, Arthur Gilligan and Maurice Tate at
Edgbaston. At Auckland I used four to bowl twenty-seven overs,
and it has been said that had I kept Tyson and Statham on, the total
would have been even smaller. There is no way of knowing, but the
key dismissal was Bert Sutcliffe, who made 11, before I introduced
Wardle to bowl Chinamen – the leg break to the left-handed
batsman. Sutcliffe went for a big hit and was bowled. Appleyard
came on at 14 for 4 and took 3 wickets in four balls, and all but
had a hat-trick when a catch fell inches short of Graveney in the leg
trap.

The fact was, any combination of bowlers was strong enough,
and I felt Tyson and Statham had earned the right to be in at the

kill. One over from Brian, however, was enough. Geoff Rabone, second top scorer with 7, went to his fourth ball, and the middle stump of the last man Hayes was sent cartwheeling through the air. After Sutcliffe and Rabone, Henry Cave scored 5, so 23 of the total of 26 came from three batsmen. Five failed to score, and three scored singles. The bowling figures read:

	O	M	R	W
Tyson	7	2	10	2
Statham	9	2	9	3
Appleyard	6	3	7	4
Wardle	5	5	0	1

To win by an innings after having a lead of only 42 was extraordinary and, delighted as I was with my bowlers, I could not help feeling sympathy for the New Zealanders, Rabone, their captain, and their faithful followers. I saw a minister of the cloth in tears, but a captain's duty is to strike hard and keep the pressure on. I do not believe there was a side in the world capable of withstanding the English attack for long, and it was not a disgrace for New Zealand to be knocked flat.

My last innings for England was 53 from the No. 5 position, the only half-century of the innings and it was 53 more than my first Test match, also against New Zealand, so many years before.

At the time I did not know it was to be my last Test, but, in retrospect, it was not a bad time to go. Right at the top. And I was spared the emotional upset of a sentimental farewell. Who could forget Bradman's last Test at the Oval in 1948 when the whole ground stood and cheered him all the way to the wicket. I am not suggesting I would have had – or deserved – a similar tribute, but as I watched Bradman take guard I could see the warmth of his reception and the occasion had got to him, and he was bowled second ball by Eric Hollies.

As he said: 'It's not easy to bat with tears in your eyes.'

9

Sad Farewell

As Old Masters go, Hutton was young enough; the sadness is that physical disability put an end to his career in its prime. . . . Hutton's batsmanship in its evolution from an early to a late period presented no marked divisions; it was never raw, unprincipled or embryonic. He batted grammatically from the start, choosing his strokes as carefully as a professor of logic his words . . . and whether or not he was putting into practice his wide repertoire of strokes, he was the stylist always; rarely was he discovered in an awkward position at the crease, rarely was he bustled or hurried. . . . As a captain he was shrewd but courteous; he knew the game's finer points, and though he was unlikely to give anything away, was too proud to take anything not his due. Sometimes he may have turned thoughtfulness to worry; but this is a natural habit in the part of the world which Hutton comes from. Hutton certainly showed that a professional cricketer can wear the robes of leadership in the field with dignity. At first, no doubt, he appeared at the head of his troops not wearing anything like a Caesarian toga, but rather the uniform of a sergeant-major. But he moved up in rank and prestige until he became worthy of his command. . . . A Yorkshireman has his own idea of humour, and Hutton, as great or famous as any Yorkshireman contemporary with him, relished his laugh all the more because very often it came last.
Sir Neville Cardus in *Wisden Cricketers' Almanack*, 1956

Life can be tantalizingly perverse. I was 99 when Yorkshire needed three runs to beat Glamorgan at Sheffield. My partner hit a long, safe single straight to an outfielder and as I arrived at the striker's end I saw the ball crawl through the fielder's legs and over the boundary for 4! When I returned from Australia with the Ashes held, and many of my critics silenced, I looked forward to leading

England against South Africa – the only country I had not taken on
as captain. To my gratification Gubby Allen's selectors gave me a
heartening vote of confidence by appointing me for all five Tests, an
unprecedented step at the time. It seemed that I was accepted by
those who counted. Looking farther ahead, I could reasonably
assume a chance of taking MCC to South Africa in the return series,
and even a prospect of completing a hat-trick of victories over
Australia in 1956.

But alas, the summer of 1955 was to be my last, a season of pain
and doubt, and finally the dreaded but irrevocable decision to retire.
The growing muscular trouble in my back, the legacy of years of
wear and tear, not only caused me to decline the invitation to captain
England but put me out of the series, and I managed only ten outings
for Yorkshire. (One was at the Oval where Peter May, my successor,
and I played under our appointed county captains, Stuart Surridge
and Norman Yardley – said to be unique in championship history.)
In late July I played my last county match at Bournemouth.

My back trouble started as far back as Hammond's tour of South
Africa in 1938–39 when I was fielding in the gully and had to move
sharply to my right to reach the ball. As I did so there was a distinct
click like the sound of a Spanish castanet, and thereafter I lived with
recurring pain in the small of my back. In Australia in 1954–55 I
regularly swallowed aspirins to ease the pain, and at Adelaide I
never thought I was going to see the Test through to the finish. By
the end of my last season, before I went into hospital at Leeds and
was put in a plaster cast from neck to waist, I was taking as many
as sixteen pain-killers a day.

Once, when I pulled out of a Test with lumbago, I had over five
hundred sympathetic letters, all suggesting remedies. A popular cure
was to place a nutmeg in my pocket and I was sent enough nutmegs
to start a business! Unfortunately nothing worked and at the Oval
I once fielded in an appliance which grew hotter and hotter as I ran
around. Mercifully, as it was becoming intolerable, Appleyard began
taking wickets and I was relieved of the torment.

Eventually arthritis developed. The doctors told me it was due to
the abnormal strain on my back. My frame ideally should have been
bigger for my job, say 5 feet 10 inches in height and a weight of 11
stones, and doubtless I overdid it when I was young for I spent every
free hour in the summer, and many in the winter, crouched over a
bat. Also no one practised harder than I did as a professional player,

and if the time I spent with my back bent over a bat, or stooped in a catching position in the field, could be counted, it would surely amount to a large proportion of the first thirty-nine years of my life.

On my return from Australia I could not play until late May and understandably my form was inclined to be as spasmodic as my appearances. In July I noted the gates were closed at Headingley with 35,000 inside the ground for the home match with Surrey, and the aggregate attendance was 60,000. In the last week of the month I took 194 off Nottinghamshire at Trent Bridge, which, at that point, was the highest individual score of the season. My last 94 came in sixty-five minutes, and I ended with three 6s and twenty-four 4s, but my exhilaration was all too short-lived. From Nottingham, Yorkshire went to Bournemouth and when I woke the next morning I could not move. I was virtually a prisoner in my own bed. Somehow an osteopath got me onto the field, and it was hardly surprising my scores were 0 and 2. Even worse than the physical pain, however, was the realization that it was the final curtain on my playing career. Long before I left Bournemouth I had come to terms with the fact that I could not carry on, and so, for the second time, there was a long, sad trek back to Leeds from the south coast. The first had been from Hove just after war was declared, and the team stopped at Leicester for a last meal and drink together. The last supper of a great county side about to break up; some might go as far as to think the glory of Yorkshire cricket has never been quite recaptured since.

I knew at Bournemouth I could not continue my addiction to tablets or play in a plaster or apparatus similar to the one I had tried out at the Oval. The plaster cast put on my back at Leeds brought me instant relief. Within an hour and a half the pain disappeared, but there was no question of changing my mind about retiring. I knew something was radically wrong, and I could not change the course of fate. Sir Jack Hobbs, I was repeatedly told, scored a hundred first-class centuries from the age of my retirement, but he had the supreme fortune to remain fit and possibly to play in an era when outside pressures were less severe. Obviously, I would have liked a few more seasons if I could have enjoyed my cricket. But there it was. We are not masters of our fate and I had the rich consolation of passing on a stronger England side than when I first took over the captaincy.

I am often asked if I regret not having been appointed captain of

Yorkshire. The brief answer is no for I cannot, in truth, declare it was an unfulfilled ambition. For most of my career the captaincy did not come within the sphere of a pro's reckoning, so the thought was not germinated. Later I came to know what captaining Yorkshire entailed. With its proud traditions and constantly high expectations, Yorkshire is the hardest of all counties to play for and, accordingly, the hardest to lead. Only the highest level of performance is acceptable. Also, it might be remembered Lord Hawke was from Yorkshire and it was Lord Hawke who uttered his famous and often-misunderstood words that he prayed God no professional would ever captain the England side. He was speaking at the annual meeting of the club in 1925 and he went on: 'I love professionals, every one of them, but we have always had an amateur skipper. If the time comes when we are to have no more amateurs captaining England, well, I don't say England will become exactly like League football, but it will be a thousand pities and it will not be for the good of the game.'

It was an ironic turn of fate that in the course of time his beloved Yorkshire should provide England's first professional captain. Would that fact have mellowed his opinion? I doubt it, for he lived in an age of vastly different social standards, and I would be the last to pour scorn on his sincerely held beliefs which seem impossibly dated in these times. Lord Hawke was far from being anti-pro – indeed, Louis Hall, a pro, captained Yorkshire when his lordship was away in the 1885 season and was made assistant captain – but he believed strongly in the system of his time. Lord Hawke was one of the many amateur captains and amateur cricketers who made a magnificent contribution to the game both at national and county level. Most pros can cite instances of invaluable advice and encouragement given to them by captains early in their careers and I am no exception. In my first season I was sent as a nervous messenger into the Kent dressing room at Headingley to have a bat autographed by Percy Chapman, latterly England's captain. Frankly, I did not know what to expect, but he welcomed me and made me feel it was a pleasure for him to sign a bat for me. I had made a few runs and he went on to compliment me and wished me luck in the future. To an awe-struck youngster, his words were music and meant a great deal to me. I am sure such figures as Lord Hawke and Lord Harris did much to set standards which the game will be ill advised to despise and ridicule as old-fashioned nonsense. They gave cricket a healthy base, both at home and overseas and, as I have already said, MCC could not have treated me better or more fairly when I was made captain; had Lord Hawke been on the committee I doubt he would have misunderstood the situation.

Wisden speculated on what he might have thought of the knighthood conferred on me in the Queen's Birthday Honours of June 1956, but I am certain he would have been delighted, albeit, perhaps, surprised at the changed social order, and would have sent his congratulations. The letters I received, both on my captaincy appointment and the knighthood, represented a remarkable cross-section of society, ranging from what might be called the pillars of the cricket establishment like Sir Pelham Warner, to fellow cricketers, past and present, and members of the public. But, if I may be forgiven, the letter I cherished above all others came from George Hirst who, at the Winter Shed at Headingley so many years before, had started his teaching with the advice which to all young cricketers should be a veritable commandment: 'Remember, always, the more you put into the game the more you take out of it.' George did not live to see me as a Knight of the Realm, but I know he would have chuckled and thought back to the days when I used to meet him to carry his bag onto the tram to my coaching sessions. We talked of cricket and cricketers until our throats were dry, the old master and his pupil, but never was there a thought of the captaincy of England or a visit to Buckingham Palace to kneel before the Sovereign. That would have been pure fantasy, and George was too good a Yorkshireman to indulge in dreams.

When I received a letter from Sir Anthony Eden, the Prime Minister – and it has always been understood that the recommendation came from Downing Street and not Lord's – to ask if I would accept a knighthood, I could not have been more surprised and it took time for the fact to sink in. Unfortunately I never had the privilege of meeting Sir Anthony.

I was in somewhat of a daze when, accompanied by Dorothy and our sons Richard and John, I went to Buckingham Palace for the investiture. The solemnity of the occasion and the splendour of the great room in which the ceremony took place were awe-inspiring. In such surroundings and amid such company, I felt insignificant and humble. The Queen spoke a few words to me which I am sure must have been gracious and appropriate, but I was too bemused for anything to register and I am ashamed to say I have no idea

what Her Majesty said. I was in a whirl, but Dorothy and the boys
had an unforgettable experience. A knighthood brings its advantages
and disadvantages, but nothing can diminish the inner pride at being
singled out for high honour. I know it to be an awful platitude to
suggest cricket shares my distinction, and I would like to think
that somewhere on high George Herbert Hirst looked down with
approval and understood I remembered him in one of my proudest
hours.

Both the boys went to Repton, and Richard, a chartered accountant, gained his blue at Cambridge, played for Yorkshire and five
times for England against India and Pakistan in 1971 – hence my
excusable use of the phrase 'one of my proudest hours' about going
to Buckingham Palace. I am immensely proud of my family, but
watching Richard in the Varsity match and for England was an
infinitely more trying ordeal than going in to face Lindwall and
Miller. At the Oval (where else for a Hutton?) Richard took 81 off
India's famed spinners and maintained the family reputation for
quick scoring with a stand of 103 in sixty-five minutes with Alan
Knott! At the time it was a record for the seventh wicket for England
against India, and was the perfect answer to an outspoken critic
who had told me to my face that Richard wasn't good enough.

Richard and I were the sixth father and son to play for England,
following C. L. and D. C. H. Townsend, Fred and Maurice Tate,
Jim Parks Sr and Jim Parks Jr, Frank and George Mann, and 'Old
Joe' and 'Young Joe' Hardstaff. It is always harder for son to follow
father in sport as usually only father's better days are remembered,
and an above average performance is all too often expected as the
norm. One evening the Hardstaff family sat for dinner after Young
Joe had been dismissed attempting a risky shot. Old Joe, with solemn
face, looked down the table and announced: 'I am sad to have
discovered today that my son is a gambler!'

Ironically, I am inclined to think John had more natural talent
than Richard. Certainly he had a better bowling action and some
pointer to his ability came when he bowled Peter May in a match
in the Cricketer Cup. Stan Cullis, then manager of Wolverhampton
Wanderers, also had a son at Repton, and he was so impressed with
John as a centre half that he wanted to sign him. John also hits a
golf ball like a pro. But promising as he was, he did not have
Richard's devotion to cricket. From his early childhood Richard was
passionately interested in the game and he still turns out for MCC,

Repton Pilgrims and the Courage's Old England side. He also toured Pakistan with Mike Brearley's Under-25 side and it was no mean feat to become one of Yorkshire's principal all-rounders in his career.

The welfare of the boys was one of the reasons for the family moving south to Surrey. There was a time when it was quite something to be a Yorkshire cricketer – the glamour might have worn thin in the last quarrelsome decade or so – and some of it rubbed off onto the son. An old player once feelingly advised me to have daughters! There was always the possibility of the sons of a Yorkshire cricketer becoming well known without having accomplished anything by themselves, which cannot be good for them. While we had every confidence in Richard and John remaining level-headed, Dorothy and I wanted them to strike out independently and make their own way. Sir Don Bradman's son John actually changed his name in an effort to seek his own identity and life, and though I would shrink from putting myself in the same category of fame as the incomparable Don, we knew the risks in cricket-loving Yorkshire and felt the boys would benefit from being in a fresh environment.

I trust I will not be misunderstood for I am Yorkshire to the core, and I long for the day when the giant stirs again, but there were times when I found it impossible to have a private life in Yorkshire and to converse on any subject other than cricket, which, with the best will in the world, can be wearing. There is nothing I like better than to sit with old cronies and relive the past, but I am equally happy at times to strike up a casual conversation with a stranger who doesn't know I am an old cricketer able to cure Yorkshire's ills with devastating insight. In London and the south I can be more anonymous than in Pudsey and Leeds, which, it goes without saying, I still love dearly. The weather in the south is a little kinder to my arthritis, and there are some excellent golf courses!

Golf is a relaxation which has given me infinite pleasure. When I was playing cricket I could steal away for a few hours, forget the pressures and make as many bad shots as I liked without half the world reading about my mistakes the next morning. My golfing days actually started as a result of playing in an annual two-day match at Malton, the home of Lord and Lady Milton. On the first evening I was in a cloakroom and looking at a bag of clubs deposited in a corner, when Lord Milton arrived and asked: 'Do you play?'

'Not yet,' I replied, 'but I'm thinking of taking it up and am about to buy a set of clubs.'

To my surprise Lord Milton waved his hand at the bag and said: 'You can have those.'

At breakfast the next morning I told Hedley Verity and Arthur Dolphin of my chance encounter and the promise of the set of clubs. Arthur jokingly said: 'When his Lordship comes down we'd better get the conversation going on golf to jog his memory!' We all laughed, but when Lord Milton arrived he did not need to be reminded of his promise and I left with the clubs. I started with an 18 handicap and, at my best, went down to 3.

In 1948 I started business as a sports outfitter in Bradford. The shop property belonged to the Bradford Corporation, but in the fifties they wanted it to extend the Town Hall. The old city centre has since been transformed. The council offered me an alternative site, which I duly inspected, but after a lot of thought I decided against accepting and it remains one of those decisions which might have been right or wrong. But it was made, and in 1959 we moved to Surrey, intending to stay no more than five years. Dorothy likes Kingston-upon-Thames and the boys, now married, live nearby at Tunbridge Wells and Twickenham.

Another factor in the move south was the number of engagements in hand in London, which involved considerable travelling. I was also writing for the London *Evening News*. I became involved with J. H. Fenner and Co. (Holdings) Ltd, the power transmission engineers, and on their behalf I have travelled to Australia, South Africa, the United States and India primarily on the coal mining interests of the company. Dr Sidney Hainsworth, now president and former chairman and managing director, is a keen and knowledgeable cricket supporter. As a vice-president of YCCC, he has organized matches for county beneficiaries. And, of course, the Fenner Trophy, promoted by the company, was a feature of the season in the north.

For a while I went to Hull, Fenner's home base, and became immersed in the severely practical world of pulleys, feed belts, gear boxes – indeed everything connected with the transmission of power from a motor to a machine. A far cry from Headingley and Lord's, but fascinating and rewarding. I never believed that a sportsman is owed a living once his playing days have ended and I would not have enjoyed batting if my skill had gone into decline.

Fenners, I think, were agreeably surprised by my ability to get on with the mining fraternity both at home and overseas, but Pudsey is not all that far from the Yorkshire coal fields and I had a natural affinity with colliers, many of whom were keenly interested in cricket. I have some wonderful friends from the pits. In America, in the coal mines of Pennsylvania and the potash mines of New Mexico, I was surprised to find a percentage of the work force had, by law, to be women. They oiled the machinery and so on, but a British engineer, responsible for thirteen collieries near Pittsburg, discovered one of his employees had set up her own business in the world's oldest profession. American enterprise knows no limits!

On a visit to India I had the privilege of meeting Mrs Gandhi at New Delhi. The British High Commissioner was concerned that a Prime Minister and a former cricketer might find conversation difficult but, to say the least, his fears were groundless. For an hour Mrs Gandhi spoke of the world situation, of Russia, the United States, the Middle East, and her own political problems with fascinating candour, before moving to the subject of cricket. This, I thought, is where I come in, but I was impressed by her knowledge of the game and the leading players. Clearly she was not a casual follower and told me she recognized the importance of cricket as a great pastime, giving pleasure to millions and having a valuable unifying effect in India's national life. When in 1983 Kapil Dev's team won the Prudential World Cup I thought it was no bad thing for cricket at large.

Ever since Mr Fisher, Pudsey's appropriately named wet-fishmonger, presented me with Ranji's *Jubilee Book of Cricket* (the Jubilee marking Queen Victoria's reign) I was drawn to Indian cricket – an interest no doubt nourished by my being an avid reader of *Magnet* and Greyfriar's match-winning batsman Gamset Ram Singh! Unfortunately I never toured India but I can claim to have played an innings on the subcontinent. My visit to Bengal Colliery coincided with a cricket match starting after lunch and the message came: 'Will Sir Len play?' In borrowed gear and wearing my street shoes I went out to bat, but the heat was so stifling that when I'd scored 34 I'd had enough. The enthusiasm of the players, officials and spectators was rewarding enough and I regretted that it had not been customary in my time for MCC to send full-strength sides to India.

At Bombay on the same business trip I had tea with the great Kumar Shri Duleepsinhji, Ranji's nephew, who played for England with such distinction before India was granted full Test match status. I heard so much about Ranji and Duleep from Rhodes and Co. that

I felt I almost knew them. 'Eyesight!' Rhodes would declaim. 'Ranji could count the stitches on the ball.' And yet, F. S. Jackson had to be pressurized into giving Ranji his blue in his last year at Cambridge because he was unconvinced at the time that he could bat!

Duleep, by all accounts, must have been a joy to watch, and I often wonder how he would have coped with the modern barrage of short-pitched bowling and if he would have worn a helmet. Methinks not. Frank Chester was umpiring on the day Duleep scored 333 for Sussex against Northamptonshire at Hove. In the middle of the onslaught 'Nobby' Clark, the fast left-arm bowler, who was not noted for keeping a tight rein on his temper, turned in despair to Chester and asked: 'What can I do?'

'Simple' replied Chester. 'Pull a muscle and spend the rest of the day on the beach!'

Clark was once having a rough time against Yorkshire and a second slip chance went down off his bowling. He strode back to his bowling mark muttering furiously and, looking up at a skylark overhead, suddenly shouted: 'What the hell have you got to sing about!'

Duleep would have gone to Australia with Jardine's team but for ill health. The Nawab of Pataudi went instead, and I notice in the official photograph his hand rests on the player in front of him in a clear gesture of friendliness. The player: Hedley Verity. In 1950 Duleep went to Australia in the capacity of Indian High Commissioner and although some of Freddie Brown's MCC team, playing at Canberra, went to see him, unfortunately I was not one of their number. When I did meet him at Bombay I was profoundly impressed by the man, his modesty, his genuine friendliness and his deep love of cricket and cricketers. Maybe it was just as well he was spared the bodyline bitterness.

In 1958–59 I went to Australia in my new role as newspaper correspondent, sharing the general confidence that my successor, Peter May, had a winning team. I genuinely felt he had a stronger side than I had taken to Australia four years before. Yet May was routed, losing four of the five Tests, and long before the end England were demoralized and shattered, laid low by the fierce controversies centred on throwing, dragging and umpiring. Looking back, it is not difficult to plot the cause of the disaster, starting with MCC's decision to withdraw their invitation to Johnny Wardle, who had been involved in a flare-up at Sheffield and became the author of sensational articles in the *Daily Mail* critical of Yorkshire and his captain Ronnie Burnet, who had been appointed to instil discipline in the side. It is not for me to sit in judgement on Wardle in this issue, but the sequel of events was unfortunate. Only three days after he had been chosen for Australia, Wardle was sacked by Yorkshire. MCC, taking the view that they had the responsibility to regard the matter in the wider interests of the game as they saw it, rescinded their invitation. I do not argue that MCC had a perfect right to take this line, but, having done so, they failed to replace Wardle and left England with only two spinners. True, they were the redoubtable Surrey pair, Lock and Laker, but a third slower bowler was imperative. In due course their error was recognized and Gloucestershire's John Mortimore was sent out, together with a batting cover in Ted Dexter. Had I been in May's position, I would have been dismayed by Wardle's absence following an internal Yorkshire domestic wrangle. Finally Wardle went to Australia as a newspaper critic; he should have been a valuable member of the team.

May was like a captain of a ship caught in a sudden storm. To begin with, I think, England made the mistake of assuming that the throwing controversy around the world had largely blown over. But they had the rudest of awakenings and there were so many suspect bowlers in Australia that Tommy Andrews, an Australian Test player of the twenties, surprised me by saying: 'If they stop throwing, cricket in Australia will die.' To their credit, Australia tackled the problem with characteristic vigour – albeit after the series – and, of course, cricket did not die any more than the breed of fast bowlers, which was confidently predicted in some quarters when the front-foot law was introduced to stop dragging. At one stage or another in the series, Australia played four bowlers with suspect actions, and there were others in the state sides. Nor could one be happy with Tony Lock's action, and he wisely took his own remedy after seeing himself on film. Throwing was by no means a new problem and generally authority had turned a blind eye.

In the opinion of MCC players in South Africa in 1948–49, fast bowler Cuan McCarthy had a bent arm, an opinion later reinforced by Frank Chester. At Nottingham in 1951 Chester went to two leading members of the MCC committee at lunch on the day of England's first innings and told them that, in his opinion, McCarthy had an illegal action. Chester sought assurances that if he no-balled

McCarthy he would, in principle, be supported by MCC. He was bluntly told that if he did no-ball McCarthy for throwing, it was unlikely he would remain on the Test umpires' panel. Chester, relying on umpiring for his bread and butter, prudently stayed quiet, took no action and, understandably, South Africa countered any suspicions thereafter with the fact that he had satisfied Chester. In those days MCC took the view that they were hosts and harmonious relationships were paramount.

I did not mind batting against McCarthy or, for that matter, any bowler with a suspect action. Washbrook and I shared a record first-wicket partnership at Ellis Park, Johannesburg, in 1948 when McCarthy spearheaded South Africa's attack. If I faced a right-arm thrower I had the comforting thought that he did not move the ball away from the bat. That suited me, but I cannot recall facing a left-arm bowler with a doubtful action. Ian Meckiff, the main bone of England's contention, was left-arm, which made him a different proposition. He made the ball leave the right-hander's bat and, therefore, if he pitched the ball in the right spot he was very dangerous. Apparently when MCC players first saw Meckiff loosening up before the start of their match with Victoria, some favoured an official protest there and then. The argument was that it would be difficult to lodge a complaint once the Test series had started, particularly if England were on the losing end.

May was clearly in an invidious position, but I cannot believe any satisfaction would have been gained from the Australian Board, who merely had to retort that Meckiff had been passed on a previous tour of South Africa and by their own Australian umpires. Peter would have had to accept the fact that umpires were there to interpret the laws of the game. Further, if a protest had come to public notice, England would have earned the ridicule of the Australian press. Of course, throwing offends the law, and has largely been stamped out, but, in my opinion, England's players were at fault for allowing themselves to be upset by throwing and umpiring decisions. As a generalization, it can be said English cricketers have a tendency to be put off their game and poise if they are convinced something wrong and irregular is going on.

One of the indisputable facts of cricket life is that a moderate umpire cannot be transformed into a good umpire by beefing about him. Nor can the behaviour of a crowd be changed by resenting their apparent partisanship. Umpiring mistakes, crowds and other upsetting distractions have to be overcome. I can honestly claim not to have complained of a bowler's action and, it might be added, if the thought had occurred to me in my early Yorkshire days there would have been scant sympathy and plenty of outspoken advice from my seniors. Verity and Bowes were never heard to grumble about a pitch. Yet I have known players make such a habit of grumbling that they would moan if they bowled on a corrugated iron roof.

Bad umpiring mistakes have to be accepted, maddening though they are to the victim. Nor is it possible to expect the general high standard in England to be found elsewhere, which is not to suggest the absence of first-class umpires around the world. But every batsman has a shocker at some time or another.

I have never thought much of the speculative appeal with the excuse that it's up to the umpire to make a decision. If umpires were infallible the argument could be tolerated, and I sincerely believe they should be helped, not challenged or intimidated. May's team had some dispiriting breaks, not the least being the disputed catch at Brisbane (Brisbane again!) which went against Cowdrey at a crucial stage. Some of the Aussie fielders sportingly told Colin to stay and he left the field slowly as he expected to be called back. Poor Colin lost out both ways, as he was criticized for his reluctant departure.

My advice to cricketers is to try to avoid making umpiring an issue. I know I had the problem in the West Indies where there was a special difficulty at the time, but it is all too easy for the rot to set in if players start thinking and brooding about questionable decisions instead of getting on with the game. At the same time, it has to be said that excessive and organized appealing, designed to pressurize umpires and put off the batsman, has crept in like an unwelcome tide. It is a deliberate ploy and is much to be deplored. Unfair and incessant appealing, particularly by a heavily protected posse of close-in fielders, is an ugly development on a par with so-called 'sledging', the violent abuse of opponents, also sometimes known as 'the verbals'. Fortunately abuse was not part of the game I knew and I am puzzled by captains who stand aside and let it all happen – unless they are part of the conspiracy.

There have been times in recent years when I have become so bored with the nonstop frivolous shouting that I have thought it might be better if appealing could be eliminated completely. But when all is said and done, appealing is part of cricket and something would be lost without it. Fair appealing generates sudden excitement followed by a moment of agonizing suspense. I have heard Trueman appeal with such righteous passion that a ripple of laughter circled the ground. But organized appealing is quite different. One might say it is one of the most unappealing aspects of modern cricket.

Cheating, verbals, intimidation and the other undesirable elements of the game can be defeated by firm captaincy and umpiring, and, in turn, both need to be supported by the various Boards. Boards have also to learn over again that no player is greater than the game. I preach old-fashioned principles, but a return to basic standards of behaviour is necessary as the game accelerates into becoming a branch of showbiz with total commercialization.

Television, which has changed the habits of nations, let alone sport, has turned cricket into a branch of showbiz which, in itself, might be no bad thing if it added to the popularity and support of the game. Showbiz, of course, demands drama and constant action, and if players are conscious of cameras being upon them, they are tempted to overreact in the most absurd fashion. Some of the passionate appeals might make for good, lively television, but they are bad for cricket and an irritating bore to the knowledgeable watcher. Undeniably, fashions and manners change, but I never feel there is any logical reason why the cricketers of today should not be every bit as skilled and entertaining as in days gone by. Yet the stage has changed, and sport, it should be remembered, is the only part of entertainment without the players having a prepared script. One of its endearing fascinations lies in its unpredictability. Success can never be ordered. My private fear was to go first ball of a Test! Success and failure often comes when you least expect it. Bruce Cairns, the New Zealander, in 1983 in England was Man of the Match at Headingley, contributing largely to England's defeat, and in the next Test at Lord's missed a sitter, which arguably led to New Zealand's defeat. The game is a great leveller. Television has introduced a new type of tension but, if cricket becomes secondary and a platform for exhibitionism, it will lose its special charm and identity. And possibly its sponsors.

I am not among the older brigade who cannot accept limited-over cricket. I would have enjoyed playing in the one-day internationals and the major domestic competitions, particularly in front of a full house at Lord's. The possible exception would be the forty-over contests, which deny basic abilities, with bowling run-ups restricted and fielders scattered around without slips. There is something wrong when it is as valuable for bowlers to keep the runs down as to take wickets, and I do not think it possible to have a real cricket match in less than fifty overs a side. Unlike the far-seeing 'progressives', I do not anticipate a time when one-day internationals will replace the longer Test match, but I am worried by drawn matches. The public want to see a result. Personally, I did not welcome the introduction of the five-day Test as I always believed four days should be long enough in normal conditions to achieve a result. Generally speaking, the longer the time, the slower the tempo of play.

One-day cricket is offered as the prime excuse for a decline in technical skills. That there has been a decline is seldom in dispute, and English cricket is becoming depressingly familiar with the story of young players of rich promise who fail to progress or actually go backwards. I am inclined to think, however, that cricketers ought to be able to adapt to the various forms of the game. Golfers have to play on a variety of courses and cope with the differing paces of greens. There is no reason why cricketers should not be able to master the various conditions of the modern competitions. In my time we played six days and rested on Sunday – provided we were not engaged in benefit games – and the routine of the county championship was broken only by Test matches and a few representative occasions like Gents *v.* Players. The season was rounded off with the festivals.

Now there is infinitely more variety, which surely creates wider public interest and should stimulate the players. Yorkshire were a privileged county as they were invariably involved in the championship honours, but for the majority of clubs there was no competitive edge to the season by mid-summer. Year after year they merely made up the number, with no higher ambition than to end in a respectable position in the table. How much better it must be with a chance in four competitions. The Prudential World Cup has been an inspiring innovation and I would have relished the chance of being one-day champions when I captained England. The National Westminster Bank brought the 1953 players together on the eve of the 1983 Cup and I said at the time I thought a squad from that set of players would have been champions, a view I stand by.

Fortunately sponsorship in England has been splendidly handled.

The sponsors have supplied a cash flow, without which the books could not be balanced, and the administration the knowhow. A happy combination. The Australian scene, which I saw first-hand in 1982–83 when I combined a business visit with comments on the cricket for the *Observer*, is much different, and it is hard to avoid the conclusion that commercial television is the dominating factor. Showbiz razzmatazz, coloured clothing and the rest are a new dimension of cricket which would not go down well in other parts of the world. At least I would not be happy to see English cricket follow suit. Too much of the best of the game is sacrificed. Cricket can be part of the business of entertainment without becoming brash, and as long as the sponsors continue to stand apart from the actual running of the game, I believe one-day tournaments, which are the financial crutch and, in any case, have come to stay, provide a vibrant and interesting dimension to the more serious matches.

I am totally in favour of players earning as much as they can during their short careers, which end at an age when in other fields the ladder of promotion is being climbed with prospects ahead. Cricketers should be seen as people with responsibilities to their families, with mortgages and school fees to be met, but a few of the elite in the top-earning bracket must guard against the temptation to be too greedy. Test fees, with the extra incentive of bonus and prize money, benefits, payment for overseas tours, and general commercialization of talent and names have soared rapidly. Therefore I cannot see the point of squeezing more from ventures gaining comparatively little reward. I have heard of payments being sought for team photographs, which I find degrading. Nor do I like advertising on clothing. The worst thing that could happen to cricket would be a commercial takeover weakening the attitude of players to the game. Loyalty should remain paramount, and while it may be possible to take on authority by legal action, the outcome can be a Pyrrhic victory.

I cannot believe a wise cricketer puts his position in jeopardy by going on unofficial tours, particularly like Graham Gooch, Geoff Boycott and John Emburey at a time of peak reputation. When I was dropped after the Lord's Test in 1948 it hurt and, on the odd occasion when I was injured or ill, I was genuinely disappointed. When Boycott decided he would not play for England, I automatically concluded that was the end of his Test career. I was a selector during his self-imposed (and never satisfactorily explained) exile and supported the policy of chairman Alec Bedser not to woo him to return, despite the outside pressures to do so – particularly after a bad match for England. Bedser's conduct in remaining available to Boycott if Boycott wished to contact him was correct. Ken Barrington, purely on his own initiative and I am sure for the best of motives, approached Boycott at Worcester. He had not gone with that precise intention but the other selectors, myself included, did not find out until later that he had sounded him out. Personally, I thought it was up to Boycott to make his own decision and I would never have made an overture to him. I was surprised when eventually he made himself available again and, to my mind, he was doubly lucky to have a tolerant set of selectors and not to find his position had been usurped by a younger batsman.

I did not make a fortune out of cricket. Far from it. My first payment was a five shilling piece from an elderly gentleman after my first 50: 'Never spend it until you're down to your last five bob,' he smilingly advised the young lad in knickerbockers. Not yet being reduced to such straits, I still have it, though it was not conspicuously lucky for me when I used it to toss with when I was captain in home Tests. In fact I won the toss only seven times out of twenty-three. I remained faithful to my five shilling piece, although literally scores of guaranteed 'lucky' coins and talismen of every description were sent to me.

I never had an agent, not because I was against their use, but simply because there were not many around at the time, and the opportunities to exploit commercial avenues were very limited. In any case, Denis Compton was the No. 1 personality and attraction, and not even he did all that well from his most famous advertisement. There was the Len Hutton Autograph Bat but, apart from a couple of years, the revenue from that venture was small – indeed, trifling would be the word if put against today's contracts for endorsing equipment and clothing. While I have no possible objection to the good agent, I have reservations about American-style agents, and the attachment of lawyers and accountants. Perhaps they have become necessary for the commercially geared top liners, but there must be a danger of losing sight of the fact that the main function of a player is to play cricket consistently to the highest level of his ability. Unfortunately, to meet the high fees and cost of maintaining first-class cricket, far too many Tests are played. The magic of the Test match is disappearing amid a welter of matches and series.

The brilliantly organized benefit has hit the roof. Even ordinary county players, whose names have never passed the lips of selectors, have raked in huge sums. In 1950 my benefit of £9713 was considered to be in the 'bumper' class, and it was the practice of the day – a legacy of a time when the pro was not trusted to deal competently with large sums of money – for the club to keep two-thirds of the amount to invest in gilt-edged dated stock on behalf of the beneficiary. Eventually we were all paid out in full and the total was the same as when it was originally invested.

At Yorkshire the pros had no contracts as such. Our caps were our contracts, but there was nothing in writing. My cap was awarded in 1936, which was regarded as swift promotion. I was on the standard pro's pay, and in 1949, when I aggregated 3429 runs, the fourth highest of all time, I received the same as the other capped batsmen, who didn't score half as many runs. The same pay-scale arrangements remained in the fourteen years I topped 2000 runs. I do not complain, but merely point to the changed financial circumstances of the county player. In *Barclays World of Cricket* it is recorded that I hit eighty-five centuries and scored almost 25,000 runs for Yorkshire, and I made myself ill with the cares of Test captaincy in exceptionally demanding circumstances. 'For Yorkshire Hutton played in an isolation of technical superiority as the county's one assurance of logical and masterful batting.' I wonder what use an agent might have made of that compliment in the commercial field!

Perhaps I missed my main chance when a smartly dressed stranger approached me in the pavilion at Lord's in 1947 and asked me if I backed horses. I am not a betting man, but at the time there were several in the Yorkshire dressing room not averse to an inside tip. The horse recommended to me was Friar's Fancy in the 3.30 at Sandown Park. I duly passed on the information and decided to have a go myself. Maurice Leyland, having failed a fitness test, was told to take a break and he left for the afternoon at Sandown. I saw Friar's Fancy listed at 4 to 1 and asked Maurice to place the bet for me on the course. Friar's Fancy duly won, and the next morning I went to collect my winnings, only to be told he was sorry, but he had forgotten all about it!

From then on every visit to Lord's by Yorkshire was eagerly anticipated by the punters of the side, and I was given some splendid information by my unknown contact. I never knew his name and our conversations were brief and to the point; if he should still be around and read these words, I would not object if he contacted me again! At Lord's there was an annual visitor from Los Angeles, who had emigrated from London when very young and built up a reputation in America as a fitness expert. One of his jobs was to look after the health of film stars and he promised me he could make me throw away the years and be rejuvenated. Naturally I listened intently, but his advice did not make me feel any younger, or enable me to run quicker between the wickets!

After the war I often felt I was beginning again. The surroundings were the same but the associates had changed. Verity had not returned, and Bowes, Leyland, Barber and Turner did not remain long. The face of Yorkshire cricket changed and many of the accepted traditions and attitudes disappeared with the older stalwarts. Knowing what Yorkshire meant to them, I am thankful Rhodes, Hirst, Sir Stanley Jackson and many others were spared the undignified squabbling and public disputes of the last decade or so. The more I read of the goings-on, the personality clashes and the tug-of-words by the various factions, the more confused and saddened I become. For me it is like seeing a well-loved family being torn apart, and I would not pretend to know when or where the rot started, its cause, or how to put it right. One basic trouble must be the lack of success on the field, which is hard to take after so many generations of dominance. Yorkshire began to believe they had an almost divine right to the championship.

Events, too, have conspired against Yorkshire since the influx of overseas stars. While Yorkshire doggedly, and rightly, stuck to their policy of playing only Yorkshire-born players, other clubs bought their way to success. If Yorkshire, for instance, had imported a strike bowler from the West Indies, New Zealand, South Africa, Pakistan or Australia, the recent history of failure would surely have been rewritten. At least Yorkshire can have a clear conscience as far as national interests are concerned as they have not made a single contribution to a situation which has caused a serious decline in England's Test standards. As a selector I experienced at first hand the damaging effect of too many overseas players occupying the key batting and bowling positions in county teams; it will take many frustrating years to regain acceptable standards. Perhaps, as the natural balance of the championships is restored – and it has to be considered in the national interest – Yorkshire will come into their own again. But it is often overlooked that even in the thirties Yorkshire took some hammerings when the side was weakened by Test calls and injuries. I have every confidence players will come along as they did in the past. The well of talent cannot have run dry, but results will not come unless everyone pulls in the same direction. Unlike other team games, in cricket there can be a conflict between self-interests and team needs. Cricket can breed a degree of selfishness, perhaps as high as 75 per cent self and 25 per cent for the team, and to switch from thinking about one's own performance to putting the team first needs character of a high order. But unless the individual works for the team, there isn't much chance of sustained success. The quick captaincy changes provide surface proof of Yorkshire's problems, and it was a desperate throw to hand the reins to the fifty-year-old Ray Illingworth. He must now feel he could always get a job in a circus putting his head in a lion's mouth.

Was it not Harold Macmillan who said: 'Only a fool would want to be Prime Minister'? I often thought the same could be said of cricket captaincy. The best player in the side does not necessarily make the best captain, one reason being that the job entails considerable concentration, whether batting, bowling or fielding, and the extra burden of captaincy is often too much to carry, especially when criticism begins to bite. The disappearance of the amateur made the lot of the pro that much harder.

By sheer chance I was browsing through Ranji's *The Jubilee Book of Cricket* when Bob Willis's diary of the 1982–83 Australian tour was published. With amusement I read Ranji's words: 'A man who is engaged in heavy brain-work, such as writing a book on cricket, or trying to matriculate at a Cambridge college, cannot be expected to be at his best on the cricket field.' I leave it to others to judge the ethics of a tour captain commenting on the performances of team-mates immediately after the event – in my time there was a sensible interval of two years before going into print – but, drawing on my own experience as a captain in Australia, I would never have had either the time or the inclination to prepare a book. I was so preoccupied with the manifold tasks on and off the field that I scarcely had a moment to myself, and if one came, I was invariably too tired to do anything but relax with a glass of ale. If I wasn't planning tactics, I was at the nets, talking to my manager and players, answering questions from newspaper and radio men – television was less prominent at the time – and cooperating in public-relations stunts like dressing up in a driver's outfit and being taken through the streets of Bunbury in a spider after a trotting meeting.

Speaking in public did not come easily to me, at least at first, and I went to a lot of pains to try to strike the right note. No doubt some of the chores of touring captaincy have disappeared since my day as tours are much shorter and there is a second manager to look after the playing side, organize the nets and so on – a job, it might be added, once done without fuss by the senior pro. Many of the obligatory functions have gone; but I beg leave to doubt if pressures on the players are any greater, or that the standard of cricket has improved, with fielding perhaps as the exception. As a general observation, I believe the one necessity of the modern game is a return to basic techniques.

I would give a lot to listen to the reactions of the immortals if a wand could be waved for them to return to survey the spectrum of cricket in the eighties. Touring must have been tough, with long sea voyages, often around the coast of Australia to and from matches, primitive hotels without air conditioning, cold beer and having to wear thick suits and high collars in the middle of the Australian summer. Touring, like the game itself, changed dramatically even in my time. For a start, the equipment is different. George Hirst never paid more than twelve shillings and sixpence (62½p) for a bat. The cricket balls to commemorate his outstanding feats were larger than the present ball, with very little seam. Modern bowlers would refuse to use them. I find it impossible to imagine England's selectors recalling a forty-eight-year-old bowler for a critical Test as they did with Rhodes in 1926 – with success, too! Rhodes was fond of telling me of his first visit to Lord's at the turn of the century: everyone was scared of W. G. Grace and the pitch was so bad that there were little pebbles on the surface.

Since my retirement in the mid-fifties there have been fundamental changes in style and techniques. Today's batsmen do not have to deal with the variety of bowling I and my contemporaries had to face. What could have been more contrasting and challenging than series against Lindwall and Miller and Ramadhin and Valentine. Lamentably, the trend has been towards almost unrelieved speed, with spin as the secondary weapon. I have often wished the bowling success of recent West Indies teams had been founded on a more balanced attack, for the worst condemnation of nonstop fast bowling, often pitched short, is that it produces dull cricket.

India and Pakistan's Abdul Qadir have provided exceptions to the rule, and the English batsmen's inability in 1982 to pick Abdul Qadir's googly from his leg break demonstrated all too well how untutored the modern player can be against wrist spin. The Bruce Dooland, Doug Wright, Ces Pepper, George Tribe and Johnny Wardle vintage wrist-spinning has become unfashionable, and the England captain Bob Willis voiced modern thinking when he said leg-break bowlers do not win Test matches. I would enjoy seeing the theory put to the test if another Grimmett–O'Reilly partnership emerged, or Abdul Qadir could have a bowler to complement his skills at the other end. One bowler cannot do it on his own.

Constant and short-pitched fast bowling, without even the No. 11 being spared the bouncer, is unwelcome and tedious. Lest any should regard my view as the pot calling the kettle black, there can be no fair comparison with my tactics and the current practice of four fast bowlers. While it is true I put my trust in speed at both ends in Australia in 1954–55, Appleyard and Wardle provided invaluable support. At the time I had the two fastest bowlers in the world, and they had the pitches to bowl on. On the two occasions, Brisbane and Kingston, when I played fast bowlers, there were sound reasons for my decisions, as I have explained elsewhere. At home in 1953, when the Ashes were recaptured, my principal bowler was Bedser, who certainly did not bowl bouncers and was a shining example of a bowler succeeding with all the virtues of his craft.

Far be it for me to make sweeping condemnations. Not everything is wrong; far from it. Yet I do not believe there can be as much enjoyment playing at Test and county levels as there once was. We played hard, but the bowling lengths and speeds, the incessant appealing, even perhaps the extra cash, have given rise to a new intensity. Speak to any umpire and he will deplore the language and sharp practices. Yorkshire, it was always said, didn't play for fun, and maybe we didn't, but we had our fun in our own way, and our humour was true to our environment. The character of Yorkshire cricket was made great by great players, totally dedicated to a cause, and there were some marvellous men and players.

Who knows? I might have played in a different way if I had been born at Canterbury or St John's Wood, or been an amateur. Or my mentors had been Patsy Hendren and Walter Robins. But I was born in the north, and was a pro. We are what we are.

Not all the so-called 'hard' cricket was played north of the Trent, as I was reminded by a letter in which the writer apologized for a dimly remembered incident in which I was run out in peculiar circumstances at Taunton many years earlier. I harboured no grievance, but the matter had obviously preyed on the mind of the lone appealer who was the cause of my dismissal. I very much appreciated his letter.

A short third man had been placed to save the single to the bowling of the left-arm spinner Horace Hazell, and I duly played a shot in that direction without attempting to run. The rest should have been a formality, but the return came straight towards me and I stepped aside and moved just out of my ground to allow Walter Luckes, the wicketkeeper, to gather the ball unimpeded. By a mischance he did not collect it cleanly and it hit my pads and rolled onto the wicket dislodging a bail. As I was in the act of picking up the ball I heard an appeal and, looking up, saw the raised finger of the umpire. Technically I suppose I was out, and I did not argue, but I half-expected to be recalled, as I ought to have been after that notorious dismissal at Melbourne in 1950.

Washbrook, my partner in a Test at Christchurch in 1951, was brought back after being given out leg before off a thick edge. Wallee Hadlee, the home captain, consulted with some of his fielders and raced after Cyril, who had almost reached the pavilion rails. He invited Cyril to resume his innings. I wonder if a similar example of fair play would be re-enacted today? Many years later, on the same ground, Derek Randall was run out by a bowler while backing-up without the time-honoured warning. Times have certainly changed.

I have the doubtful distinction of being the only batsman in Test history to have been given out for obstruction. The game was against South Africa at the Oval in 1951. Frank Lowson, my Yorkshire colleague, and I were going steadily towards the 163 runs England needed to win. We had reached 53 when Athol Rowan pitched a ball to me just outside the leg stump which turned an inch or so. By then the pitch had lost some of its pace and, fractionally early, I got a top edge (all the versions that I was hit on the glove and that the ball ran up my arm were wrong). I saw the ball leap up in front of my eyes, and my first reaction was to think that if it hit the ground it could spin back onto my stumps. Instinctively I put my bat up to fend off the ball.

There was no way of my knowing that wicketkeeper Russell

Endean was poised to take a catch – indeed the whole affair was over in a flash – and the moment my bat made contact with the ball there was an appeal from several fielders. There was never any intention on my part to prevent the wicketkeeper, or any of the fielders, taking a catch. Nor had I any thought of going for a run. Umpire Dai Davies, supported by Frank Chester, who seemed to take immediate charge of the situation, gave me out. Amid the resultant confusion Peter May came and went for a duck, and in the end England scrambled home by 4 wickets, thanks to some bold hitting by Freddie Brown.

The 1951 season brought my hundredth first-class century at the Oval. I well recall the final stroke, a drive off a juicy half-volley for which I duly thanked the Surrey bowler John Wait. Previously, in a Test at Old Trafford against South Africa, I had finished 98 not out, making the winning hit with a 4 which fell just inside the boundary. *Wisden* said that most cricket-lovers hoped that I would not regret missing my objective as there was some criticism that Jack Ikin and Reg Simpson manipulated the bowling to give me as much of the strike as possible. If true, surely that was not a crime, and I am certain that if I had been the non-striker with my partner edging towards as notable a record as one hundred centuries, I would have been content to let him have the bowling. I may not be believed when I write that I was not all that concerned with the record then and there, for, barring miracles, it was likely to come before the end of the season.

In the first innings there was some snide sniping that Ikin took much of some short-pitched bowling by McCarthy at the beginning on a pitch made difficult by rain and a drying wind – in fact it was one of the most difficult I played on in a home Test match. What was overlooked was Jack's trouble against Geoff Chubb, who was able to move the ball away from the left-hander, and who bowled exceptionally well. In some circumstances there are those who see what they want to see, and you just can't win. There was certainly no deliberate intent on my part to stay at one end, and I remember long singles and a 3 being taken which made nonsense of that particular theory.

As I have written earlier, I made it my business to find out as much as I could about opposing bowlers, not only what they bowled but what they were like as people. The value of knowing your enemy is drummed into young batsmen. Freddie Gardner was in his first season with Warwickshire and the time came when he had to play against Kent and Doug Wright, about whom he had been told so much. He had been batting for a long time when he turned to the slip fielders at the end of an over and asked: 'When's Wright going to bowl?' To his astonishment the answer was: 'Doug Wright? That's the chap just putting his sweater on. He's been bowling to you for the last half an hour!' Who was the poet who said that if ignorance was bliss, it is folly to be wise?

Also in his first year, Gardner took 53 off Gloucestershire and was complimented on the way he had handled Tom Goddard. 'Oh, was he playing?' was the innocent answer. Another time he arrived at Taunton and asked if Alec Bedser would be bowling. On being told that Bedser played for Surrey, not Somerset, he muttered: 'I knew it began with an S.'

Gardner had what John Arlott might have described as a comfortable girth. He was injured while batting at Old Trafford and had to be carried to the dressing room across the field and up the stairs. On arrival he gasped: 'Brandy.' Brandy was hastily brought, but he said: 'Not for me — them,' pointing to his exhausted 'stretcher bearers'.

Another time at Headingley we could not get him out even though it was a flier and Trueman was bowling. Gardner bravely took frightful punishment and at last Trueman, hands on hip, loudly declaimed: 'What does he think he's doing?' Whereupon a Yorkshire voice was heard to say: 'He thinks you're an off-spinner!'

The laugh was on me at Lord's in 1953 when I forgot Tom Graveney's name as the England players were being presented to the Queen. For some unaccountable reason — perhaps because Her Majesty had stopped to talk to the player next to him — my mind went blank and even if I had been threatened with banishment to the Tower I could not put a name to my partner in a stand of 168. Fortunately the Queen spared my further embarrassment by moving on after shaking hands.

But the mental block remained and I'm darned if I didn't introduce Tom to a high church dignitary at Port-of-Spain as Tom Goddard. The right county, but the wrong Tom!

How I would have liked them all to have gone! Helping a fast ball to
the leg-side boundary. The bowler was Surrey's Alf Gover

Australia has produced many outstanding left-handers but none better than Neil Harvey. *Above*: He falls to a catch by me at slip off Doug Wright in a match at Arundel Castle. We weren't always so lucky! Wicketkeeper is Billy Griffith, as well known as an MCC secretary as he was as a player

'The Barnacle', alias Trevor Bailey, was the answer to my dreams when I captained England. He did everything asked of him. I successfully converted him into an opening batsman, to the surprise of the pundits

Sonny Ramadhin and his 'calypso twin' Alf Valentine, came from nowhere to rout England. They were a formidable spinning combination, but I felt Ramadhin sometimes had a bent arm, a theory which is supported by this picture taken in 1957.

e menace of speed as exemplified by four
ssies. Keith Miller never allowed me a
ment's relaxation. I never knew what to
ect from him, and he would be my first
ice for an all-time XI

nnis Lillee, something of a firebrand on the
d. His hostility was matched by his
trol and speed. One of the greats of
time

It was wonderful how the mind was
concentrated when Ray Lindwall ran into
bowl. He had a gloriously smooth, athletic
approach, a superb action and the guile of a
slow bowler

With his back arched like a bow string,
Jeff Thomson caused havoc in his prime with
the ball just short of a length which rose
steeply at express speed. A really difficult
bowler to handle

Joy and despair in the differing faces of modern cricket. Despondency by
the dismissed batsman Kiwi Bob Anderson; elation by Mike Brearley
and Ian Botham. In my view, Botham should never be saddled with
the responsibilities of captaincy, at least at Test level. Brearley had a
remarkable record as England's leader

Viv Richards showing the strength and power of his on-side play.
Exquisitely balanced, Viv believes in attack, and the West Indies
have produced no more exciting a batsman

India's little master, Sunil Gavaskar, has reeled off records in the
Bradman manner. And, in my judgement, it is not impertinent to put
him close to the Australian champion. Here is a splendid study of
Gavaskar following through a drive. Note his balance with the
weight distributed on his toes

Bob Willis does a lot that the purists might find technically wrong, but his performances supply the perfect answer

In its comparatively short history, Pakistan have had many gifted players. Imran Khan ranks as one of the world's best all-rounders – a batsman of high class and a bowler of genuine pace. Also a fighting and able Test captain

I regard Michael Holding as the deadliest of the brilliant array of West Indies fast bowlers. With his classic action and strength he is one of the best of his breed I have seen

David Gower has the gift of natural timing and a wide range of strokes. Perhaps the best batsman England have produced since Peter May and Colin Cowdrey – and in full cry he is entrancing to watch

10, Downing Street,
Whitehall,

Personal and Confidential   May 8, 1956.

Dear Mr. Hutton,

I have it in mind on the occasion of
the forthcoming list of Birthday Honours
to submit your name to The Queen with a
recommendation that Her Majesty may be
graciously pleased to approve that the
Honour of Knighthood be conferred upon you.

I should be glad to know if this would
be agreeable to you, and I will take no steps
until I have your reply.

Yours sincerely,

Anthony Eden

Leonard Hutton, Esq.

Left: A knighthood for
services to cricket: the
letter from No. 10 Downing
Street from the Prime
Minister, Sir Anthony Eden

Below: A chat with India's
Prime Minister, Mrs Indira
Gandhi, during one of my
business visits to New Delhi.
Mrs Gandhi showed an
intimate knowledge of cricket
and players

My younger son, John, then aged fourteen. Unlike Richard, he did not follow up his career with regular cricket after Repton, but he has always been a fine games player. Now he is a golfer

Much to my joy, Richard, my elder son, followed in my footsteps and played for England and Yorkshire. He also won his cricket blue at Cambridge

The next generations of Huttons – Richard's two sons. Benjamin was seven when this photograph was taken

Oliver, aged four and a half

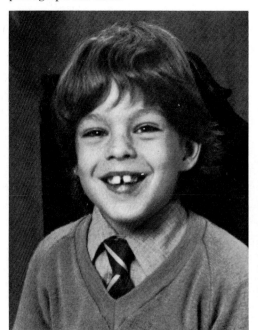

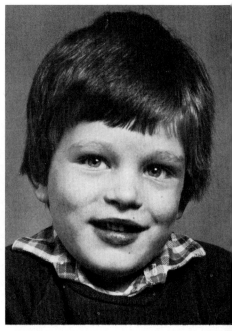

10
Gavaskar and Other Greats

And now that I have gone through the whole of my career, and look back to the time I was a young man, I am far from regretting that I have been a cricketer; and he who has never indulged in this noblest of pastimes, be he prince or peasant, has missed one of the great enjoyments of life.

Richard Daft, a member of the legendary
Nottinghamshire and All-England teams (1893)

Richard Daft's simple sentiments, written all those years ago, are still re-echoed by every cricketer. Alternatively, I could have quoted my erstwhile Pudsey St Lawrence partner, Edgar Oldroyd, who used to say in broadest Yorkshire: 'Lad, if I were coming ageean I'd want t'do same. I've enjoyed my cricket.' I had my good times; I had my hard times – it wasn't nice to finish before my time and have to start a new career at an age when most businessmen are forging ahead. Fortunately I had some business acumen, but not every cricketer is so lucky. I couldn't see myself as an umpire or a school coach. Being a cricketing knight put me apart, but, if anything, I have always tended to underplay that side of my career.

Cricket can be a cruel taskmaster, and the critics and the public overdemanding, but the game has given me an entrée into a world that, in all likelihood, would have been closed to me. Yes, indeed, I would like to be sixteen again, on the threshold of a career. But I wouldn't want to start with the knowledge I had when I retired, for half the fun of cricket, like life itself, is in finding out for yourself by trial and error and pitting your wits against the next fellow. I am assuming that I would have the same love and interest in cricket as when I first set out to play for Yorkshire half a century ago, and I should feel as inwardly invigorated as I do when I go to New York. New York has that effect on me. I hope I would be fit and not undergo the pain and heartbreak of an arm injury a second time, and be spared the medicals I had to undergo every two or three years to ascertain the extent of my disability. Nor, obviously, would I want a sizable chunk of my career to be lost by war.

I would have liked to have played more brilliantly. Every now and again everything seemed to come together, and an innings is etched in the mind. There was the 62 not out on the Brisbane sticky of 1950, 174 in three hours against a Transvaal attack, including Athol Rowan and Geoff Chubb, at Johannesburg in 1948, the 205 which took so much out of me at Kingston in 1954, and 100 in a county game against Worcestershire at Huddersfield in 1953. Reg Perks had got me out so many times that he was beginning to think of me as his rabbit, and I was determined to show him, in the only way I could, that it was time to put the record straight! Such innings make spectators sit up, but in your heart you know it can't be a standard performance. Only Bradman sparkled most of the time. And even he had his failures; but he reached the stage when a failure was even more spectacular copy for the critics than a big score!

One of the joys of regular Test cricket is the opportunity to study at close hand the master batsmen and bowlers of the world and, in later years, I have watched them with equal fascination from the press box. Rhodes's ultimate accolade was to say quietly: 'This chap is a good player.' One to have won his ungrudging admiration would surely have been Sunil Gavaskar. I have a feeling that if he had been born English or Australian, many of the better judges would have been tempted to bracket him with Bradman. Gavaskar is not as good as Bradman, but very close, which automatically puts him in the very highest class of batsmen of all time. He is a small, compact man, thicker set than Bradman, but of a similar height, and, like all the true champions, can play off both feet with equal facility. He uses a medium-weight bat and hits the ball hard enough with precise accuracy to beat the fieldsman, but not hard enough to knock it out of shape. He cuts, pulls and drives the half-volley beautifully, often through mid-wicket, and to back his natural accomplishments, he has the concentration, willpower and temperament of a record-breaker. I admire too, the positive and quick movements of his feet and the almost feline grace with which he gets into position to deal with the bouncer.

I have had the good fortune to have seen many memorable double centuries in Test matches, and Gavaskar's 221 at the Oval in 1979 should, at the very least, be bracketed with Stan McCabe's 232 at Trent Bridge and Wally Hammond's 240 at Lord's, particularly bearing in mind the important fact that India started their second innings in the seemingly impossible position of needing 438 runs in 500 minutes to win. They reached 429 for 8, and I am tempted to think, thanks mainly to Gavaskar, India's cricket came of age during that tense and gripping last day. For once English partisanship was abandoned as half the country longed for India to win. Gavaskar was by far the best batsman of either side in the series – and England had Boycott, Gooch and Gower – and at his peak was undeniably the world's leading No. 1.

Bombay is a far cry from Pudsey, but I see a lot of myself in Gavaskar's early years. The same irrepressible forces drew us to cricket. We came under its spell almost as soon as we could walk, and Sunil broke records at every level, including becoming the first Indian to score 5000 Test runs, and the first of his double centuries for India came in only his fourth Test. In four Tests in the West Indies he scored 774 runs – and that in his maiden series. At thirteen he scored a century in a Bombay schools' tournament, and a year later was in the Air-India schools' competition. Some of my generation might stand by Vijay Merchant as India's greatest, and Alec Bedser insists he remains the finest Indian batsman he has seen on all types of pitches, with none from overseas better in difficult English conditions. But I do not think in my span of playing and watching I have seen a better Indian batsman than Gavaskar, who probably had more relish for the big score than Merchant, as well as having a technique which gave bowlers less chance.

Certainly Gavaskar has a model technique. If I were to recommend a schoolboy to copy a modern master, I would go for Gavaskar rather than Viv Richards who, though a great player in every sense, depends enormously on his eagle eye. I have seen Richards play many innings and score many runs, and I have never banished the feeling that he could miss a straight ball. That might seem a naive observation, but he hits the ball so often off middle and leg stumps that I think, against a bowler able to hold the ball up, he might be in a bit of trouble. Richards's technique is based on a remarkable

eye, footwork and powerful forearms and is extremely effective on
the on-side. Most of today's topline batsmen are predominantly on-
side players and, as most bowlers try to move the ball in, it is easy
to understand why. It made a refreshing change to observe the young
Essex bowler Neil Foster in his first Test against New Zealand at
Lord's in 1983 deliver the ball close to the stumps instead of wide
of the crease. I would dearly love to watch Richards against a quality
out-swinger or leg-break bowler. Richards is immensely strong and
a joy to behold when he is on song and timing the ball sweetly, but
I do not think he is quite as correct as Gavaskar. Gavaskar plays
straighter and more like Bradman. If I were captaining a side against
Richards I would pray for an out-swing bowler and set the field
accordingly – certainly with a mid-wicket on the leg side – but
Richards might well answer me: 'As long as they make the ball move
in to me, I shall hit them to leg.' For a well-built man, Richards is
light and nimble on his feet, which almost goes without saying for
a batsman of his stature.

Having aired my one suspicion about a weakness in his technique,
I would not hesitate to put him alongside George Headley, Everton
Weekes, Frankie Worrell and Clyde Walcott as the first five batsmen
to come out of the West Indies. I put Gary Sobers apart for the
moment. I would not dare to put the specialized batsmen in order
of merit, and I am never sure whether to put Headley as the supreme
champion. In the 1939 home series he had me totally absorbed by
his methods. For a comparatively small man, he surprisingly used a
long-handle bat, and though he wasn't a particularly good driver,
at least by comparison with his other strokes, his pulling and square-
cutting, he was as near to Bradman as it was possible to get, and
he was positively brilliant off his back foot. I never saw any batsman
play the ball as late as George. Sometimes his stroke was delayed
so long that you felt certain he had been bowled, but he was so well
positioned that his bat would come down and he would complete
his intended shot with consummate ease. Many a bowler strangled
a cry of exaltation. The ability to have so much time and play so
late was one of the hallmarks of his genius.

Apart from an inward breath of sheer disbelief that the tiny island
of Barbados could produce three such batsmen – all born within a
mile of each other over an eighteen-month period – there are two
observations I would like to make about the three Ws. First, I would
never argue vehemently to put them in any order of ability; second,

as an opposing captain, I do not believe it was possible to contain them once they were set. All three had so many shots, were able to improvise so readily, and basically were so good that no captain could logically set a field to close them up. I would look around and think I could do with four or five more fielders! Worrell was the most stylish – indeed, his elegance faithfully reflected the innate culture of a man whose attainments off the field were equally distinguished – Weekes the hungriest run-gatherer, and Walcott arrived at No. 5 or 6 (surely no side has ever had a better No. 6!) when the bowling had usually lost its freshness, to attack with his heavyweight strength. He hit the ball with the power of a mule's kick, particularly off the back foot.

Walcott once modestly said that if his name hadn't started with the letter W nobody would have thought of putting him in the same class as the other two, but such an assessment can be brushed aside with a Test record of fifteen centuries, the same as Everton, against Worrell's nine. The vagaries of cricket are endlessly fascinating, and it still comes as a surprise to be reminded that at one stage Clyde kept his place by keeping wicket. He was behind the stumps when I first faced Ramadhin and, as I took guard, he said to me: 'You'll have trouble with this fellow, Len. I am still trying to pick him, and I'm standing two yards further back than you.'

All the Ws made a tremendous impact on world cricket. Worrell's death from leukaemia was a tragic loss in every respect. By example, he unified the islands as no man, cricketer or politician, has done before or since, and I cannot think of a cricketer anywhere who possessed his serenity – he declared himself to be a fatalist – or his genuine friendliness. His match temperament was ideal. Before an innings he would take a nap, and often he played a Test innings as free of care as in a friendly. Frankie will never be forgotten for his marvellous ability and polished style, his captaincy, and as a man whose character far transcended such divisions as colour. Walter Robins, when managing MCC in the West Indies, asked him bluntly if he ever thought he was disadvantaged being black. 'I only notice I'm black when I'm shaving,' he replied.

If Weekes reached 20 or so, I used to fear the worst for experience taught me he would take some getting out and would not be satisfied with a first 100. Everton, compact, so quick on his feet, had the mentality of a big-score man with the difference that he had so many strokes that the runs came rapidly.

Rohan Kanhai suffered by comparison with Weekes only because of his inconsistency. But when in the mood he was savagely brilliant, even within touching distance of Bradman. Clive Lloyd? Well, some may argue with justification if my list of five specialist batsmen from the Caribbean could be extended to six he would automatically be there. I confess I do not know where to put him. Undoubtedly a fine, aggressive and dominating player, he shone at both Test and one-day international level – particularly in single-innings matches. I often felt, however, that he was prone to take more of a chance than the three Ws and would lose his wicket when in full flight.

West Indies fast bowlers, despite the triumphs of recent years, have not, in my opinion, been in the same class as Australia's. I was never terribly impressed by them though I go back to Martindale, Constantine and Hylton. As an example, Martindale was highly rated but I would much prefer to have to deal with him than Lindwall. Constantine, a spectacular hitter at times and a fielder on every occasion, had the extraordinary habit of looking up at the ball in his hand just as he was about to release it, and now and again he bowled a slow googly. His bounding and infectious enthusiasm had an electrifying effect on spectators and he was adored in the leagues. How joyously he would have responded to knockout cricket and what a crowd puller he would have been! Yet I could never put him in the category of Jack Gregory, Ted McDonald, Ray Lindwall and Dennis Lillee. Fast and dangerous as he was, I never felt Wes Hall was quite sure where he was pitching the ball, although his strength and stamina were almost awesome.

As a general criticism, I have always been inclined to doubt whether West Indies fast bowlers made the utmost use of their intelligence. They have concentrated on all-out speed, admittedly with singular success, and length and accuracy have often suffered. In recent series they scored by having a quartet of speed in Andy Roberts, Joel Garner, Mike Holding and Colin Croft, with Malcolm Marshall and Sylvester Clarke joining the battery. Garner, 6 feet 8 inches tall, typifies the modern Caribbean pace man. He is a short-of-a-length expert and because he tends to deliver far wide of the crease, he owes a lot to the changed LBW law (I realize it has been changed for a long time now), but I mention the fact to underline how hard it is to make comparisons of individual performances.

Holding, in my view, is the best of the West Indies fast bowlers, past and present, and he would be even better with ten yards or so knocked off his prodigious run. I would not have thought he needed to run any longer than Richard Hadlee. I have never understood why so many pace bowlers need to charge to the wicket from distances around twice the length of the pitch and, all too often, end by bowling well wide of the off stump. Such a waste of effort. There is no substitute for accuracy at whatever pace the ball is bowled. Holding's run, it has to be said, is graceful as befits a natural athlete, and contrasts vividly with Bob Willis's approach. Every so often cricket, praise be, throws up the complete individualist, the exception to every coaching rule. Bob is strictly of the non-classical school. He is, to be blunt, all wrong. He runs too far, with a suggestion that his limbs must be in eternal protest, and his action is not right. When I have watched his laboured run and delivery I have been at a loss to account for his huge success of over 300 Test wickets. In comparison with Larwood, Lindwall, Holding and Trueman, he is the shire horse to the Derby thoroughbred, but no one has had a bigger heart or more determination. As he got older he became more accurate, which is a telling factor in his favour.

Willis has emerged from dark passages of injury and non-success with his spirit and resolve fiercer than ever, which speaks volumes for his character. He must have unusual depths of willpower and is entitled to much credit and respect; he has become the symbol of the player who triumphs over adversity. And it takes a strong man to do that. Whether he could have stood up to the old programme when 1200 to 1500 overs was the norm is open to doubt but, in the final analysis, Willis has been a pillar of strength in an era when England have relied heavily on the efforts of a handful of players. As a captain, Bob will not be remembered as a leading tactician and he had no talent to spare in his teams. Invariably he was inhibited by a shortage of runs, but at home and abroad he does not seem to have put a diplomatic foot wrong, an achievement in itself. He showed thought for his players; an excellent sign. His action at Lord's in 1983 in giving Foster a go at New Zealand's tail when he could have conceivably added to his own tally of wickets was generous. He has had his cool moments with the media, which surprises me. On that score, speaking from personal experience, I don't think Bob knows the half of it! He ought not to worry. So often he has had the last laugh.

I was not in Australia in 1974–75 when Lillee and Thomson were at their belligerent best, but I have seen enough of both to appreciate how close they challenged Lindwall and Miller. Lillee, representing the modern Australian image of aggression, and Thomson, able to make the ball lift off just short of a length, were always magnificently supported by Max Walker just as Bill Johnston backed up Lindwall and Miller. There have been things done by Lillee which did not impress me, but as a bowler none could be other than profoundly impressed by him. Maybe he enjoyed the macho-type role; maybe it was all part of his psychological build-up against batsmen. It must have been a harsh ordeal to face him on the less-than-perfect pitches on the Mike Denness tour of 1974–75 with the new-style Australian crowds baying 'Kill, kill, kill.' It would be difficult to fault Lillee's action, and hard to name a more aggressive opponent. Yet he had so many skills that I am reminded of another Rhodes story. Rhodes and Sydney Barnes shared a taxi to take them to Lord's for a Test with South Africa during the triangular tournament of 1912. On the way Barnes announced: 'If we lose the toss today I'll bowl in-swingers. They have never seen me bowl them before and it'll surprise them.' South Africa batted, and Barnes duly had three out with in-swingers. There has to be an awesome admiration for a bowler, so gifted and totally devoid of personal doubts, able to turn to a style of bowling for tactical reasons, or almost as a personal whim. Lillee's well-publicized belligerence ought not to hide the fact that he is one of the finest bowlers Australia has produced.

If I were asked to nominate a classical style to copy, Lindwall (despite his low arm action), Miller, Trueman, Lillee and Bedser would spring to mind, and I would certainly recommend aspiring fast bowlers to seek out old newsreels and action photographs of Gubby Allen. At the crease you saw only Allen's left shoulder pointing towards you. He ran a sensible, energy-conserving length, and he was one of my reasons for disliking Lord's in my early years. Because of his business commitments Gubby had the advantage of avoiding the day-to-day chore of county cricket, and whenever I played against him he was authentically fast. In 1937 he struck me on my left thigh with a ball which came like lightning 'down the hill' and even today when the weather is damp and cold there is pain on the precise spot where I was hit.

The one broken finger I suffered – many players who are repeatedly hit on the hand and fingers have the wrong grip – was at Lord's, but over the years my attitude changed from dissatisfaction to warmth and affection for the ancient ground. My attitude to

Lord's was not helped by Jack Cowie, who made my Test baptism a misery. New Zealand does not produce many good fast bowlers because the pitches are generally too slow, but Hadlee and Cowie, whose career straddled the war, can always be cited as the shining exceptions. If Cowie, like Grimmett, had gone to Australia and bowled on pitches of pace and bounce, he would, I am sure, have been even more highly regarded. Sir Plum Warner went as far as saying he might have been the bowler of his age. At Lord's on that far-off morning he bowled fast off-breaks, as I can vouch to my cost.

New Zealand's batsmen have been more prominent than their bowlers and, starting with 'Stewie' Dempster, there have been Martin Donnelly, Bert Sutcliffe and Glenn Turner in a company any country would be proud to name.

Since the halcyon period of Bradman, Morris, Hassett and Co. after the war, Greg Chappell has by a comfortable margin been the best of Australia's batsmen. Greg had the advantage of playing straighter than most recent Australians. Some of Australia's heavy scorers in the past may not have conformed to purist styles, but invariably the bat was straight in the last, decisive movement. Pakistan have not had a better bat than Zaheer Abbas, a truly beautiful stylish attacker with so many strokes at his command. He positions himself perfectly, and there must have been many a captain wishing he had an extra fielder or two. His driving is superb. Zaheer Abbas is high on my list of best batsmen, along with the South Africans, Graeme Pollock and Barry Richards.

I cannot believe the true cricketer anywhere fails to deplore South Africa's banishment. I was upset by the original dispute over Basil d'Oliveira and I have continued to be upset that the dispute has dragged on. As I write, it shows no sign of being satisfactorily solved. Broadly I believe that internal policies must be determined by the country concerned and, though we may dislike it, it is not for us to interfere unless we become politically involved. My belief is that it is human nature for any ostracized country to stand four square against outside opinion, and the tighter the squeeze the more counter-productive it becomes. All I wish to say is that, purely from a cricket viewpoint, it was a pleasure to play against South Africa, and I enjoyed my two tours there as much as any tours I made. Freed of the shackles of politicians, cricketers, who have never been cursed by prejudices of colour or creed, would settle the issue in no time and, further, I am sure they would play with and against each other quite happily. The failure to find a solution to the problem, or even a measure of goodwill, is a major calamity. Cricket, so vulnerable, is victimized by power politics. To be denied the talents of Richards, Pollock, Proctor and Co. is sad enough, but the split ever widens and the bitterness deepens. The cancellation of a Test match at Georgetown in the 1980–81 series because Robin Jackman coached in South Africa was followed by the West Indies pulling out of a one-day practice match before the 1983 World Cup on the grounds that Yorkshire had two players, Geoff Boycott and Arnie Side-bottom, who had been members of an unofficial tour of South Africa. If the policy follows its logical course, the West Indies and others will not accept players of English parentage born in South Africa and England will, at some future date, face exactly the same dilemma which brought the original dispute to the fore – a refusal to allow the politicians of a foreign country to interfere with selection. The mind boggles.

Cricket, at large, is made immeasurably poorer by the absence of South Africa, which might justly lay claim to have had a powerful a side as any country in the last decade. South Africa, the West Indies, Australia or England at full strength would considerably raise the present mundane standard of Test cricket. The Springboks have always produced vintage players. In my playing days there were very few batsmen of Dudley Nourse's quality. His Test record included 231 in less than five hours against Grimmett and O'Reilly and 208, with a broken thumb swelling by the hour, at Trent Bridge in 1951. The previous year on a notorious pitch at Old Trafford, Hines Johnson, the fastest of the West Indies bowlers at the time, gave me a nasty blow on the hand. I congratulated myself on scoring a few runs virtually one-handed, but Dudley stuck it out for 550 minutes and set up South Africa's victory. His father, 'Old Dave', was recognized as South Africa's first established international batsman and Dudley enhanced the family reputation. Eric Rowan, who scorned gloves, was as gutsy a batsman as ever I encountered, and Alan Melville and Bruce Mitchell were as stylish and correct as any. Bruce seldom smiled or spoke during an innings, but after the teams had been presented to the late King George VI at Lord's, I noticed he was chuckling to himself. 'The King,' he explained, 'asked me how my war wound was!' Apparently Bruce was wounded in the buttocks during his army service and the suspicion was that the King's briefing on the matter was something of a legpull on Bruce.

Athol Rowan, as an off-spinner, was second only to Laker, and Neil Adcock and Peter Heine excelled as an aggressive fast-bowling partnership. I have little doubt that if the war had not intervened Norman Gordon would have made a big name for himself had he toured England. At medium pace he bowled remarkably well against Hammond's side. It has been a tragedy that Graeme Pollock and Barry Richards, who belong to a very exclusive band of batsmen of all ages, have been outlawed. Imagine the impact they would have had on the World Cup. A fair parallel would be to picture the competition and Test cricket without Viv Richards or Clive Lloyd, or even Gary Sobers restricted to playing only in the Caribbean. Sobers, like Hammond, was the complete cricketer able to do everything – bat with the same genius as Headley and the three Ws, open the bowling with as deadly effect as any new-ball bowler in the world, turn to spin, either orthodox or Chinamen, and catch superbly. He was uniquely versatile, though I have seen Hammond bowl leg breaks and googlies to the highest standards. I will avoid the trap of trying to compare Sobers and Hammond!

On the odd occasion, I suspected that if Sobers had a batting weakness it was outside the off stump, but he rarely got out in that area and when in form, which was normally the case, he was practically impossible to bowl to. Like all beautiful strikers of the ball, he had a high pick-up and follow-through, and I was always fascinated by the fact that he was every bit as good a driver as he was a puller and hooker; in fact he seemed to like nothing more than to drive straight and through the off side. Gary had all the basic requirements of eye and footwork, and he was so positive – either well forward or back. I cannot recall seeing him indecisive and caught in two minds, and he had that inbred confidence that comes from being brought up on pitches always to be trusted. If Gary hadn't taken a wicket for the West Indies, he would have still been extraordinarily successful with 8032 runs, twenty-six centuries, including the highest individual Test score, and an average of 57.78. Yet he also took 256 wickets, which made him a bowler of the highest quality. His action was perfect; his accuracy so sustained that it was impossible to fault him. Cricket might see another Sobers, though I doubt it very much. If one should appear, I trust he will be born in Yorkshire and, in this dire moment of my county's fortunes, I'll push my luck and pray for twins!

Sobers was finally defeated by a knee injury, as was Compton, and with more and more Tests being played it is small wonder that limbs are protesting. There are some fine all-rounders like Kapil Dev, Imran Khan, Richard Hadlee and Ian Botham, who play the year round and every year. The quality of Test cricket is lower and must not be cheapened further. But a Test match is still a Test with all the attendant strains, and there is a real danger of having too much of it. I know too well the demands of playing summer and winter nonstop, and the present international programme is nothing short of feverish. By the end of the 1983 English season, Botham had played in sixty-three Tests since 1977, including twelve with the extra responsibility as captain. Hobbs, in contrast, had sixty-one Tests between 1909 and 1930 with a four-year break in the first war, while my seventy-nine were spread over eighteen playing years.

Botham's nonstop schedule is not helped by having to bowl in Pakistan, India, the West Indies and Australia where, as a general rule, the pitches are not really suitable for his medium-pace style; it should not be an occasion for surprise when he runs into barren periods, at least by his own exacting standards. I know only too well from personal experience what a strain it can be living up to the expectations of critics and the public, and Botham's early achievements were nothing short of incredible. To be an instant success as Ian was incurs special penalties; sometimes I am grateful that I didn't rocket to the skies in my first Test which produced 1 run in two innings! England's captain, Walter Robins, lifted me from my depression with the remark: 'Don't fret. But whatever you do, don't do that against Australia next year.' The words reminded me that there's always a tomorrow, and Ian is so talented that runs and wickets are always in the offing. The trouble is that he is expected to be a Keith Miller every time he bats and bowls. Also it ought to be borne in mind that, unlike the bowlers of the past, he has done his bowling on covered pitches, and I cannot imagine the legendary Gilbert Jessop ever batted more spectacularly than Botham in his match-winning centuries against Australia at Headingley and Old Trafford in 1981. Trumper himself would have been riveted by the power and range of his strokes. Headingley's crowd, more accustomed to the circumspect Boycott, watched in utter amazement and I confess that during the two innings – the Old Trafford effort was the better with less playing and missing – I pinched myself that it really was England versus Australia and not a light-hearted Sunday frolic. One hooked 6, played with closed eyes, was unforgettable coming from the meat of his heavy bat. There cannot have been many more astonishing innings in the annals of the game at any class, and I would cross mountains and swim rivers to be present to see its like again. Frank Woolley always told me he couldn't see enough of Gary Sobers, and I would say the same of Botham. On occasions, admittedly, he can appear infuriatingly casual or careless, and that left-handed sweep is anathema to my eyes; but, that apart, he should be left alone to play cricket in his own natural way. I would dearly love to see him in a powerful England side, with the threat of a failure less important. Miller didn't have Botham's responsibilities, and few know better than myself how heavily responsibility can rest even on the broadest shoulders. If I were Ian I would put regaining the Test captaincy aside. I know he thinks he has something to prove and, being Botham, that nags his thoughts. But if I were in his place, I'd let the ambition drift away and concentrate on thoroughly enjoying myself. Boycott allowed the captaincy issue to envelop his thoughts and, in my opinion, cloud his judgement. Test captaincy is a great honour, but it can also be a weight around the neck.

David Gower is the best home-grown batsman since May and Cowdrey in the fifties and is another to have crowded what used to be a lifetime career into a few years. He has all the proper ingredients – a good background, footwork, the eye to see the ball fractionally earlier than most, and exceptional timing. In form, he can make batting look effortless and absurdly simple, even to the point of inviting criticism that he is too casual. But his method can be misleading and many elegant batsmen – Graveney was a typical example – are wrongly faulted for alleged carelessness. For some unexplained reason it looks worse when the graceful stroke-maker is bowled, or is caught off a mistimed stroke. David has a quiet manner off the field. Some years ago I met him at an MCC dinner and was impressed by the way he talked of the game and what he aimed to achieve. Then he had yet to play for England, and he had the luck to begin his Test career against teams weakened by the Packer dispute. His quiet confidence is reflected in his batting approach; in fact, he was so unaffected by the occasion that he might have been taking a net on a sunny afternoon on a school ground. I could not recall a young cricketer for England, or for that matter any country, being less awed. I have some doubts about his technique to make runs consistently against bowlers of the highest quality on pitches giving them help, but he is clearly intelligent and, if he has the determination, he will finish in the top class of England's batsmen since the war. And, in the long-term future, a successful captain.

11
Oh! My Beloved Yorkshire

Let it be said that the Yorkshire spirit is one of cricket's most precious
ingredients.
  H. S. Altham and E. W. Swanton in *A History of Cricket* (1938)

Nothing in my cricketing life has saddened me more than the decline
and fall of Yorkshire. A hard-won inheritance handed down by
generations of dedicated players and officials has been squandered,
and the only hope in the bankrupt present is that the traumas and
blood-letting will lead to a revival of 'the Yorkshire spirit'. I weep
for my old county. Yorkshire's tragedy must be England's tragedy.
Never was there a greater national need for a powerful and vibrant
Yorkshire.

Alas, it has been all too predictable. Years of in-fighting and
mischievous gossip filtering from the dressing room came to a head
in 1983 when Yorkshire – for the first time – finished last in the
championship, and Geoffrey Boycott, who epitomized to me the rise
of the personality cult, was not re-engaged. I could tolerate with a
measure of understanding the indignity of failure on the field, though
the thought would never have occurred to me in the high noon of
success – I refer to the thirties and the late fifties and sixties which
I followed personally.

I appreciated some extenuating circumstances. In the much
changed format of the county game Yorkshire have become disadvantaged by sticking to their long-established principle of not going
outside the county's boundaries for players. In recent seasons one
strike bowler from overseas would surely have made all the difference. I could also have tolerated the almost obsessional hero-worship

of Boycott by a vociferous self-appointed group, though I might not have understood it.

But it is far less possible to bear the collapse of the team spirit which made Yorkshire what they were and the envy of every club in the land. A major cause of this collapse in my view was the lack of success – Yorkshire's bowlers did not have the necessary class to bowl other sides out. It is also difficult to bear the shame of open warfare and the challenge to the club's elected authority conducted with an almost religious fervour. It was not to be wondered at that the rest of cricket looked on with growing disbelief and distaste. I had a dull despair that a minority should have the pompous nerve to call themselves Yorkshire Members 1984 and seek to overthrow the officials of the club. Beyond a purblind loyalty and enthusiasm for Boycott, they did not see the danger their actions might cause either to the club or to the player himself.

Seldom, if ever, have properly and democratically elected representatives of a club been so openly abused, or a county put to so much tribulation by so few. The decision to end Boycott's contract was not lightly taken, and it was interesting that the eleven-man cricket committee had a combined total of 162 Test matches for England and over 2000 appearances for Yorkshire. I could never believe laymen (if I can use the word) had superior judgement and experience in matters of cricket and cricketers. For example, I wonder how a chartered accountant would react if a cricketer told him he did not know how to audit accounts? Boycott has always insisted on his loyalty to England and Yorkshire, and though he has at times gone a strange way about it, I do not disbelieve him. I was a Test selector when he opted out of England's team for three years. To this day I can only guess his reason. In India in 1981–82 he did not last the tour – on the grounds of 'physical and mental tiredness'. I doubt if Geoffrey could have exceeded the 'physical and mental tiredness' I often experienced on overseas tours. But that is neither here nor there. Loyalty to a team involves the presence and participation even of those not actually playing.

Since I started attitudes have changed. I was brought up in the proper belief that the team, and not the individual, came first. As captain I expected an automatic response without compulsion on my part. I recall my surprise and upset at the end of a bad day in the West Indies in 1953–54. Entering the hotel, I was met by one of the MCC party *not* playing in the match.

'What a terrible day,' he began. 'Well, you saw it,' was my tired response. 'Oh, no,' he replied. 'I've been listening on the radio.'

At that I blew my top. As a Yorkshireman I had automatically expected everyone to be at the ground, and the non-players to be in the dressing room to lend moral support.

David Denton, one of the old Yorkshire stalwarts, once told me that he 'never thought much of "Lordie" '. But he seemed to be in a minority opinion about Lord Hawke, who is generally credited with instilling that 'precious ingredient' of team spirit into the Yorkshire dressing room. When asked for the secret of. Yorkshire's success, Lord Hawke gave the simple explanation: 'We all try and work for each other.' It's easy to scoff and stress that cricket is harder and life has changed (which I am the first to admit), but what would Yorkshire do for a Lord Hawke today! He established the precept of team spirit which worked for so many decades. Yorkshire have never lacked strong individualists and characters, but, in the main, they played within the framework of the team. If they strayed out of line there was a captain to pull them back. It is my profound belief that today's paramount need is for a captain to display an old-style amateur-like authority backed by the committee.

I sometimes wonder how Boycott, with his statistical record of a run rate of 1·1 an over, would have fared under a Brian Sellers. First, he would have had to share some of the public adoration – he would not have been the only fish in the pond; second, there would have been stiffer competition for places and more explicit instructions on what was expected of him – he might well have been transformed from a match-saver into a match-winner and become an even better player; third, I believe he would have responded like the rest of us to firm leadership. As it was, Geoffrey became identified with Yorkshire's brilliant past. The more runs he stockpiled the more a section of the success-starved public separated him from the rest of the side and put him on a pedestal. If they were not able to support a winning side they could support a successful player. I can think of no other reason for the emotions that Boycott arouses; he is a contradictory personality and often very hard to watch as he gathers runs at his own speed and time.

Clearly, he has a problem being part of a team, and the abiding criticism among his fellow players is that he has put himself above the county. There can only be one sequel – an undermining of morale.

The changed attitudes in players is a fact to be reckoned with in modern cricket and during my span as a player. They are summed up in the words of K. M. Kilburn in *A History of Yorkshire Cricket*. He wrote:

In Hutton's Yorkshire training individual concerns were community concerns. Help in a period of struggle was as freely given as it was readily accepted, not necessarily in the form of direct instruction as from tutor to pupil, but perhaps as an oblique reference, or a demonstration, based on understanding of a common language. Hutton's hints were allusive.

The Yorkshire of Hutton's later career never seemed to acquire this unity. Hutton had learned much of his own cricket by listening and watching and thinking how suggested solutions could be applied to his own problems. He was surprised and dismayed to find the tradition being abandoned in the new cricketing world of easy self-satisfaction and, being an introvert, he tended to withdraw rather than to initiate apparently unwanted assistance.

Cricket revolution with the introduction of knockout competitions and overseas stars left Yorkshire and its demanding following with special problems. I recall a match at Sheffield in the fifties when the team were constantly barracked by part of the crowd. At tea Lady Worsley, the wife of Sir William Worsley, asked me why the spectators were so angry. I tried to explain that for a week or so we had not played well as a team and when that happened it became a personal issue to some of our followers. They expected the highest standards to be maintained. In many instances they were in creative jobs themselves and got tired of watching Yorkshire playing below their best, and it was a responsibility every Yorkshire team had to carry. I went on to tell Lady Worsley that there were times when batsmen couldn't get runs, bowlers take wickets and catches were dropped, no matter how hard the players tried. Lady Worsley was more satisfied than the crowd on that occasion. The fact is that Yorkshire followers have become disappointed and bemused by the failure of modern teams to emulate the achievements of the past. Yorkshire were pre-eminent for most of the century.

In the ten years up to the second war only Lancashire, twice, and Derbyshire, in the wet summer of 1936, broke the pattern of Yorkshire championship triumphs. It was a decade of great players and great teams, a decade in which it was pardonable to believe that it was Yorkshire's birthright to dominate English cricket and to be the mainstay of England's Test side. The old observation that a strong Yorkshire meant a strong England was not an idle boast.

I was in four title-winning teams between 1933 and 1939 and, when the competition was resumed in 1946, Yorkshire, with many new faces, won again, which meant four championships in a row. In 1949 Yorkshire, collecting maximum points from their last six fixtures, and Middlesex tied for first place. Soon Surrey came along with their Test-standard attack of Alec Bedser, Peter Loader, Jim Laker and Tony Lock to monopolize the championship for seven successive seasons, and by the time Yorkshire started winning again in the sixties I had retired.

In the seventies Boycott was captain for eight years without marked impact – indeed nothing was won. I am sure he was handicapped by a dearth of high-quality wicket-taking spinners and the adoption of limited-over matches by the leagues was not in the county's interests. Inevitably that form of cricket leads to defensive measures and the use of medium-paced bowlers to the exclusion of spin. And, equally, the gulf between the standards of the leagues and the county championship have widened. While Yorkshire persisted with home-grown talent, other counties went into the international marketplace in search of ready-made players to bring swift, short-term success. I am not against overseas players being employed, but one has only to look at the options open to the Test selectors to realize their numbers needed to be controlled.

I am also sorry to say that I constantly heard tales in later years of a lack of discipline in the Yorkshire ranks. No matter how long I think about Yorkshire's fall from grace, I come back to the essential and basic truth that nothing will be accomplished in either the short or the long term until the pride and strength of teamwork is restored. Team spirit makes a moderate team into a good one, and a good one into a great one. My every constructive thought points to the captaincy. I am sure that is the key to the present problems and future prosperity. David Bairstow is a positive, combative enthusiast, and he has some of the assets which made it a pleasure for me to play under George Mann in South Africa in 1948–49, and provided the spark for Colin Ingleby-Mackenzie's exciting leadership with Hampshire. I cannot believe it is right to judge a captain on the mistakes he might make, but on his intentions. Bairstow, and every future Yorkshire captain, should expect all the support and help that is his due. All Yorkshire captains and players are under pressure.

It is the price to be paid for the privilege of playing for a county with exacting standards. Some are uplifted and respond to the challenge; others find it too difficult and beyond them. The same can be said of Test cricket.

Maybe the modern cricketer is better educated, more sophisticated in a worldly sense, and expects more from life than when I started fifty years ago. At least in the top bracket he is far better off financially, which leads to a measure of independence; but whatever the pattern, there are still golden rules to be followed. One is that without love for and dedication to the game the most talented are unlikely to progress. Basic talent is not enough. Maybe, too, it is tougher for batsmen as most of the law changes have been made to help bowlers. I am sure too that some of the sparkle of county cricket disappeared with the amateur. Without a light touch the game can become laborious. Technical perfection is much to be admired, but it is not the be-all and end-all of cricket. But, for all the difficulties, the young cricketer of today does not lack encouragement. More cash is available, facilities have improved and Yorkshire Second XI have an excellent fixture list. Even at school level there are overseas tours.

In every club, the captain, manager, coach and scorer have vital roles to play – possibly the scorer sees more than anyone, and his contribution can be invaluable. There must be a strict understanding of the responsibilities of captain and manager. Their duties cannot overlap. As a general observation of managers, I do not see them as one-man selection committees. The captain must be left to captain the side. Clearly, every cricket committee must be left to run the cricket, and the general committee to run the club. In my experience of cricket committees for the selection of Test teams and overseas tours, all are conducted with scrupulous fairness and with a fetish to study every aspect of the question at hand. Yorkshire is not an exception.

If, in the long term, Yorkshire can be seen as a caring club with a united dressing room and everyone, including the press and the public, pulling in the same direction, is it more than likely that better young players will begin to emerge. The fact has to be faced that since the thirties and sixties there has been a shortage of genuine class, especially in bowling. The importation of overseas players would obviously meet the needs of the moment, but the very idea is anathema to most Yorkshire hearts. I would not like to see it happen for it would be against long-held principles and, in practical terms, against the interests of county and country.

I have been constantly asked what course of action I would take if I had become captain in Yorkshire's troubled times. It hardly needs saying that I would regard it as a daunting task and extremely important, as the position holds the key to Yorkshire's future. I would start with the cold facts of the situation: a recognition that the old dressing-room atmosphere has perished with many other admirable qualities of life that I took for granted when I began my career. I would accept that some of the necessary self-discipline has gone, and that the character of the crowds has changed. There is often evidence of a built-in resentment against the failures of recent decades. It is understandable.

I would try to lead by example, and break down the urge for self-preservation which leads to a drab side and drab cricket. I would *not* try to be one of the boys. You would not often find me drinking beer in the tap room. There would be times to mix, and though I would not be in complete isolation, I would, in everyone's interests, be a little apart. Though Lord Hawke was the first to insist on amateurs and pros using the same dressing room, there is a case for a separate room for the captain.

I can hear indignant voices protesting that I am advocating putting the clock back fifty or more years. Perhaps – but I am sure Yorkshire's members and the public would not object to having a team as good as they had in the days of amateur leadership. The amateur captain led the side and allowed the professionals to get on with their job, and he did not allow drabness or permit discipline to sag. The system functioned well for Yorkshire. If a captain has the secret of welding the different talents and personalities into one effective unit, he is worth his place. Many of Yorkshire's captains were modest players, but that mattered little if they brought the best out of the others.

I firmly believe that if Yorkshire could find an amateur-type captain, able to devote his summers to playing county cricket and gain the respect of the players, a new dawn would break, and once again it would be the ambition of every county to humble the white rose.

As for the personality cults and the challenges to the club's authority by dissident factions, I can only say the activities severely damage the club's reputation both inside and outside the county.

The only place for fighting is on the field, and the sooner Yorkshire concentrate on cricket, the better the chance of restoring lost glories.

I was, therefore, dismayed when the members at the historic meeting at Harrogate backed Boycott's reinstatement and threw out the general and cricket committees. Chill blew the January winds on that bleak afternoon in 1984, but, to me, chillier still were the portents for Yorkshire cricket. I believe tragic mistakes were made and, far from healing the wounds, the dagger was thrust deeper. The long-running crisis, which threatened the very fabric of the club, was by no means resolved.

Within forty-eight hours the members of the two committees, containing many distinguished ex-cricketers and loyal officials, resigned en bloc as they were honour bound to do after the 'no-confidence' votes, and so departed one of the best administrations the club had had for many years. Power was transferred to a rebel group, but whether the upheaval heralds a new dawn of success, peace and prosperity for Yorkshire remains to be seen. As I saw the situation, the membership remained divided, the reasons for the original decision to part company with Boycott had not changed, and surely I was not alone in my sad forebodings that a great county would tear itself apart with such savage intent over a single issue.

My fears were borne out by the words of the retiring president Norman Yardley and chairman Michael Crawford. Both said they could not see the light at the end of the tunnel.

I make no apology for having cast my vote against all three resolutions. I was in the minority, and I accept the democratic process without being converted to the belief that in this instance the majority was right. In the matter of Boycott's contract, I saw no advantage to be gained by rescinding a decision arrived at by competent officials armed with all the facts. They had agonized long and hard and, rightly or wrongly, sought to invest in the long-term future without Boycott and with a new captain.

Having ventured so far, it seemed to me singularly unwise to turn back. The omelette could not be unscrambled without further breakages, and it was necessary to back the club and its officials. I am old-fashioned enough to believe the club to be bigger than the individual, no matter now eminent a player or strong a personality he may be. This is an elementary but golden rule which often escapes modern thinking. It is the age of the personality cult. Excessive hero-worship of one player can be unhealthy and act against the general interests of the club.

Perhaps Geoffrey, who has given Yorkshire such outstanding service in a long innings with the county – and I wish him well with his testimonial – is the prisoner of circumstances. At another time he would have been one of several titans, each enjoying a share of the public adulation. At Yorkshire he has had the limelight virtually to himself. Yorkshire seems to breed a peculiar type of fanatical supporter whose emotions tend to overspill and muddle loyalties. There were occasions during my own career when I experienced some of the fervour which has surrounded Geoffrey over the years. I was highly embarrassed, and had it been with me all the time I would have been deeply worried.

Certainly I have no wish to minimize Geoffrey's considerable achievements, but his supporters do go overboard. No doubt it can be argued that he cannot be held responsible for that, but had I been in a similar situation I could never have allowed it to develop into a club-splitting issue. We were obviously cast in different moulds, but I don't think I could have slept again if I had been a rallying point for an argument with the authorities.

The weakness of the case of his supporters is that there are two sides to every argument, even with Geoffrey, and as Michael Crawford sadly said: 'People these days, not only in cricket, take diametrically opposed views and will not budge.' I look at the names of those who led the crusade against the so-called establishment – a word guaranteed to raise the temperature, as Kerry Packer discovered to his advantage – and wonder at their credentials. If there are former players of note among their numbers, it has escaped my notice. Their enthusiasm can not be questioned, but some, to judge by their public utterances, have bees in their bonnets about Boycott. Harmless enough in the ordinary way, but surely carried to excess over the last decade. It must be a worrying aspect of the whole unhappy affair that some of the big and respected names of Yorkshire cricket have become casualties.

In particular I think of Norman Yardley, president since 1981 and a real stalwart on and off the field for the best part of fifty years, and Michael Crawford, chairman and committee member for twenty years. I played under Yardley for England and Yorkshire, and a kinder or more considerate captain never walked onto a field. Players of the calibre of Trueman, Wardle and Appleyard will testify to his help and understanding in their formative years. Yet his strained face on the television screens when announcing his resignation encapsulated Yorkshire's agony and loss. As an old player, I wondered how the members could do such a thing. The chairman also placed himself unreservedly at the disposal of Yorkshire although the calls on his professional life must have been severe. I cannot imagine two more able and conscientious servants. They were tremendous assets and Yorkshire can ill afford to lose them. Yet lose them they did; as if such men were freely available.

Both the general and cricket committees had my firm support for the simple reason that I believed the administration in the last twenty years or so has been as sound as at any time of my long experience. Understandably the public are apt to judge a club by performances on the field and in Yorkshire there is an impatience to recapture the old glories. But matches are won on the field and not in the committee room. The vital matter of not engaging an overseas star, which would make all the difference, still has overwhelming public support. Perhaps if Yardley, Crawford and Co. had thrown away the old principles and taken on an all-rounder of the calibre of Imran Khan – even against the general wish – they would still be in office and enjoying the fruits of success in the championship!

In my considered opinion, it will be a long time before Yorkshire can expect to have a better administration. I deplore the break-up of the committees. I think perhaps a general committee of twenty-nine is overweight and could be profitably streamlined, and I would make it a cardinal principle to limit the selection committee to the lowest possible number and to be comprised of ex-players.

The emotive nature of the resolutions at Harrogate defeated any possibility of a desparately needed aura of compromise and conciliation. All those who wanted to take the heat out of Yorkshire cricket politics must, like myself, have been much troubled by the personality clashes, the boos and insults, the general intolerance and charges of incompetence made against the club's administrators. Sober judgements were never going to be made. In public wrangles of this nature a club fights with one hand tied behind its back. Accusations are easily made, while the club is obliged to be more circumspect.

Boycott's supporters were always going to make it hot for the club. His loyal band held meetings, collected cash from members and had the financial backing of a Bradford businessman. The *Sunday*

Telegraph commented that a campaign had been run which would not have shamed a by-election. They also wrote to each of the 10,000 members on two occasions. Would that such energies be put to better use on behalf of the club, which, in turn, had to spend an estimated £25,000 in its own defence. Money down the drain. And cash which could have been put to so much better use.

Now the die is cast. I and my fellow thinkers have already been typecast as diehards. Be that as it may, but I firmly hope the voice of experience will not be drowned in the uncertain future. Frankly, I would not care to be in Geoffrey's shoes knowing I dare not put a foot wrong and that a considerable chunk of the membership were still behind me, or at least were prepared to stand by the committee decision. His position is without parallel in county cricket but, recognizing his stubborn determination, I would not put it past him to thrive on it. I pray for the old club to emerge from the current mess, and that in due course sanity will return.

Postscript

Customs are constantly changing. The game is never quite the same from one season to the next. As has been said before now, it never has been what it was. To those who love it, though, cricket remains, despite the politicians, an incomparable pastime.

Wisden Cricketers' Almanack, 1983

Anyone in the business of cricket prediction is on a Brisbane-type sticky wicket. Fifty years ago I would have rated the odds of a boy from a Yorkshire village becoming a knight of the realm and the first professional captain of England about on a par with the waters of Lake Windermere catching fire in a snow blizzard. I would have been very wrong about Sunday play, which I considered a nonstarter, and I could not have anticipated the time would come when Yorkshire players signed contracts, had a loyalty-bonus clause, and actually left the club by choice. The thought of Yorkshire finishing last in the county championship, and the domestic scene being dominated by overseas men, would not have entered my head. Or that countries by the name of Pakistan and Sri Lanka would be a force in the international programme, and not South Africa.

The only contract I signed was for overseas tours. With Yorkshire my cap was my contract. I had complete faith in Yorkshire's doing right by me; as I would do by them. In any case, I did not want a contract, for a contract can work both ways. Yorkshire cricket was the cornerstone around which I built a major part of my life, and it did not occur to me that the disciplined traditions inherited from the days of Lord Hawke were wrong. That spirit worked well enough for me to be in four championship sides from my debut to the outbreak of war. Perhaps Lord Hawke's concepts lasted too long and Yorkshire became too comfortable and inflexible for their own good. Some odd decisions were made, but in my time players were generally on the best of terms at county and national level. When tours were twice as long as they are today and players could not afford to take their wives as a matter of course, I suggested to Lord's that it would be appreciated if a Christmas card could be sent officially from MCC to wives and families. On the next tour the cards were duly sent. Relationships were friendly.

Nevertheless, the formation of the Professional Cricketers' Association was commendable if only because it gave the players an official vote. If anything, the sensible liaison between the Association and the various bodies appears to have cemented rather than weakened attitudes between authority and the players. All commonsense points to the fact that they need to work together.

As an old player, I would like to see the Association take the lead in curbing incessant and unfair appealing and in helping umpires, who nowadays have a murderous job. To try to cheat out a fellow pro must be against the spirit of cricket and the Association.

When I first went into the Yorkshire side I was much impressed with 'Ticker' Mitchell's fairness when he fielded close to Verity. Mitchell was an uncompromising character, but he scorned to cheat and instantly ruled out a catch if he was not satisfied with its fairness. To my sorrow, the old standards have gone, and there are concerted appeals for anything that goes in the air close to the bat. I can't believe the modern game is *all* about money and winning.

There is a clear need for stricter captaincy. Joe Hardstaff once told me that in his young days he was fielding on the boundary and missed an instruction from his captain Arthur Carr, who used to clap his hands to get attention. Joe was unwise enough to tell him that there was a man behind him who came from his village. He was promptly told he could have the next three matches off to talk to him. Obviously, I do not want to see that form of discipline reintroduced, but there is a middle ground. Somewhere between the extremes would benefit the game enormously.

Without sponsorship, the first-class structure as we know it could not survive. Cricket is not alone in today's facts of economic life, but I am sure it has the advantage of much goodwill. If that goodwill is eroded by exhibitionism and cynicism, a prime commercial asset will disappear. I hope all cricketers who might be thinking I am sermonizing will bear this fact in mind.

Sponsorship is also attracted by television coverage, and it is up to the players to protect their livelihoods by making it as compelling as they can. Other games and pastimes are fast-emerging as there is more leisure for the masses. By asking for it to be compelling, the last thing I am advocating is trivializing the game. One of the lessons of Packer's World Series Cricket was that contrived cricket is no substitute for the real thing. Fortunately the BBC's coverage of the game has been respectable. Long may it remain so.

One disquieting area is the loss of interest in the county championship. Instant cricket in an instant age has become the vogue. The public have been served with a form of the game more to their liking, and, to many, the championship represents the dinosaur of cricket – belonging to a different age. Of course the view is wrong. County cricket can be good, and it is the necessary training ground for Test matches. To put players into five-day matches after an exclusive diet of single-innings fiestas would be patently absurd. Possibly the situation will have to be accepted that cricket's three-day competition will have to be heavily subsidized by the other forms. Rather like classical music living off pop. The hope must be that a sponsor might be found who looks on his contribution as a service to cricket. As a commercial investment it would not be entirely lost. Far from it.

If the championship did have to go – and perish the thought – a different form of competition would need to be substituted. As long as there are five-day Tests, there has to be some equivalent to the championship in order for players to learn techniques and develop the mental stamina needed for long innings. The only alternative would be a truncated version of the present championship with perhaps the country divided into regions with fixtures like North v. South. The day of the amateur might dawn again. I do not believe the championship would be revived by creating two divisions, with promotion and relegation. There are some visionaries who see a future consisting only of limited-over cricket. They may be right, but I hope there will always be a place and support for all forms of the game.

Against the problem of the championship is the encouraging fact that more cricket than ever is being played by villages and clubs, and the grassroots are being caringly nurtured by the National

Cricket Association. Equipment manufacturers report ever rising sales, and if I ever suffer a moment of despondency I recall playing in a Test at Old Trafford when the old *News Chronicle* devoted much space to an article on the theme: 'Is Cricket Dying?' If this was so I wondered why the match in progress was given so much coverage, and in the end it was the newspaper, not cricket, which died an untimely death.

Whenever I hear complaints about the number of overseas players in the county ranks, and the multinational nature of England's team, it occurs to me that the situation would never have arisen if our own home-born men had been good enough. As soon as the door was opened wide to the world, it was a safe prediction that counties would grab ready-made stars in the quest of one of the domestic prizes. The major mistake was not to limit further the number of overseas cricketers permitted in county sides. Now the system has had to be put into reverse, and it will take a number of years to redress the balance. I do not wish to single out Derbyshire as an extreme example of what has been happening, but it was somewhat bizarre that a county famous for its pace bowlers of the ilk of Bill Copson, Les Jackson and Cliff Gladwin, went to Copenhagen for an opening bowler. Are there no more bowlers from Derby and Chesterfield?

With West Indian- and South African-born players now regularly making the Test side, it is cynically suggested that England will have to play under a new name in the future. The call is for the qualifying rules to be tightened. English authorities have invariably tried to look at the game's interests from a wide angle, and tried to be fair to individual players. Clearly it is manifestly unjust that a player should be deprived of cricket's greatest honour because of political mischance. Yet I think it reasonable to expect that all England players should have learned their cricket in England, and/or hold a British passport.

Though I express the hope that every England player wants to play for England as a privilege rather than for what he can get out of it, a position has arisen in which a professional needs to be constantly in the top bracket from a financial point of view. Earnings from Test and county cricket have widened to the point that it is arguable that the difference is too wide. Unfortunately, the competition for places is small and there are too many moderate players around. Selectors have a thankless task.

I would like to see a fresh dedication and attitude in the first-class game with everyone uniting to try to put the best possible national side in the field. The old Australian ideal produced results, though it is possible that ideal will be put to severe test in the post-Packer era with its TV gimmickry. The English counties ought to think in terms of how they can best contribute to rebuilding the strength of the Test side, and not hide behind the excuse that their first duty is to look after their members and public. Genuine class has been absent in depth too long, and the long-term answer cannot be in the further recruitment of players not eligible for England.

Television has now such an influence that not only schoolboys but club cricketers copy the manners, styles, technique and field placings of the leading players and teams. My son Richard went to a Whitbread village competition final at Lord's and said all the batsmen played like county pros. I am not certain that this is a good sign, but I am convinced of the need for composite pitches at junior stages. I also think up to the age of ten or so a soft ball (not a tennis ball because its bounce is too high) is better than a hard ball. When I was of a similar age I was hit by a hard ball which lifted off a length on an uncertain pitch, and I was not only hurt but a little frightened. Even for a boy with a passion for cricket as I had, it took a bit of nerve to play on, and I believe many victims of a hard ball at an early age lose interest in the game. Artificial pitches reduce the risk of injury, and of the ball misbehaving, and encourage confidence and shot-making. If a lad is occupied in defending his person because of an erratic bounce on a poor pitch, he is unlikely to develop. Bowlers are also required to learn the basics of line and length. The composite surface, which has served Australia so well, is the ideal way to start to learn to bat and bowl.

Despite all the counter-interests, cricket still has a large and affectionate following. I am certain it will adapt to any future society with its extra leisure and cable television in the same way that it has moved into the latter half of this century. Whatever system there is in the end, it comes down to the players: their attitude; their enthusiasm; their skill, and, above all, how much they are prepared to put back into the game.

I often think old George and I must have appeared an unlikely pair as we made our way on dark winter evenings to Headingley in those far-off days, but I have never ceased to admire his selfless devotion and sheer love of cricket. 'Theer's nowt like a green field on a summer's day with wickets pitched,' he used to say.

George would have cast an interested eye on the news that Texaco's important sponsorship was announced by an American from Virginia who had never seen a ball bowled.

A pity that on the same day as a spokesman for the company praised the game in ringing terms Boycott had to be sacked by Yorkshire. That's life, but if the next fifty years are as colourful, interesting and compelling as the last fifty, a future editor of *Wisden* will be re-echoing John Woodcock's truth that, for all its faults, cricket is the 'incomparable pastime'.

CAREER RECORD
Compiled by Geoffrey Copinger

Batting (All First Class Matches)

Season	Inns	Not out	Runs	100s	50s	Highest inns	Average	Catches
1934	28	2	863	1	5	196	33·19	8
1935	23	3	577	1	1	131	28·85	6

YORKSHIRE IN JAMAICA

Season	Inns	Not out	Runs	100s	50s	Highest inns	Average	Catches
1936	5	2	123	0	1	59	41·00	0
1936	49	6	1282	1	8	163	29·81	26
1937	58	7	2888	10	12	271*	56·62	26
1938	37	6	1874	6	5	364	60·45	12

MCC IN SOUTH AFRICA

Season	Inns	Not out	Runs	100s	50s	Highest inns	Average	Catches
1938–39	19	1	1168	5	4	202	64·88	7
1939	52	6	2883	12	8	280*	62·67	38
1945	16	0	782	2	4	188	48·87	3
1946	38	6	1552	4	7	183*	48·50	13

MCC IN AUSTRALIA

Season	Inns	Not out	Runs	100s	50s	Highest inns	Average	Catches
1946–47	21	3	1267	3	8	151*	70·38	5
1947	44	4	2585	11	7	270*	64·62	23

MCC IN WEST INDIES

Season	Inns	Not out	Runs	100s	50s	Highest inns	Average	Catches
1947–48	10	1	578	2	3	138	64·22	6
1948	48	7	2654	10	13	176*	64·73	23

MCC IN SOUTH AFRICA

Season	Inns	Not out	Runs	100s	50s	Highest inns	Average	Catches
1948–49	21	1	1477	5	7	174	73·85	8
1949	56	6	3429	12	17	269*	68·58	40
1950	40	3	2128	6	11	202*	55·99	24

MCC IN AUSTRALIA AND NEW ZEALAND

Season	Inns	Not out	Runs	100s	50s	Highest inns	Average	Catches
1950–51	25	4	1382	5	7	156*	65·80	18
1951	47	8	2145	7	9	194*	55·00	33
1952	45	3	2567	11	12	189	61·11	31
1953	44	5	2458	8	10	241	63·02	15

MCC IN WEST INDIES

Season	Inns	Not out	Runs	100s	50s	Highest inns	Average	Catches
1953–54	12	2	780	2	4	205	78·00	3
1954	28	2	912	2	4	163	35·07	7

MCC IN AUSTRALIA AND NEW ZEALAND

Season	Inns	Not out	Runs	100s	50s	Highest inns	Average	Catches
1954–55	25	2	1059	2	6	145*	46·04	7
1955	19	1	537	1	4	194	29·83	5
TOTALS	810	91	39950	129	177	364	55·56	387

* Signifies not out

Aggregates

	Inns	Not out	Runs	100s	50s	Highest inns	Average
In England	672	75	32116	105	137	364	53·79
In Australia	63	9	3425	10	18	156*	63·42
In West Indies	27	5	1481	4	8	205	67·31
In South Africa	40	2	2645	10	11	202	69·60
In New Zealand	8	0	283	0	3	69	35·37
TOTALS	810	91	39950	129	177	364	55·56

Test Matches

	Tests	Inns	Not out	Runs	100s	50s	Highest inns	Average
Australia	27	49	6	2428	5	14	364	56·46
South Africa	19	34	4	1564	4	7	158	52·13
New Zealand	11	17	0	777	3	4	206	51·51
West Indies	13	24	3	1661	5	6	205	79·09
India	7	11	2	522	2	2	150	58·00
Pakistan	2	3	0	19	0	0	14	6·33
TOTALS	79	138	15	6971	19	33	364	56·67

County Championship Matches

	Inns	Not out	Runs	100s	50s	Highest inns	Average
1934	25	1	801	1	4	196	33·37
1935	19	3	411	1	0	131	25·68
1936	43	6	1108	1	6	163	29·94
1937	36	5	1728	5	7	271	55·74
1938	17	3	631	1	3	107	45·07
1939	40	4	2167	9	6	280*	60·19
1946	26	4	1112	3	5	171	50·54
1947	23	1	1551	6	4	270*	70·50
1948	22	5	1565	8	4	176*	92·05
1949	38	5	2098	6	11	269*	63·57
1950	21	2	1125	4	4	156	59·21
1951	26	5	1222	5	4	194*	58·19
1952	26	1	1482	7	6	189	59·28
1953	21	1	1149	4	4	178	57·45
1954	19	2	676	1	4	149*	39·76
1955	18	0	535	1	4	194	29·72
TOTALS	420	48	19361	63	76	280*	52·04

Test Matches

	Inns	Not out	Runs	100s	50s	Highest inns	Average
1937 (v. New Zealand)	5	0	127	1	0	100	25·40
1938 (v. Australia)	4	0	473	2	0	364	118·25
1938–39 (v. S. Africa)	6	0	265	0	2	92	44·16
1939 (v. West Indies)	6	1	480	2	1	196	96·00
1946 (v. India)	5	1	123	0	1	67	30·75
1946–47 (v. Australia)	9	1	417	1	2	122*	52·12
1947 (v. S. Africa)	10	2	344	1	1	100	43·00
1947–48 (v. West Indies)	4	0	171	0	2	60	42·75
1948 (v. Australia)	8	0	342	0	4	81	42·75
1948–49 (v. S. Africa)	9	0	577	2	2	158	64·11
1949 (v. New Zealand)	6	0	469	2	2	206	78·16
1950 (v. West Indies)	6	1	333	1	0	202*	66·60
1950–51 (v. Australia)	10	4	533	1	4	156*	88·83
1950–51 (v. New Zealand)	3	0	114	0	1	57	38·00
1951 (v. S. Africa)	9	2	378	1	2	100	54·00
1952 (v. India)	6	1	399	2	1	150	79·80
1953 (v. Australia)	9	1	443	1	3	145	55·37
1953–54 (v. West Indies)	8	1	677	2	3	205	96·71
1954 (v. Pakistan)	3	0	19	0	0	14	6·33
1954–55 (v. Australia)	9	0	220	0	1	80	24·44
1954–55 (v. New Zealand)	3	0	67	0	1	53	22·33
TOTALS	138	15	6971	19	33	364	56·67

For MCC Touring Teams (Excluding Tests)

	Inns	Not out	Runs	100s	50s	Highest inns	Average
In Australia	35	4	2255	8	11	151*	72·74
In South Africa	25	2	1803	8	7	202	78·39
In West Indies	10	2	510	2	2	138	63·75
In New Zealand	2	0	102	0	1	69	51·00
TOTALS	72	8	4670	18	21	202	72·96

Mode of Dismissal

Bowled	207
Caught	372
LBW	94
Run out	21
Stumped	19
Hit wicket	5
Obstructing the field	1
TOTALS	719

Test Match Hundreds (19)

v. Australia (5)
364   at the Oval, 1938
156*   at Adelaide, 1950–51
145   at Lord's, 1953
122*   at Sydney, 1946–47
100   at Nottingham, 1938

v. South Africa (4)
158   at Johannesburg, 1948–49 (Second Test)
123   at Johannesburg, 1948–49 (Fourth Test)
100   at Leeds, 1947
100   at Leeds, 1951

v. West Indies (5)
205   at Kingston, 1953–54
202*   at the Oval, 1950
196   at Lord's, 1939
169   at Georgetown, 1953–54
165*   at the Oval, 1939

v. New Zealand (3)
206   at the Oval, 1949
101   at Leeds, 1949
100   at Manchester, 1937

v. India (2)
150   at Lord's, 1952
104   at Manchester 1952

Bowling

	Overs	Maidens	Runs	Wickets	Average
1934	103	17	379	11	34·45
1935	22·1	5	79	2	39·50
1935–36	7	0	45	1	45·00
1936	173·3	44	479	21	22·81
1937	315	56	1025	28	36·60
1938	227·1	51	576	20	28·80
1938–39	24	1	108	2	54·00
1939	220·7	38	822	44	18·68
1945	35	0	167	5	33·40
1946	58	11	173	9	19·22
1946–47	18	1	116	2	58·00
1947	109	18	344	12	28·83
1947–48	5	1	20	0	—
1948	26	5	102	0	—
1948–49	1	0	7	0	—
1949	102	29	286	7	40·86
1950	28	5	90	2	45·00
1950–51	3·6	0	11	1	11·00
1951	11	1	44	4	11·00
1952	10	1	43	1	43·00
1953	31	8	129	0	—
1953–54	6	0	43	0	—
1954–55	00·6	0	2	1	2·00
TOTALS	1293·5	292	5090	173	29·42

and   243·3 eight-ball overs

These figures exclude one first-class game in 1957 in the Old Trafford Centenary match (MCC *v.* Lancashire, scoring 76 and 25), and two in 1960 – 0 for Colonel L. C. Steven's XI *v.* Cambridge University at Eastbourne; and 89 for MCC *v.* Ireland at Dublin.

Index